NATIONAL
PARKS *of*
EUROPE

Contents

NORWAY

SWEDEN

RUSSIA

Scotland
10

33
Glasgow ● Edinburgh

North
Sea

DENMARK

60 ● COPENHAGEN

Baltic
Sea

RĪGA ⭐ 20 LATVIA

Smolensk ●

Northern
Ireland
● Belfast

LITHUANIA

VILNIUS ⭐

14
Kaliningrad
Russia

● MINSK

13
30
Irish Sea

DUBLIN
IRELAND ⭐

Manchester ●

Hamburg ●

Gdańsk ●

BELARUS

Brest ●

Vistula

27

53
Wales
40   9
Cardiff ●

39
UNITED
KINGDOM

THE
NETHERLANDS
AMSTERDAM
THE HAGUE ⭐

Elbe

BERLIN ⭐

WARSAW ⭐

POLAND

KYIV ⭐

Dnieper

England ⭐ LONDON

Odra

Kraków ●

Lviv ●

UKRAINE

15

NORTH
ATLANTIC
OCEAN

English Channel

Le Havre ●

BRUSSELS ⭐
BELGIUM

LUXEMBOURG

Frankfurt ●

GERMANY

Dresden ●
49

PRAGUE ⭐
CZECH REPUBLIC

55
51

Dniester

MOLDOVA

CHIŞINĂU ⭐

11

ROMANIA

PARIS ⭐

Seine

Rhine

SLOVAKIA

VIENNA ⭐ BRATISLAVA ⭐

24

Loire

FRANCE

Munich ●

Danube

8

AUSTRIA

BUDAPEST ⭐

47

7
LIECHTENSTEIN
23
SWITZERLAND 54
BERN ⭐

HUNGARY

BUCHAREST ⭐

Bay of
Biscay

Bordeaux ●

Garonne

Lyon ●

Rhône

Geneva ●

6

56
SLOVENIA
LJUBLJANA ⭐

ZAGREB ⭐
CROATIA

BELGRADE ⭐

Tisa

Danube

5

42
Bilbao ●

46

18

Milan ●

Venice ●

Po

44
38
28

BOSNIA &
HERZEGOVINA
SARAJEVO ⭐

SERBIA

BULGARIA

41

36   3

ANDORRA
ANDORRA ⭐

MONACO
Marseille ● MONACO ⭐

45

12

FLORENCE ●

SAN MARINO

SAN
MARINO ⭐

17

57
31

MONTENEGRO

KOSOVO

SOFIA ⭐

SKOPJE ⭐ 43
MACEDONIA

MADRID ⭐

Duero

Ebro

● Barcelona

Corsica

ITALY

ROME ⭐

2

TIRANA ⭐

Adriatic Sea

Thessaloniki ●

PORTUGAL

Tajo

SPAIN

Balearic
Sea

4

ALBANIA

LISBON ⭐

● Valencia

21

Naples ●

59

● Cordoba

Sardinia

Tyrrhenian Sea

GREECE

34

Aegean
Sea

16
● Seville

Palermo ●

Ionian
Sea

ATHENS ⭐

50

Mediterranean Sea

Sicily

19
Catania ● Mediterranean Sea

● Gibraltar

The medieval fishing village of
Manarola in the Cinque Terre.
Dartmoor National Park.
Plitvice National Park.
Picos de Europa.

Introduction

My first sight of Italy's Cinque Terre National Park (p56) was through the train window as I headed south along the coast from Genoa. It was painfully brief. And the same could be said for my second… and third looks. Mere glimpses of the beautiful Ligurian coast, each a fleeting snapshot between the blinding darkness of lengthy rail tunnels. My upset with the subterranean tracks didn't last long, however, as I was soon gaping at the full coastal splendour of the Cinque Terre from the village of Vernazza's splendid natural harbour. Cliffs plunged into the sea, forested hills marked the horizon and ancient drystone walls formed twisting terraces above town. And there was not an unsightly train track in view.

The stunning vistas only grew in magnitude over the coming days as I ran the steep and precipitous coastal trails linking the Cinque Terre's five medieval villages. Mix in some lovely beaches, great Italian seafood and gelato, and the park was a truly rewarding experience.

This diversity is carried through to Europe's national parks as a whole, and that is what makes them so special. They protect areas of coast, high-altitude peaks in the Pyrenees and Alps, and even parts of the frozen Arctic, with wildlife ranging from Carpathian squirrels and fin whales to peregrine falcons and polar bears. Setting out to choose Europe's top 60 national parks was no easy task, so we called on our expert writers and well-travelled Destination Editors. We asked them to tell us which parks provide the best experiences and why. The final selections were those that offered something truly unique, often an enthralling mixture of stunning natural beauty, incredible wildlife, fulfilling activities, local culture and (occasionally) a compelling history too.

But this book is intended to be more than just a celebration of Europe's top national parks – it's also a practical introduction to each of them. We highlight the best activities and trails – in the case of Port-Cros (p226), one of the trails is actually below the Mediterranean's surface! – explain how to get there and where to stay, show you the wildlife to watch out for, and even suggest itineraries.

We hope the following pages inspire you to explore more of Europe's wild and wonderful spaces.

Matt Phillips

01

Abisko National Park

Beyond the Arctic Circle, Abisko is the northern gateway to the legendary Kungsleden (King's Trail) that takes you across 440km of wild Sweden.

Getty Images | Johner Images

Abisko National Park

If you stand on top of the alpine massif of Mount Kebnekaise – Sweden's highest mountain – you're looking down at a pristine landscape wrestled from the grip of an ice age. Glaciers still stretch across the flanks of the neighbouring mountains and, while their larger brethren have retreated from the valleys that they once filled completely, the deep, narrow canyons and steep rock walls testify to a violent geological past. Everything is on a larger scale here. You hike for an entire day and realise that you're not even halfway along the Tjäktjavagge valley. Lakes Torneträsk and Akkajaure are like two inland seas. The birch and spruce forests that cover the foothills seem endless.

Abisko National Park came into being in 1909, making it one of the first in Sweden. Forming part of Sápmi, the historic roaming lands of the Sámi that span a large part of northern Sweden, Norway, Finland and Russia's Kola Peninsula, Abisko has been home to Sweden's only indigenous peoples for thousands of years. Their hunter ancestors followed the retreating ice into Abisko's valleys after the last ice age, 10,000 years ago, and remains of ancient hearths and pit traps used to capture wild reindeer and elk can still be found today. Centuries ago, the Sámi switched from hunting to herding, and reindeer husbandry is still prevalent in Abisko, divided between the forest Sámi and the mountain Sámi communities and dictated by the seasons. Forest reindeer herding is more stationary, with the forest Sámi moving their reindeer between foraging grounds in the wetlands and coniferous forests. The more nomadic mountain Sámi follow their reindeer along ancient migratory routes from low-lying

birch and coniferous forests to summer pastures in the mountains, corralling them along the edges of the Kebnekaise range.

⬆ Abisko National Park is an ideal place to go dog-sledding.
Previous page: cross-country skiing is another way to get around.

Toolbox

☼ When to go
Hike under the midnight sun between late May and mid-July. Prepare for mosquitoes in July and August, the warmest, most popular months for hiking. September and October paint the trees gold and red. Ski under the northern lights from November to March.

🧭 Getting there
Abisko is the northern entrance to the 440km Kungsleden (King's Trail) in the very north of Swedish Lappland. The town of Abisko is a 10-minute drive from the trailhead. Kiruna is the nearest airport, two hours' drive away.

Park in numbers

77

Area covered (sq km)

2106

Highest point:
Mount Kebnekaise (m)

10,000

Years that the Sámi have lived in the park area

Stay here...

Icehotel
Starting as a small igloo–art gallery in 1989, the Icehotel has grown into a winter extravaganza built of ice blocks, its corridors decorated with extraordinary ice sculptures and its rooms created afresh each year by artists. Sleep on beds of compact snow, reindeer skins and army-issue sleeping bags. The main building is surrounded by satellite bungalows with skylights for watching the northern lights, and the restaurant is one of Sweden's best. Dog-sled pickup is available from Kiruna airport in winter.

STF Kebnekaise Fjällstation
This mountain lodge has a picturesque location at the foot of Mount Kebnekaise. Superb meals are conjured from locally sourced ingredients. In summer, arrive by helicopter; in winter you can opt for reindeer sled or snowmobile.

STF Abisko Turiststation & Abisko Mountain Lodge
The gateway to Abisko, this lodge draws backpackers with simple dorms and the rest with hotel-style rooms. Guests can treat themselves to three-course gourmet dinners.

Do this!

Seeing the northern lights
One of the best places on Earth to experience nature's most spectacular light show, with eerie streaks of green, white, red and yellow streaming across the night sky, is the Aurora Sky Station. Chairlifts run to the lookout tower on top of Mount Nuolja between November and March, and its location away from any city lights makes viewing conditions particularly favourable. In winter, Lights Over Lapland runs nightly Aurora Borealis photography tours from Abisko Mountain Lodge, with professional photographers teaching you how to capture the winter night magic.

Experiencing Sámi life
The Sámi village of Rávttas teaches visitors about nomadic Sámi life, which revolves around reindeer. You'll learn to distinguish between individual deer, ride a sleigh (in winter) and indulge in Sámi dishes around an open fire in a traditional *lavvus* (teepee).

Going husky sledding
Imagine yourself on a sled, shouting commands to your team of baying huskies. They surge past the frozen river and over the pristine landscape, snow flying from under their paws. Brothers Tomas and Andreas at Abisko Fjällturer can teach you everything about mushing.

What to spot...

Illuminated by the northern lights in winter and the midnight sun in summer, Sweden's northernmost national park is marked by surprisingly mild winters, due to the region's microclimate, and brief, warm summers. Habitats include subarctic forests, alpine rivers, subalpine grasslands and quaking bogs. Larger mammals such as reindeer and moose are diurnal and spotted year round; in winter, tracks on the snow reveal shy wolverines, foxes and lynx. Feathered denizens include golden eagles, buzzards, falcons and a wealth of wading birds.

ELK (MOOSE) This immense, solitary herbivore is best spotted at dusk or dawn, when it forages for food. Moose are extremely good swimmers, can dive for underwater plants and can run up to 6okm/hr.

REINDEER These herbivores can find food even under snow, digging for lichen with their hooves. Domesticated by the Sámi, they graze all over Abisko. Like human fingerprints, no two reindeer antlers are the same.

WOLVERINE This solitary omnivore that looks like a bear but is the largest member of the weasel family is both diurnal and nocturnal. It feeds on plants, berries and rodents and takes on weakened moose.

Hike this...

O1 Mount Kebnekaise
Reaching the summit of Sweden's highest mountain (2106m), this strenuous 12-hour-return, 20km hike rewards you with all-encompassing views of the surrounding tundra.

O2 Puddus Nature Trail
This easy 14km hike takes you to a reconstruction of a traditional Sámi camp and a former Sámi sacrificial site with awesome Lake Torneträsk views.

O3 Abisko to Nikkaluokta
The park's longest hike, this 105km, six-day trail leads you past pristine lakes, along verdant valleys, over the scenic Tjäkta Pass and around the iconic Mount Kebnekaise.

⬇ Photographers gather beneath the spectral glow of the northern lights; Abisko is one of the best places on Earth to see the lights.

Itineraries

Survey the Arctic north from the top of Sweden's highest mountain and hike part of Sweden's longest hiking trail. Staying awake under the midnight sun? That too.

➔ Staying in Jukkasjärvi's otherworldly Icehotel is a once-in-a-lifetime opportunity.

01
Two days

Get a taste of the park in the least amount of time by taking the gently undulating, 8km trail from Abisko Turiststation along the Ábeskoeatnu River and then along the left fork of the signposted Kårsavagge trail through birch and pine forest to the tumultuous Kårsa rapids. Then, in the evening, cap the day with a chairlift ride to the Panorama Café at the top of Mount Nuola and watch the midnight sun cast a pearly glow over the lake and forest. Spend the night at Abisko Turiststation, rent a bicycle the following day and take on the 39km-long Rallarvägen (Navvy Rd) to Riksgränsen. It runs parallel to the railway line from Abisko towards the Norwegian border and was used by railway-construction workers in the early 20th century. Or, for a shorter biking adventure, take the train to Låktatjåkka and do the 10km return trip to the enormous boulders and rock formations of the Kärkevagge valley, with Trollsjön (Sulphur Lake) its showpiece.

02
Three days

One of Abisko's highlights is following the 19km trail from the park's eastern entrance, Nikkaluokta, to the foot of Mount Kebnekaise. The trail passes Lake Laddjujavre; you can cut 6km from your hike by catching a boat across the lake in summer. From STF Kebnekaise Fjällstation you have a choice of two trails to the summit of Mount Kebnekaise. The Vastra (western) trail is gentler but longer (25km return), while the last part of the shorter Ostra (eastern) route (20km return) involves a steep scramble to the summit and sometimes crampons to get across the glacier. The western trail takes you into the Kitteldalen valley and involves fording two streams. Ascend the steep track to Vierramvare, with the summit on your left. If you have the energy on the way down, you can visit the lesser Toulpagorni peak. Recuperate at STF Kebnekaise Fjällstation and either retrace your steps to Nikkaluokta or take the daily Kallax Flyg helicopter.

03
A week or more

For the park's longest hike, take the Kungsleden from Abisko Turiststation. The trail follows the rapids of the Ábeskoeatnu River as it gushes along a narrow canyon, before passing through a vast, gentle valley and then dense beech forest, where wooden boardwalks carry you over bog land and bridges help you traverse streams. You pass several small lakes en route – ideal for skinny-dipping first thing in the morning or if no other hikers happen to be passing by! Around 35km from the start, the trail climbs to a mountain ridge, from which you'll have fantastic views of the countryside you've just tramped across. There's a sauna here at Alesjaure cabins to take care of your aches and pains. The highest point of the five- or six-day trek to Mount Kebnekaise takes you over the Tjäkta Pass (1150m), where you'll occasionally find snow even in June. Take a day to hike up Mount Kebnekaise and then either carry on south along the Kungsleden or walk out to Nikkaluokta.

02

Parco Nazionale d'Abruzzo, Lazio e Molise

For centuries this was Italy's most isolated wilderness, and notoriously shy bears and wolves still roam amid its towering peaks, silent green valleys, cobalt-blue lakes and thick forest.

500px | Daniele De Rubeis

Wild poppies flame from the foothills in spring as you approach the Parco Nazionale d'Abruzzo, Lazio e Molise. Gentle hills give way to steeper slopes, rearing up to the highest points of the Apennine range. Glacial and fluvial gorges trace the violent geological activity that has created these peaks, troughs and chasms. Remote sanctuaries punctuate forgotten-feeling high-altitude valleys, ideal points to contemplate the vastness of nature and your smallness within it.

Mountain-edged valleys cup lakes that reflect the peaks in their mirrored waters. The small scoop of Lago Vivo partly freezes in the winter chill. A herd of deer scatters as you follow a path upwards. Occasionally you'll pass snub-roofed drystone huts, still used by farmers and shepherds as their livestock roam across the hills. Beech trees dominate the forests, their leaves turning gold, rust and terracotta-red in autumn.

Such was the isolation of the area that it was for a long time almost inaccessible. Tratturi (long grassy paths) weave across the countryside, linking the Apennines to Puglia in the south. These still-in-use routes were used by the pre-Roman Samnite population and later the Romans. From the 1400s to the 1970s shepherds drove their flocks along these twice annually. In autumn they travelled from the highlands to balmier grazing in Apulia in Italy's deep south, returning up to the cooler pastures in summer. This was the annual transhumance, and today walkers can trace their footsteps across these ancient routes.

In 1922, the (then) 5 sq km park was founded to protect the area's rare natural riches, from bears to orchids, born of its isolation and inaccessibility, but

the Fascists abolished the park in 1933. Following the park's re-establishment in 1950, it was gradually expanded to cover the vast, epically wild and diverse 500 sq km of today.

⬆ Cycling below Monte Amaro (2793m) – one of the highest Apennine peaks – in nearby Maiella National Park. Previous page: Monte Marsicano (2242m).

Getty Images | N Eisele-Hein / LOOK-foto

Toolbox

⚙ **When to go**
Wild flowers carpet the park from April to June, while in similarly temperate September to October the vast forest turns magnificently gold and red. July and August are hot, and winter's cold and snowy, prime time for winter sports.

🧭 **Getting there**
In central Italy, the park is accessible via bus from Avezzano (for connections to L'Aquila, Pescara and Rome), to Pescasseroli, Civitella Alfedena and other villages. The A24 and A25 highways are the closest major roads.

Park in numbers

440
Area covered (sq km)

2249
Highest point: Petroso (m)

60
Percentage covered by forest

Stay here...

 Albergo Antico Borga La Torre
Up a stepped cobbled lane, this 18th-century town house has small geranium-laden balconies. It's in the medieval centre of Civitella Alfedena, a red-roofed, pale-walled small town that spills across the wooded landscape at the foot of a string of Apennine peaks. Rooms have pine furnishings and an old-school feel, and superb panoramas lift them out of the ordinary. The small restaurant serves hearty local dishes to set you up for the hills, usually with some homemade liquor to finish.

B&B Animali Selvaggi
In Pescasseroli, this three-bedroom guesthouse has rooms featuring polished-wood antique furniture that belonged to the owners' grandparents. It's also eco-friendly, and all the food for breakfast is organic, plus it caters for vegans.

B&B La Sosta
This whitewashed B&B is on the main road below the small town of Opi, which cloaks a hilltop below higher peaks. It's run by a welcoming elderly couple who take pride in their hospitality, offering smart, well-cared-for rooms with balconies.

Do this!

Bear watching
One of the many thrilling adventures to be had in the park is to take bear-watching excursions with local operators. Some offer middle-of-nowhere accommodation for better bear spotting, in remote mountain lodges set amid snowcapped peaks and emerald-green grassy hills. At dusk or in the early morning, as the sun rises and turns the surrounding colours golden, you'll venture out to track and observe bears with an expert local guide, exploring the ancient woodlands, grassy clearings and hidden crevices that are the favourite spots of these retiring creatures.

Wolf howling
Wolf howling was a technique used by hunters in the past, and local operator Ecotur has adopted this method as a way of discovering more about wolves, offering evening treks to hear the howl of the wolf.

Horse riding and donkey trekking
Exploring the park's pristine wilderness on horseback or taking it slowly by donkey feels like a link to the past as well as a way to cover a lot of ground while enjoying the unmotorised peace.

What to spot...

The park is two-thirds forest, mostly beech, with other foliage including black pine and silver birch. Species such as the chamois, the Marsican brown bear and the Apennine wolf roam the inhospitable-seeming landscape. The densely forested hills hide wild boar, and roe and red deer, while smaller mammals include martens, otters, badgers and polecats. You're most likely to see squirrels, dormice, hedgehogs, moles, weasels, hares and foxes. Whirring above are sparrow hawks, kestrels, buzzards, peregrine falcons and golden eagles.

ABRUZZO CHAMOIS Part goat, part deer, this variety of chamois had almost died out when the park was established, with just a few dozen left, but the population now numbers over 2000.

MARSICAN BROWN BEAR
This quiet, solitary, imposing creature, which can weigh up to 200kg, feeds on fruit, plants, insects, honey and small animals. There are around 100 in the park.

ITALIAN WOLF A grey-wolf subspecies, this wolf is particular to the Apennines. Roaming in smaller packs than their foreign relatives, by night they feed on chamois, roe deer, red deer, wild boar, hares and rabbits.

Hike this...

01 Val di Rose to Rifugio di Forca Resuni

A gentle, waymarked three-hour walk, this popular trail runs through glorious, goat- and deer-dotted forested countryside.

02 Monte Amaro route

The climb to this peak (2793m), just outside the park, takes 2¼ hours and offers soul-stirring views over the woodlands and gullies of Valle di Sangro, and a strong possibility of spotting chamois.

03 Monte Tranquillo and the Rocca Ridge

This route up Monte Tranquillo (1658m) is around a 2½-hour walk, and from here you can continue north along the challenging, top-of-the-world Rocca Ridge, a 19.5km circuit.

Itineraries

Take trails deep into this wildest and most untouched-feeling of Italian landscapes, listening out for wolves, tracking bears or gliding serenely across mountain lakes.

← Just outside the protected area is the beautiful Lago di Scanno.
→ The stunning hill-town of Scanno was immortalised by the photographer Henri Cartier-Bresson.

01
A day

Despite the impenetrable atmosphere of the park, you can explore a thrilling swathe of its mountains, forest and lakes in a day. Start your exploration from the headquarters of the national park, the town of Pescasseroli, which lies in the upper valley of the Sangro River, backed by thickly wooded hills.

After parking your car in the car park, try one of the short trails cobwebbing out in all directions (maps are available from the town). You'll soon be immersed in the peace, birdsong and sumptuous natural splendour of the national park, with towering peaks plummeting down into forested valleys.

After your walk is done, hop back in the car for the 7km drive to Opi, a medieval town perched on a rocky promontory with views over the surrounding thickly wooded countryside, and eat a meal featuring local mountain produce, comprising ingredients such as lamb, truffles and wild mushrooms, at one of the local restaurants, or unwrap a picnic lakeside at your next destination.

Finish your day trip at Barrea, 13km further on, a magical-looking red-roofed town that clings to the steep, wooded lakeside. The deep blue waters of vast Lake Barrea appear to have been here for millennia, but the lake was created by damming the river after WWII.

There are lake beaches or you can hire boats so that you can complete your day gliding across the water, walls of mountains on every side.

02
Four days

For this slower route around Abruzzo National Park, once again start at the small town of Pescasseroli, where you can consult the local visitor centre to help decide which of the park's 150 walking trails you fancy, or arrange wolf- or bear-spotting excursions. Next, head on to Opi. From this town you can take a 2½-hour walk through Valle di Fondillo, past thickly wooded areas alive with wildlife – there's a chance you'll see chamois, and possibly bears (they're shy, but keep quiet, calm and at a distance). You could also climb Monte Amaro (Bitter Mountain; 2793m), one of the highest Apennine peaks (it lies just outside the park, in Maiella National Park), for heart-in-mouth, moonscape views. At your third stop, make a base in Civitella Alfedena, a higgledy-piggledy village on a wooded hilltop above Barrea Lake. Choose a walking trail from the town, such as around the Val di Rosa, a forested valley that offers the best chance of spotting the park's graceful herds of chamois. On your final day, take a beautiful journey to Scanno, just outside the protected area, past the Lago di Scanno, a rippling mirror of blue-green lake. The road from the lake runs through the Gole di Sagittario, a chasm hemmed in by vast walls of rock, and snakes above the turquoise waters of the Sagittario river. If the villages clinging almost surreally to the hillsides remind you of works by Dutch artist MC Escher, you're on to something: he drew the town of Castrovalva near here.

03

Aigüestortes i Estany de Sant Maurici National Park

If you imagined the Pyrenees as piercing peaks and crystalline lakes of singular beauty, you were probably thinking of Spain's Aigüestortes i Estany de Sant Maurici.

'Aigüestortes i Estany de Sant Maurici' may sound more like a Catalan riddle than a national park, but few labels are quite so apt, describing as it does this splendid world of winding streams (aigüestortes) and lakes (estany). The Pyrenees are home to an estimated 1000 lakes, and 300 of these fall within the park's boundaries. So expansive are these bodies of water – which owe their presence to the impenetrable granite substrata that serve as foundations for the peaks – that, remarkably, 15 percent of the park's surface area is water.

Evidence of human settlement here dates back more than 8000 years, but this is a place where nature holds sway, where the human story is a mere footnote to altogether more compelling tales from the natural world.

Sculpted and forged by glaciers over two million years, the park is essentially two U-shaped, east–west valleys that begin at an altitude of 1600m and don't stop climbing until they approach a dizzying 3km high. Against a backdrop of jagged granite shards, transparent mountain waters, forests of pine and fir, and high pastures carpeted with spring wildflowers, are found natural features stranger than fiction: free-roaming horses that wear cow bells, a century-old bonsai pine tree growing straight from a rock, fields of wild saffron, places with mythic names like Agujas Perdut (Lost Peaks) and Estany Perdut (Lost Lake), mountains where Atlantic and Mediterranean weather systems collide... and such is the drama of the park's topography and the accessibility of its inner reaches and hiking trails that it has been described as Yellowstone, Canada and the Alps all squeezed into one 'miniature' package.

Toolbox

When to go
Most of the high valleys and certainly the hiking trails remain inaccessible for much of the year, making the park primarily a summer experience. May and June are the best months, because the streams fill with water at this time, while flowers bloom from June until late July.

Getting there
The park lies in the Pyrenees in the northwestern Spanish region of Catalonia, close to the border with Aragón, and north of Lérida. It's about a day's drive from Barcelona.

Park in numbers

141.2
Area covered (sq km)

3033
Highest point: Pic de Comolaforno (m)

300
Number of lakes (estanys) within park boundaries

Estany de Sant Maurici is just one beautiful lake in a park full of stunning lakes.

Stay here...

Pensión Santa Maria

In the mountain village of Taüll, this lovely place looks out over the town's fabled Romanesque churches and sweeping pre-Pyrenean valleys. Through a shady entrance, a grand stone archway leads into the quiet courtyard of this rambling country haven with its rose-draped balcony. The rooms are tastefully furnished and the building oozes timeless character. Owner Alex is warm, welcoming and a fount of information on the area.

Alberg Taüll

This is everything a hostel should be: the stylish rooms feature large beds with orthopaedic mattresses, there's underfloor heating for those crisp mountain mornings and you'll find a large map of the park in the common area to help you plan your hikes.

Roca Blanca

This small hotel in Espot has contemporary art on the walls, caring personal service and lovely rooms with plenty of space. Some have balconies, and there's a gym, sauna and a relaxing garden space.

Do this!

Hiking

There's no better way to explore the park than by hiking the trails that connect one mountain with the next, pausing to explore the deep valleys and gin-clear lakes as you go. Crossing the park in a single day is possible, but most walkers restrict themselves to one or two of the main valleys – Llong and Llobreta – thereby gaining a much more intimate picture of the park. Remember that the weather can be fickle and that snow is possible up high on any day of the year.

Tracking down trees

Close to the Estany Llong, perhaps the loveliest of the high Pyrenean valleys, you can find a famous dwarf pine thrusting out of a rock; there's also a 600-year-old black pine with a girth of 6m that predates Columbus.

Exploring villages

Just outside the southwestern entry to the park, the Vall de Boí hosts Unesco-listed Romanesque churches – small, unadorned stone structures that were constructed between the 11th and 14th centuries.

Hike this...

01 East–west traverse

You can walk right across the park in one day. The full Espot–Boí (or vice versa) walk is about 25km and takes nine hours. It's a tough trek but worth every blister.

02 Marmot Trail

The Marmot Trail, a return trip of three to four hours, begins next to the impressive Cavallers dam and ends at Estany Negré (Black Lake) – the views are exceptional.

03 Estany Llong

Traverse the Aigüestortes Plateau, explore the park's inner sanctum around Estany Llong and finish it off with a climb to Estany Redó, a hike of 2½ hours one way.

What to spot...

Roe deer, fallow deer and chamois are the most common large mammals, although alpine marmots and stoats keep them on their toes. Birds of prey are something of a park speciality, with the golden eagle, griffon vulture and lammergeier the standouts. Other important birds you may see include the turkey-like capercaillie, rock ptarmigan and black woodpecker. At lower altitudes, deciduous forests (such as oak and ash) and open grasslands dominate, but these yield to mountain pine, rhododendron and silver fir.

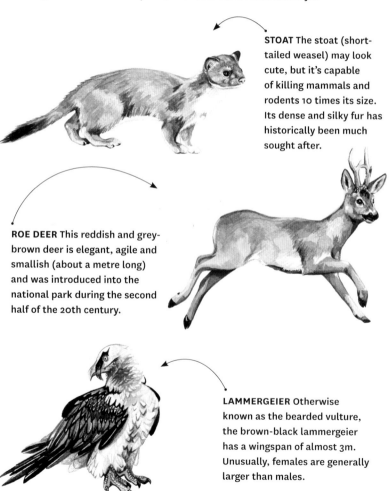

STOAT The stoat (short-tailed weasel) may look cute, but it's capable of killing mammals and rodents 10 times its size. Its dense and silky fur has historically been much sought after.

ROE DEER This reddish and grey-brown deer is elegant, agile and smallish (about a metre long) and was introduced into the national park during the second half of the 20th century.

LAMMERGEIER Otherwise known as the bearded vulture, the brown-black lammergeier has a wingspan of almost 3m. Unusually, females are generally larger than males.

Itineraries

Cross the park on foot, then circle it on four wheels. Put the two together and you have one of Europe's finest high-mountain experiences.

◄ Aigüestortes i Estany de Sant Maurici loosely (and very aptly) translates to 'The winding streams and St Maurice lake'.

↑ The park is home to herds of semi-wild horses.

↑ Sant Climent de Taüll is an exquisite Unesco-listed Romanesque church.

01
A day

You *could* cross the park in a day, and who are we to advise against it? The views as you cross between east and west are some of the most spectacular anywhere in Spain and possibly even Europe. But you don't have to go to such lengths to enjoy the park's best scenery and you'll be amply rewarded if you spend your day exploring Llong and Llobreta, the two main valleys in the west. Llong in particular captures the essence of the park's appeal: lammergeiers soar above on the thermals and

the valley's bowl – at once vast and intimate – feels like a natural amphitheatre.

Climb the moraine off the lake's northeastern tip and watch for the fortress-like outcrops of Agujas Perdut away to the southeast. It's here that you'll find the iconic 600-year-old black pine; the equally celebrated dwarf pine is trackside en route back to Estany de Llobreta. Llobreta is fed by the Cascada de Sant Esperit waterfall and its shoreline turns autumnal yellow in September.

02
Two days

After the exertions of day one, sit back and enjoy a drive. Base yourself at Taüll and spend the morning exploring the Vall de Boí and its unforgettable Romanesque churches. Follow the valley's southwestern descent along the L500, then veer south on the N230 and east on the N260. As you shadow the park's southern boundary, the hamlets of Perves and Peramea look for all the world like Tuscan hill towns.

Detour north up the L503 to Cabdella, which is

surrounded by mountains. Back on the N260, the road turns north, with a detour into the park along the LV5004 from Espot, then climbs, following switchback upon hairpin bend all the way to the Puerto de la Bonaigua. Further on, the Vall d'Aran is a pretty ski centre, while the final southward sweep offers magnificent views of the park's Besiberri Massif, which includes the Pic de Comolaforno, the park's highest peak, on your left as you return to the Vall de Boí.

04

Parco Nazionale dell' Arcipelago di La Maddalena

A pink-granite wonderland fringed by seas of kaleidoscopic blue, this Italian archipelago between Corsica and Sardinia begs to be dived, strolled and swooned over.

Your boat bobs below weather-beaten licks of pink granite in the Bocche di Bonifacio, the strait that draws a rich ribbon of blue between Sardinia and Corsica. As the sun beams down, you're grateful for the northwesterly *maestrale* (breezes), which have sculpted La Maddalena archipelago's rocks over millennia. Rounding a headland, you spy an island necklaced with white-sand coves and plumed with dark pines. Just as you think it couldn't get more ravishing, a pod of dolphins appears on cue, frolicking breathtakingly close in water fading from azure to deepest sapphire.

Such enthralling moments are the norm in this vast marine park, sprinkled with 62 islands and islets dropped like stepping stones between the northeastern coast of Sardinia and Corsica. The seven main islands are the heights of a valley that now lies submerged – an Atlantis of sorts. But La Maddalena's isles predate such myths. They rose up in the late Paleozoic era, some 300 million years ago, when the continents of Euramerica and Gondwana collided to form the supercontinent of Pangaea. Surprising, then, that aside from the odd inquisitive Roman, the islands lay deserted until the mid-17th century, when a few shepherds from Corsica arrived on La Maddalena.

Visit today and you can't help but think that that old warhorse Giuseppe Garibaldi was on to something when he snapped up the entire island of Caprera in the mid-19th century and called it his 'Eden'. Indeed, whether you dive in barracuda-filled waters, wander through holm oak and juniper that hum with cicada song, or drop anchor at a cove discreetly tucked amid ragged granite cliffs, you'll be inclined to agree that this national park is a little slice of heaven.

⬇ The turquoise bay of Cala Coticcio on the island of Caprera is just one of many perfect places to swim.

Shutterstock | Elisa Locci, Getty Images | DEA / P. JACCOD

Toolbox

When to go
The season runs from Easter to October. Spring and autumn are best for dolphin, whale and bird watching (this is an important trans-Saharan migration stopover). Temperatures soar and room rates skyrocket in July and August.

Getting there
The nearest airport is in Olbia, a 45-minute drive south of Palau. Frequent ferries run between Palau and La Maddalena. The crossing takes 15 minutes. La Maddalena is linked to Caprera by a causeway.

Park in numbers

150
Marine surface area covered (sq km)

7
Number of main islands (plus 55 granite islets)

2006
Year the park appeared on a tentative list of Unesco World Heritage Sites

Hike this...

01 Mount Tejalone
Pine greens and sea blues dominate on this short but memorable walk up a stone staircase to Tejalone (212m), Caprera's highest point. Look out for royal seagulls, cormorants and peregrine falcons.

02 Punta Crucitta
Starting at Arbuticci fort, this 1¼-hour ramble takes you to Caprera's northernmost corner. Look out for birds of prey as you pick your way through wind-licked formations of pink granite.

03 Punta Crucitta to Candeo
Threading the northern cost of Caprera, this 1½-hour circular trail links the sturdy fortifications in Arbuticci with the whimsical, rock-built ones in Candeo.

Stay here...

 Residenza Mordini
The welcome is heartfelt at this guest house near La Maddalena's harbour. Rooms ooze rustic charm, with 18th-century antique furnishings. After a day on the trail or *la spiaggia* (the beach), hang out in the garden or hot tub out the back.

Hotel Capo d'Orso Thalasso & Spa
A pebble's throw from Palau, this luxe beachfront number gazes over to La Maddalena. It's five star all the way, with a *thalasso*-focused spa, sea-view pools, gardens planted with juniper and olive, and a restaurant where you can dig into locally caught lobster and spider crab.

Do this!

Island hopping by boat
See the park from the water, taking in cove-necklaced Spargi, Razzoli, and Budelli with its gorgeous (and off-limits) Spiaggia Rosa, so named for the pink tint of its sands. Numerous companies offer boat trips, including Elena Tour, with time for lunch, swims and snorkelling.

 Diving
Moray eels and shoals of damselfish, scorpionfish, groupers and barracudas dart among granite rocks, drop-offs, overhangs and caves. Some of the Med's finest marine life and dive sites are right here. Looking for a school? Try PADI-accredited Nautilus in Palau.

What to spot...

Geckos and Hermann's tortoises hide among coastal macchia of myrtle, juniper, lentisk and broom. Bottlenose dolphins and fin whales glide through the sea, while Audouin's gulls and peregrine falcons swoop overhead.

FIN WHALE Measuring up to a whopping 22m, fin whales are Earth's second-largest mammal. They come to La Maddalena to feast on krill and schooling fish.

Itinerary

Island hop to pink-granite isles, swim in translucent waters and feel the revolutionary spirit at Garibaldi's residence.

01
Three days

Buongiorno! An espresso shot and you're off on the ferry from Palau, slicing through topaz waters to pink-granite La Maddalena. Get acquainted with the main island, hanging out in its harbourside cafes and cobbled piazzas. Or hire wheels to zip around the 20km panoramic road that loops the island. Pause to swim in crystal-clear bays like Giardinelli, Monti della Rena and Cala Spalmatore. Cap off the day with super-fresh seafood at Il Ghiottone.

On day two, cross the causeway to the rocky, pine-brushed isle of Caprera, where you can strike out on walking trails: hike to 212m Tejalone for broad views and to spot hovering falcons. Devote an hour to touring the former residence of Giuseppe Garibaldi, professional revolutionary and all-round Italian hero. Tie this in with a refreshing paddle in aquamarine water at temptingly nearby coves like Cala Coticcio. On your third day, either boat it out to neighbouring islands or dive deep in the marine park.

05

Atlantic Islands of Galicia National Park

The three islands of Illas Cíes dominate northwestern Spain's Atlantic Islands of Galicia National Park with wild coastal scenery, prolific birdlife and glorious beaches.

If it weren't for Galicia's rather unpredictable weather, the Costa del Sol might never have happened. Instead, beachgoers would have flown into Vigo and colonised en masse the Illas Cíes, the heart and soul of the Parque Nacional de las Islas Atlánticas de Galicia. If you happen upon these islands on a sunny day and the Atlantic winds drop, you'll find yourself wondering why this place isn't crawling with visitors. Then, in the amount of time it takes to lay your towel upon an empty stretch of sand or raise your binoculars to identify one of the islands' seabirds, you'll be giving thanks for the squally winds and scudding clouds that are surely not far away and that have preserved the Illas Cíes in a state of protected near-perfection.

Human habitation on the islands has ebbed and flowed down through the centuries. Monastic orders and pirates made the islands their own in medieval times. Although the islands' human history is a story of retreat and separation from the rest of Spain, these islands are semi-submerged mountain peaks from the same range that rises above the Galician coast, marooned at sea a mere two million years ago when the land east of here subsided and sea levels rose.

Although the national park encompasses four archipelagos – Cíes, Ons, Sálvora and Cortegada – it is Cíes that most appeals. Its three islands – Monteagudo (Sharp Mount) in the north, Do Faro (Lighthouse Island) in the middle and San Martiño (St Martin) to the south – are dramatic granite upthrusts from the sea. Wild Atlantic winds buffet vertical cliffs along the islands' western coasts – cliffs that shelter the world's largest colony of seagulls – leaving the east coast to those splendid beaches that may just amount to Europe's best-kept secret.

Toolbox

 When to go
Public boats to Cíes normally only sail during Semana Santa (Holy Week), on weekends and holidays in May, daily from June to late September, and on the first two weekends of October. Winter here, when boats can usually be found on an ad hoc basis, has its own wild-and-windswept charm.

Getting there
Atlantic Islands of Galicia National Park lies off Spain's far northwestern coast and is accessible from Vigo, Sanxenxo and Portonovo.

Park in numbers

84.8
Area covered (sq km)

197
Highest point: Alto das Cíes on Monteagudo (m)

22,000
Number of seagull pairs on Cíes archipelago

Stay here...

 Gran Hotel Nagari Boutique & Spa
Vigo is the most rewarding base for visiting the Cíes islands, and the city's compact old town and lively eating scene make it an attractive counterpoint to the wilds of the islands. Just a few blocks from the water and convenient for island departures, luxurious Nagari has a personal feel to its contemporary design and service. Rooms boast giant-headed showers, remote-controlled colour-changing lighting, coffee makers and big-screen smart TVs, and there's a rooftop heated pool and terrace with fabulous views.

Hotel América
Also in Vigo, the América has well-equipped, spacious rooms with modern art and elegant colour schemes; friendly, efficient staff; and a quiet side-street location near the waterfront. Breakfast is a buffet-style affair, served on the roof terrace.

Hotel Rotilio
Stylish and comfortable Rotilio in Sanxenxo overlooks Praia de Silgar beach. The 39 all-sea-view rooms are bright and pretty, and there's a fine restaurant. There's a five-night minimum stay from mid-July to the end of August.

Do this!

 Finding the perfect beach
Just over a decade ago, the *Guardian* newspaper in the UK announced its pick for the world's best beach. And the beach it chose was not in the Seychelles or the Caribbean but Monteagudo's Praia dos Rodas. We know what it meant: Rodas is a faultless 1km-long arc on the sandy isthmus joining Illa de Monteagudo and Illa do Faro, with dunes as a backdrop from which to gaze out to the quiet lagoon's turquoise waters.

Birdwatching
Birdwatchers love the Illas de Cíes, a haven for some of the best seabird spotting in Spain. The seagulls may get all the headlines by sheer weight of numbers, but birds of prey, petrels, pelicans and elusive Iberian guillemots are also present, with migratory species pausing here en route to/from Africa.

Walking
Walking trails skirt the shores of the Cíes islands and the Illa de Ons. One particular favourite is the climb up to the high lookout along the Ruta Monte Faro. With no climb rising 200m above sea level, hiking here is usually far more spectacular than taxing.

◀ The remarkable Monte Faro on Do Faro (Lighthouse Island), Illas Cíes.

Hike this...

01 Ruta Monte Faro
The popular, 7km-return Ruta Monte Faro is a gentle climb, save for the last push to the lighthouse, which entails a series of steepish switchbacks.

02 Ruta de Monteagudo
This is a gentle 5km-return stroll along the spine of Monteagudo, following the contours of the island's interior to ensure no steep ascents and passing through forests along the way.

03 Ruta del Alto del Príncipe
Beginning by the sands of Praia dos Rodas, this 3km walk crosses Monteagudo island, allowing you to see the transition from quiet lagoon to Atlantic hinterland.

What to spot...

Birdlife dominates these islands, whose otherwise inaccessible cliffs provide safe nesting sites for all manner of seabirds. Seagulls in particular cling to every square inch of cliff space and their vast colonies animate the dark granite walls. There are bird hides at Alto da Campa (Illa do Faro) and Faro do Peito (San Martiño).

Common trees include wild figs and Pyrenean oaks as well as plantations of pine and eucalyptus, while dolphins and more than 200 species of seaweed inhabit the waters.

SEA PINK The gloriously named sea pink is under threat in Spain but thrives on the Cíes islands. While usually pink, its flowers can also be purple, red or white. In Galicia they call it the 'love plant'.

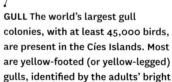

GULL The world's largest gull colonies, with at least 45,000 birds, are present in the Cíes Islands. Most are yellow-footed (or yellow-legged) gulls, identified by the adults' bright yellow legs and beak.

IBERIAN GUILLEMOT If you spot this attractive bird – with white front and black head and back – you've hit the jackpot: they're almost extinct, their population ravaged by a 2002 oil spill.

Getty Images | Jc_cantero, Jose A. Bernat Bacete, Gonzalo Azumendi

Itineraries

The islands of this national park add a whole new dimension to your exploration of Spain's stirring northwestern coast, rounding out the prevailing sense of a wild and untamed land with beauty and birdlife.

◧ Rugged Illas Cíes is famed for its sea birds and is much beloved by birdwatchers.

◨ Solar-powered Faro da Porta lighthouse was built in 1904.

◨ Idyllic Praia dos Rodas connects Do Faro and Monteagudo islands.

01

A day

If you only have one day, the choice is easy: from Vigo, make the 14km, 45-minute ferry trip to the Cíes islands. To make the most of your time, wander the Praia dos Rodas, the celebrated stretch of sand that connects Monteagudo and Do Faro.

Factor in a lie on the beach and a swim in the sea, perhaps bookended by two hikes – given the scale of things around here, the relatively fit could easily complete the Ruta Monte Faro (7km) and the Ruta de Monteagudo (5km) and still catch the ferry back to Vigo before the sun sets.

Unless you want to miss the best the islands have to offer, don't forget to pack your binoculars (for birdwatching, especially on the western side, around the turnaround point of both hikes) and your swimming costume. If you forget the latter, one cove north of Praia dos Rodas is the Praia das Figueiras, which is clothing optional.

02

Two days

Having sampled the Cíes islands, plan an overnight stay in Vigo or Sanxenxo, which has earned the sobriquet 'the Marbella of Galicia' for its upmarket marina, busy tourism scene and attractive beach. From Sanxenxo a couple of ferry operators do the 45-minute run out to the Illa de Ons several times daily from July to mid-September. The island is 5.6km long, with sandy beaches, cliffs, traces of ruined settlements, rich birdlife, and walking trails that ensure you see most of the island in a day without even breaking a sweat. The island brings to mind an outpost of Scotland, with moorland grasses and vegetation beaten into submission by relentless winds. If you're lucky enough to be here in September you might even have some corners to yourself – the beaches here rival those on the Cíes islands, so bring your swimmers. If you'd like to experience the silence (if you ignore the wind!) that reigns after the day-trippers go home, consider staying overnight – or for a lifetime.

06

Parco Nazionale delle Dolomiti Bellunesi

Skirted by pea-green valleys, Italy's lesser-known Dolomites are a humbling, heart-soaring vision. Pale-grey mountains pierce the sky – architect Le Corbusier called them 'the world's most beautiful buildings'.

A grass-carpeted valley, birds chirping in the bottle-green trees, a twinkling brook: this bucolic scene is sheltered by a castellated line of mountains, formed of an almost luminescent pale rock. The drama is heightened by the contrast between the soft, gentle curves of the pastures and the sudden eruption of vast, sculptural mountains, each prong like a cathedral tower.

This is geology as theatre. The scenic drama has been formed through the different consistency and brittleness of the rock, which has allowed erosion to sculpt it into jagged shapes, and hollow out deep, wide valleys and corridor-narrow gorges.

Before the last ice age, 250 million years ago, this area was part of a prehistoric coral reef in the primordial ocean, Tethys. As the sea disappeared, the rocks beneath rose to form the range and are consequently rich in prehistoric fossils. The Dolomites were named after 19th-century geologist Déodat de Dolomieu, who was first to analyse the rocks.

Neanderthals hunted huge mammals in this zone over 40,000 years ago, while *Homo sapiens* arrived 10 millennia later to mine flint. The first villages began to take root around 6000 BC. Later Romans, Byzantines, Lombards, Franks and Venetians all staked their claim here. In the 18th and 19th centuries the area passed from French to Austrian hands, eventually becoming part of the kingdom of the House of Savoy. However, the most recent tumultuous period of history was WWI, when the Dolomites became an unimaginably challenging battleground between Austria-Hungary and Italy. Its castle-like turrets and gully defences made

the mountains a natural, harsh fortress. Monuments to the dead and traces of many military routes remain – the famous *vie ferrate* (iron roads) consisting of metal tracks and lines across the rocks are still climbable and walkable today.

⬆ A walker pauses beneath mighty Monte Pelmo (3168m). Previous page: the Bec de Mesdi peak seems to nudge the clouds.
➡ The lakeside village of Alleghe dwarfed by Monte Civetta (3220m).

Toolbox

When to go
Spring is one of the best times to visit, with mostly sunny skies and temperate weather, and wild flowers speckling the hills and valleys. Climbing and hiking are best from June to October; ski season is from December until March-April.

Getting there
Just south of the northern Italian park, the historic town of Belluno is the main gateway to the park (two others are Feltre and Zoldo) and is accessible by train from Venice in 2½ hours.

Park in numbers

315
Area covered (sq km)

2547
Highest point: Sass de Mura (m)

2000
Population of chamois

↑ It's an easy hike to visit the 15 cool green pools of Cadini del Brentòn in Valle del Mis.

Stay here...

Alla Casetta
In a secluded setting – a lone house in a small valley on the Caorame river – this is nonetheless only 6km from the small Renaissance and medieval town of Feltre. Rooms have pine-beamed ceilings and windows framing wooded mountain views. Hosts Christian and Anna supply everything from hand-drawn trekking and biking maps to advice on where to kayak or buy cheese.

B&B Villa San Liberale
A pale-walled countryside villa with shuttered windows, this is another glorious place just outside the park gateway of Feltre. It's full of character, charm and antiques, and surrounded by carefully tended gardens with lawns and flowers.

B&B Villa Rosa
A dark-red and white Venetian villa set in lovely deep-green countryside, this has magnificent views and a choice of apartments or B&B rooms. There's a cosy family atmosphere and simple, charming rooms with wooden furnishings and take-your-breath-away mountain panoramas.

Do this!

Climbing
The steep, towering peaks of the Dolomites are a playground of rock-climbing opportunities for both beginners and experienced climbers, and the outlying Bellenesi park is far less frequented than the Brenta area of this epic mountain range. The park offers some challenging, breathtaking climbs, including five *via ferrata* routes that originated to aid military advances across these inhospitable borderlands during WWI. These metal cables fixed into the rock allow mere mortals access to some of the most dazzling peaks, but you'll need climbing experience and a head for heights.

Botanical treasure-hunting
Renowned botanically since the 17th century, the area remains famous for its rare flora. Remote grass-cloaked hills and valleys are speckled by the delicate beauty of flowers such as the black-vanilla orchid, the alpine snowdrop and the violet, star-shaped *Campanula morettiana*, the symbol of the park.

Horse riding and donkey trekking
Explore this pristine wilderness on horseback or more slowly with donkeys. Wending along narrow pathways is one of the most peaceful ways to travel through the park, with the sense of travelling here as others have for centuries.

What to spot...

The park could make a botanist weep with the abundance of rarities. High-altitude blooms include varieties of lily, crucifera, orchid and primrose. Forests knit across the landscape, including beech, conifers, pine, oak and silver fir. Chamois flit through the trees, sharing the territory with mouflon, roe deer, hares, foxes, badgers, ermines, weasels, martens, marmots, squirrels, hedgehogs and the rare Eurasian lynx. Golden eagles and rock partridges are among 115 species of bird that whir overhead or shelter in the undergrowth.

MARMOT Inconceivably ancient in origin (fossil evidence demonstrates they were in Europe around 600,000 years ago), these small, furry burrowing creatures with chisel-like teeth were hunted to extinction here but were reintroduced in 2007.

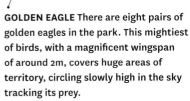

GOLDEN EAGLE There are eight pairs of golden eagles in the park. This mightiest of birds, with a magnificent wingspan of around 2m, covers huge areas of territory, circling slowly high in the sky tracking its prey.

EURASIAN LYNX Long a stranger to the area, the lynx is back: tracks have been discovered in one of the most inaccessible areas, the Monti del Sole mountains, only a few kilometres from Belluno.

Hike this...

01 Cadini del Brentòn

This 1km walk in Valle del Mis takes you past 15 translucent pools carved out by a series of small waterfalls.

02 Trail 803

This trail wends through the botanically fascinating valleys of San Martino and Fratta and takes around 7½ hours, starting at the village of Vignui (533m).

03 Alta Via 1

One of six high-altitude trails across the Dolomites, this begins at Lago di Braies in Val Pusteria to the north and ends in Belluno; it takes 13 days, covering 150km.

Itineraries

Enjoy some alpine Venetian splendour, sample high-altitude trails, enjoy adrenaline-pumping sports, and get set up for it all with some (delicious) fried cheese.

◀ The imposing walls of La Croda del Becco reflected in the serene waters of Lago di Braies.
▶ The cliffs of Monte Pelmo loom over a herd of horses.

01
Four days

Start your exploration in the major gateway to the national park, the graceful Venetian town of Belluno. It's a harmonious sprawl of red-roofed pastel palazzi dominated by a soaring and elegant cathedral spire and dwarfed by the thrilling, magnificent, silver-grey Dolomites. Once an important trading post on the way north and a favoured summer bolthole, it makes an ideal base for the park, and from here you can explore walking trails northwest into the shimmering mountains,

from easy trails to because-it's-there mountaineering, exploring areas such as the ravines and furrows of the Valle dell'Ardo. Alta Via (high-altitude trail) 1, one of eight such trails across the range, ends at Belluno. You're also well placed to fortify yourself with some particularly sumptuous cheeses, including Schiz (semi-soft cow's-milk cheese, usually fried in butter) and yolk-yellow Malga Bellunese.

After spending a couple of days exploring the countryside from Belluno,

take a short trip to explore from the other major base for the park, the town of Feltre, 20km southwest of Belluno. Feltre predates the Romans and was mentioned by Pliny. It lies on the Stizzon River and has a fine Renaissance historic centre. From here you can discover the secluded, open valleys of Lamen and San Martino – look for the small potholes eroded by the Colmeda stream – with the crowning Vette Feltrine forming a magnificent backdrop leading up to Monte Pavione (2334m).

02
A week

This circular driving route takes you through thrilling green-and-grey natural splendour – visual soul food. It cuts through the centre of the park, where the route passes through inky-green woodlands and green-cloaked hills and valleys, drawing your eyes up to the folds and summits of the pale mountains above.

Start the trip in Belluno, the Christmas card-pretty Venetian alpine town, then take the road around 20km northwest to Agordo. This mountain base is the

starting point for many trails into forgotten-feeling valleys such as the Canali, Gares or San Lucano, from where you can take a breathtaking yet easygoing walk to the Cascate dell'Inferno waterfalls.

Next you can move on to the beautiful lakeside town of Alleghe, where pointed rooftops are backed by thick forest and pale peaks, all reflected in the green-blue waters of the lake – popular for boating in summer and skating in winter. This is

a popular ski town too, with runs across the surrounding hills.

The journey continues 10km further to Selva di Cadore, a mountain village huddled around its rocket-like church steeple, with the silver and grey bulk of Monte Pelmo (3168m) looming nearby. Your final halt is at pointed-roofed Forno di Zoldo, a 20-minute drive away, which also makes for another good ski base in season. From here you can take the road back down to Belluno.

07

Berchtesgaden National Park

Be floored by mountains of myth, fjord-like lakes and lookout eyries in Germany's Bavarian hiking heartland, where views send spirits soaring like the region's golden eagles.

Many millennia ago, lore has it, King Watzmann ruled Berchtesgaden with an iron fist, striking fear into farmers by chaining them to their ploughs like lowly oxen. But the king got his comeuppance and was turned to stone for his evil deeds. He now reigns over Berchtesgaden as Watzmann mountain (2713m), terrifying only those who dare climb his notorious Ostwand (East Face). Some say it is a fate too good for such a tyrant, surveying, as he does, a canvas of glacier-encrusted peaks, torrents and wild forests bejewelled with lakes from his rocky throne.

Indeed there is something almost regal about Berchtesgaden National Park, with its procession of mountains just shy of 3000m, which wear pearly crowns of snow in winter. Here nature pulls out all the stops, with big-shouldered peaks muscling in among rugged gorges and wild-flower-freckled pastures that recall the opening credits of *The Sound of Music* – no coincidence, incidentally, as they were filmed in this neck of the woods.

Wedged into Bavaria's southeastern crook, where the Northern Limestone Alps ripple across to Austria, the park was founded in 1978, but its origins stretch back aeons. Its phalanx of peaks was created by tectonic uplift some 770 million years ago and has been shaped by glacial erosion ever since.

Wax lyrical we might, but it isn't until you explore on foot the park's wilderness that you see what all the fuss is about. Nothing can convey what it feels like to witness dawn from an alpine hut as the first sunlight creeps over the mountains, or the exhilaration of reaching a summit as sunset pinkens the sky and ibex come out to graze. '*Der Berg ruft*' – the mountain calls, say the Bavarians. And never more so than here.

Toolbox

When to go
Summer is hiking prime time, with snow-free trails, mild weather (bar the odd thunderstorm) and Alpine huts open. Hikes at lower elevations are doable in late spring, when the pastures are cloaked with wild flowers. In autumn, forests kindle into colour and game features on inn menus.

Getting there
The park nuzzles the Austrian border 26km south of Salzburg, where the nearest airport is located. A great base is Berchtesgaden, which has a decent public-transport network.

Park in numbers

210
Area covered (sq km)

2713
(m) Highest peak: Watzmann (Germany's second highest)

1990
Year the park became a biosphere reserve

⬇ This view of the Königssee is called Malerwinkel (Painters' Corner) for good reason.

Stay here...

Watzmannhaus
These rustic Alpine digs sit bang in the heart of the national park at 1930m. A bolthole for mountaineers since 1888, the lodge creaks with history and perches precariously on a rocky outcrop, commanding 360-degree views. Accommodation consists of no-frills dorms, and dinners are simple but hearty. This is the ideal jumping-off point for hikes – the four-day Watzmanntour included – and ascents of Watzmann itself. The hut opens from late May to early October.

Hotel Krone
This family-run affair in Berchtesgaden has staggering views of the valley and the Alps beyond. The wood-rich, cabin-style rooms are cosy. Breakfast on the suntrap terrace for a memorable start to the day.

Pension Seeklause
Every inch the mountain idyll, this chalet sits on the shore of Hintersee. The welcome is heartfelt, the rooms spacious, quiet and pine clad, and the terrace an incredibly scenic spot for dinner.

Do this!

Exploring the Eagle's Nest
The Eagle's Nest was built as a mountaintop retreat for Hitler's 50th birthday. It took 3000 workers two years to hack out the precipitous 6km mountain road and cut the 124m-long tunnel. The Royal Air Force destroyed his Alpine fortress, but the Eagle's Nest was left unscathed. The history is sinister, but the views are sensational.

Boating the Königssee
Mountains huddle conspiratorially above the ludicrously photogenic Königssee. Hop aboard an electric boat for photo ops of the domed chapel of St Bartholomä and to hear the captain play an alphorn towards the echo wall.

Walking the Wimbach Gorge
Nature unleashes its full force at this sheer-walled ravine, slicing through forest and mountains between Ramsau and Berchtesgaden. The river is a crash-bang spectacle, while waterfalls spill in silky threads down the rock faces. Open May to October.

Hike this...

01 St Bartholomä to Eiskapelle
This mind-blowingly scenic 6km hike leads from St Bartholomä on the shores of Königssee to the Eiskapelle, an ice cave at the foot of Watzmann's fearsome east face.

02 Watzmanntour
This challenging four-day trek delves deep into the Berchtesgaden Alps, with overnights at the Watzmannhaus, Wimbachgrieshütte and Kärlinger Haus.

03 Mitterkaseralm, Jenner
Starting at Königssee, this half-day, 9.3km hike is pure Alpine drama, leading to a 1534m mountain hut. Add 5.5km to reach the summit (1874m) for sublime views of Königssee and 100 German and Austrian peaks.

What to spot...

Berchtesgaden is pure Alpine, with montane and subalpine forests (typically plumed with spruce, larch and mountain pine), meadows, high moors, torrents, glaciers and chiselled limestone peaks. Spring brings a profusion of wild flowers, such as gentians, pulsatilla, cyclamens, edelweiss, buttercups, orchids and Alpine rhododendrons. Species to watch out for include ibex, chamois, red deer, marmots, blue hares and capercaillies. Golden eagles, hawks, woodpeckers and warblers can often be sighted flying overhead.

BLUE HARE
Also known as the mountain hare, the blue hare likes montane grasslands and is the master of camouflage, changing its fur from brown (summer) to white (winter).

GENTIAN
These deep-purplish-blue, trumpet-shaped flowers herald summer on the park's mountain slopes. They are highly prized by herbalists for their medicinal properties.

ALPINE SALAMANDER
Endemic to the Alps, this shiny black salamander lives at elevations between 700m and 2500m. Gestation is incredibly long: two to three years.

Itineraries

Putter across the jewel-coloured Königssee in the morning sun, puff up to Alpine peaks for views reaching deep into Austria and bus it up to Hitler's eyrie-like Eagle's Nest.

◧ Berchtesgaden is a great place to spot Alpine ibex.

◩ The dramatic pyramid of Watzmann is unforgettable.

◪ A boathouse on lake Obersee; Obersee was once part of Königssee, but one lake became two after a massive rockfall in 1172 created two separate lakes.

01

Two days

Go straight for the scenic bull's-eye by taking a boat across the bottle-green Königssee, gazing up at Watzmann's arrow-shaped peak. It's a tad touristy, sure, but you can't help those goosebumps when the captain plays his horn to the echo wall. Tack on a short hike from the onion-domed chapel of St Bartholomä to the Eiskapelle (Ice Chapel), the lowest-lying permanent snowfield in the Alps. Cap the day off with a meal made with locally sourced ingredients, and a cold foamy one in the beer garden at Gaststätte St Bartholomä.

On day two, begin, say, with a hike to Jenner's 1874m summit for views of the Alps rolling into neighbouring Austria. In the afternoon, take the shuttle up the windy road to the Eagle's Nest, Hitler's impossibly perched Alpine HQ. If this dark chapter in history piques your curiosity, find out more at Dokumentation Obersalzberg, 3km from Berchtesgaden, which chronicles how this sleepy village became the second seat of Nazi power after Berlin.

02

Four days

If you're fit and up for a challenge, devote the entire four days to the hut-to-hut Watzmanntour, penetrating the furthest reaches of the Berchtesgaden Alps. Otherwise, follow the two-day itinerary, then on the third day factor in a breather in Berchtesgaden. You could, for instance, head to Salzbergwerk. Once a major producer of 'white gold', the town's salt mines now offer 90-minute tours, where you whoosh down a wooden slide to a grotto and subterranean lake. Or ease trek-tired feet at the Watzmann Therme, a spa and thermal baths with big Alpine views. Dinner is in the best of Bavarian traditions, with pork roast, lashings of dumplings and Weizen (wheat beer) at the vaulted Bräustübl beer hall.

On day four, walk into the mist-laced Wimbach Gorge, where a river rages past sheer limestone walls. Go for a dip or paddle in the gem-hued Hintersee. Linger over lake fish grilled simply on the terrace at Pension Seeklause as the last sunlight creeps over the water and mountains.

08

Black Forest National Park

With glacier-carved valleys and dark spruce forests cloaking hills that seem to ripple to infinity, Germany's newest national park is every inch the Grimm fairy tale.

Morning lifts a misty veil on a forest of pine, spruce and beech as sun rays rake through the treetops to spotlight a red squirrel scampering high in the branches, velvety purple foxgloves and ferns uncoiling lazily, their fronds stretching to reach the light. The only sound at this hour is the tentative hammering of a woodpecker, the distant gurgle of a clear mountain stream and your feet falling rhythmically on rock as you stride through this forest of myth. In this lonely neck of the woods, as the forest shakes off its dewy slumber, the trail is yours alone.

Few forests have been as eulogised and romanticised as the Schwarzwald, so named because when the Romans first came here, they found a dark, murky, near-impenetrable Silva Nigra (Black Forest). Fast-forward 2000 years and the region still feels immune to time and trends. Mountains pucker above vast tracts of forest and the gentle pleats and folds of valleys. Heather-flecked moorland dips down to the icy blue-green glint of glacial lakes, and wood shingle–tiled farmhouses crouch low beside swift-flowing brooks.

Tiptoe away from the villages and you'll find pockets of pure wilderness, the finest of which are showcased in the Black Forest National Park, established in 2014. It sits astride the main crest of the Northern Black Forest, between the Murgtal valley and the Black Forest High Rd (B500), a ribbon stitching together the park's corset of mountains, valleys, high moors and cirque lakes. There is something poetic about the way the park unfolds around you as you strike out into its remotest reaches, where silence blankets the woods and the scenery is the stuff of bedtime stories.

⬆ The Black Forest's famously verdant flora surrounds a footbridge over the Neckar river.

Toolbox

When to go
The park never feels overcrowded. Go in summer for sap-scented strolls and lake swims, in winter for Christmas-card scenery and cross-country skiing. Late spring brings wild flowers, autumn the delights of fungi foraging, gold-tinged beech forests and stag rutting.

Getting there
The park sits in the Northern Black Forest in southwestern Germany, alongside the French border. The nearest airport is Karlsruhe/Baden-Baden, 41km north. The B500 runs through the heart of the park to the visitor centre in Ruhestein.

Park in numbers

100.6
Area covered (sq km)

1164
Highest peak: Hornisgrinde (m)

15,000
Years since the last glacial period

Hike this...

O1 Mummelsee to Hornisgrinde
This 1.5km hike heads from the glacial cirque lake of Mummelsee up to 1164m Hornisgrinde for knockout views over the Black Forest to the Vosges beyond.

O2 Dunkle Augen
'Dark Eyes' is a moderately challenging 16km hike that begins at Ruhestein visitor centre and embraces moorland, primeval forest and glacier-gouged lakes, and affords far-reaching views of the Rhine Plain and Vosges.

O3 Allerheiligen Falls
This 3.5km circuit takes in a ruined Gothic abbey before heading through a lushly wooded gorge to the 90m Allerheiligen Falls, spilling in silky threads over several cascades.

Stay here...

 Schliffkopf Wellness & Nature Hotel
Bang in the heart of the national park, this hilltop hotel has big views and hikes on its doorstep. Rooms are large and peaceful, and there's a spa and outdoor pool for relaxing after a day's walking. Meals play up seasonal, farm-fresh food.

 Berghotel Mummelsee
Sitting on the shores of Mummelsee, this lodge has rooms done out in modern country style and plenty of pine. The best have balconies overlooking the lake and forest. There's a little spa area, a sauna and a wood-panelled restaurant rustling up regional grub.

Do this!

Driving the Black Forest High Road
Swinging 81km from Baden-Baden to Freudenstadt, the Black Forest High Rd is a classic road trip. The vertiginous route dips into the national park and provides constant views over wood-cloaked hill and dale. Detour to Baiersbronn for lunch at one of its two three-Michelin-starred restaurants.

Foraging
Grab a basket and get foraging. The Black Forest has bountiful berries and wild herbs – buckthorn, dill, bear's garlic – in summer, and mushrooms (mostly Boletus) pop up in autumn. Ask local tourist offices to point you in the right direction.

What to spot...

Pine, spruce, larch and beech shelter red deer and pine martens. Among the birds are woodpeckers (including the rare three-toed variety), peregrine falcons, pygmy owls and capercaillie.

TENGMALM'S OWL Small, shy and mottle feathered, the Tengmalm's owl (also known as the boreal owl) likes dense coniferous forest and uses woodpecker cavities for nesting.

Itinerary

Drive to mountain lookouts, wispy waterfalls and gorge trails via mile after pine-scented mile of forest.

01

A day

Slip behind the wheel for a staggeringly scenic drive into the park on the Black Forest High Rd (B500), pausing for some cracking viewpoints en route. Start in the genteel spa town of Baden-Baden. Pause to admire Geroldsauer Waterfalls, which inspired German composer Brahms and French painter Courbet. Nearby is the 1007m peak of Mehliskopf, whose slopes attract families seeking low-key adventure. Cruising further south brings you to Breitenbrunnen game reserve for eye-to-eye encounters with deer and wild boar. An underwater king and nymphs are said to dwell in the inky, forest-rimmed depths of glacial cirque lake Mummelsee, close by. Row across it, stroll its shores or ramble 1.5km uphill to 1164m Hornisgrinde. Detour briefly west to Allerheiligen, where a 3.5km trail leads from Gothic abbey ruins through a wooded gorge to impressive falls. Push on south to the town of Freudenstadt, home to Germany's largest town square.

09

Brecon Beacons National Park

Bleak but beautiful hills and moors, historic forts, sturdy castles, lively festivals and a reputation for great food combine in south Wales' finest national park.

Bald hills stretch across south Wales in a dramatic ripple of high mountain plateaus, wild, open moorland and rolling green hills. It's a mystical landscape where prehistoric chieftains were buried on lonely hilltops and heavy stones were dragged to create stone circles that are thought to have played a part in complex pagan rituals.

The allure of the hills is undeniable and for eight millennia humans have shaped the land and the culture here, with standing stones, Neolithic tombs and Iron Age hill forts littering the slopes. Early Christian chapels lie in remote valleys, and Norman castles, such as magnificent Carreg Cennen, perch on limestone crags, mighty symbols of medieval power, wealth and territorial struggle.

It was the Industrial Revolution of the late 18th century that brought the greatest change to the area, however, with quarries and mines opening up across the landscape and the building of canals and rail lines to transport limestone, coal and iron through the wilds.

The hills are formed from ancient red sandstone, cleaved by gushing rivers that cut through the soft rock and carved the park into four distinct sections. The most remote is the wild and desolate Black Mountain region to the west, with its high moors and glacial lakes. To the south, outcrops of carboniferous limestone have been sculpted by water to form deep, wooded gorges dotted with waterfalls, caves and sinkholes, while the lowlands are a pastoral idyll of rolling green fields and lacy hedgerows.

This magnificent natural setting has become an outdoor playground for all, with elite units of the British Army training in the most wild and remote hills, mountain bikers

whizzing down steep slopes and parents of young children inspiring a love of the great outdoors on manageable walks that offer spectacular views from dramatic peaks.

⬆ The summit cairn of Pen-y-Fan (886m), south Wales' highest peak. Previous page: Carreg Cennen Castle has surveyed the rolling Beacons since the 13th century.

Toolbox

When to go
Come in May for the Hay Festival, in summer for hiking and biking, and in August for Green Man, one of the UK's best music and arts festivals.

Getting there
The Brecon Beacons are in southeastern Wales. Abergavenny, in the southeast of the park, is about an hour's drive from Cardiff airport. A good bus service connects the main centres within the park.

Park in numbers

1347
Area covered (sq km)

886
Highest point:
Pen-y-Fan (m)

8000
Years that humans have been active in the park

Stay here...

Gliffaes Country House Hotel

Experience life in a stately country pile at this Italianate mansion on the River Usk near Crickhowell. The house was built in 1883 and has the charm and elegance of the era, with period furniture, creaky floors and excellent cream teas. It's an atmospheric place at the foot of Myarth Hill, where low mists get trapped in the landscaped gardens, then burn off to reveal a stunning view. You can fish for trout in the grounds, snuggle up with a book by a roaring fire or walk right into the hills.

The Bear

With canoeing, walking and riding on the doorstep, this charming three-room B&B in Hay-on-Wye has an ideal location and oodles of charm. The 16th-century building has exposed-stone walls and original beams, offset by modern fittings.

Llanddeusant Youth Hostel

Tucked away in a remote village in the Black Mountains, this former 18th-century inn offers spectacular views and is within walking distance of Iron Age forts and Roman camps, as well as dramatic Llyn y Fan Fach glacial lake and the Carmarthen Fans.

Do this!

Caving

Riddled with caves and underground passages, the park has almost as much going on underground as above it. Ogof Ffynnon Ddu, Britain's deepest cave at 308m, is the focal point for experienced cavers and has over 50km of eerie passages. Beginners can take on the easily accessible maze of passages at Porth-yr-Ogof, while families can get in on the action with a visit to the National Showcaves Centre, which offers access to three caves, the most impressive of which is Cathedral Cave, a high-domed chamber fed by two waterfalls.

Mountain biking

Brecon Beacons is renowned for its mountain biking, and you can tackle anything from gentle off-road routes to fast descents. For experienced riders the 51km Grwyne Fawr Reservoir route offers fantastic trails through the Black Mountains.

Stargazing

Wrap up and head out under cover of darkness to enjoy big skies, bright stars and meteor showers. With the Milky Way laid before you and ancient ruins framing the view, 11th-century Llanthony Priory is an atmospheric spot to contemplate your place in the universe.

What to spot...

The park encompasses a diverse range of habitats, from exposed upland moors, dry heathland and glacial lakes to sheltered wooded valleys and slow-moving rivers and canals. This diversity provides for an array of flora and fauna, including some endemic species such as native varieties of whitebeam and hawkweed. In the birdlife-rich park, you may spot kestrels, red kites and reed warblers, and large numbers of winter migrants on Llangorse Lake and Talybont Reservoir. Otters and water voles are found along the waterways.

GREAT CRESTED NEWT
This protected species can be seen in ponds from late February to early June. They are dark brown with a bright orange underside and the males have a distinctive jagged crest.

MARSH FRITILLARY BUTTERFLY
In serious decline, this brightly coloured butterfly with orange-and-black-checked wings can be found in damp tussocky grassland, especially around Penderyn in the south of the park.

BADGER
A fat body, short legs and distinctive black-and-white-striped head make the badger instantly recognisable, but its nocturnal behaviour and underground setts make it difficult to spot.

Hike this...

O1 Beacons Horseshoe

The park's most famous hike, this challenging 17km ridge walk takes in three summits, including Pen-y-Fan, and offers spectacular views and Bronze Age cairns en route.

O2 Sugar Loaf

An easy ascent rewarded with stunning views, this is a great 6.5km family hike through oak woodland and open moorland, with only the final section a challenge for little legs.

O3 Four Falls

A magical route following rivers that plunge through wooded gorges and disappear into caves, this 6km walk takes in four waterfalls, including impressive Sgwd yr Eira.

Itineraries

Hike along high ridges with sweeping views, discover ancient ruins in empty valleys, walk behind waterfalls and explore the depths of the Earth in this magnificently diverse park.

← Walkers on the summit of Corn Du make their way to the summit of Pen-y-Fan.
→ It's only a short walk to visit the Sgwd Gwladus (Lady's Falls) on the Afon Pyrddin river.

01

Two days

If you've only got the weekend here you'll get the best overview of the park by combining a scenic drive with some time on foot in the hills.

Start your trip in handsome Hay-on-Wye with a quick browse around the bookshops, then hop in the car and head south onto the deserted moorland of Gospel Pass for epic views of the Black Mountains and the Brecon Beacons. Heading down into the Vale of Ewyas, the landscape gradually becomes greener, and the 12th-century priory ruins and 6th-century St David's Church at Llanthony make an atmospheric stop. Continue south and stop off for a drink at the oldest pub in Wales, the Skirrid Mountain Inn in Llanfihangel Crucorney.

Then pop in to see the priory church in Abergavenny before heading to picturesque Crickhowell and on to Nantyffin Cider Mill for lunch around the cider press.

Continuing north, you'll reach Tretower, with its sturdy Norman tower and 15th-century manor house with medieval garden, from where it's an easy drive back to Hay.

On your second day head for south Wales' highest peak, Pen-y-Fan. You've got a choice of routes to the top, but if you're reasonably fit and the weather holds, an all-day hike up the north side of the mountain is the most rewarding. With few hikers and superb views, the Horseshoe Ridge walk from the Lower Neuadd Reservoir is one of the region's finest; but remember to pack a waterproof jacket.

02

A week

With a week to explore you can discover the back roads and remote ruins of the park, search out its best waterfalls and caves, and find a window in the weather for some serious hiking. Once you've bagged Pen-y-Fan and driven Gospel Pass it's worth spending a day around Georgian Brecon, exploring the cathedral and castle in the morning before hiring a bike for a trip along the canal to Talybont Reservoir or hitting the Mynydd Illtud mountain-biking trail. With a base in Llandovery or Llandeilo, you could spend a day exploring the wild and remote west of the park, visiting impressive cliff-top Carreg Cennen (a medieval castle) and the Red Kite Feeding Station, and taking the tranquil hike up to glorious Llyn y Fan Fach.

Explore Fforest Fawr Geopark with a trip to the National Showcaves, followed by the Four Falls or Henrhyd Falls walks to see the area's gushing waterfalls, possibly topped off with a visit to Penderyn Distillery.

It's also worth spending a day at 4000-year-old Garn Goch hill fort for panoramic views and then walking around Usk Reservoir to Glasfynydd Forest and on to the upper moorland for superb views of Carmarthen Fans, Bannau Sir Gaer and Fan Brycheiniog. On your final day, get out on the water for a gentle paddle along the Wye or the Monmouthshire and Brecon Canal, or experienced kayakers could tackle the white water of the Tawe or Sawdde Rivers.

10

Cairngorms National Park

With a landscape forged from granite and ice, the UK's largest national park is one of the wildest places in Europe outside Norway.

500px | Neil Wakeling

It's mid-July, but despite the sunshine it's cold – very cold. A vast expanse of frost-shattered boulders stretches into the distance, sun glinting off the pink-granite crystals and sparkling on patches of snow as you hike across the tundra-like landscape. Nothing stirs except two golden eagles circling high above. But this isn't Arctic Canada or northern Norway. In fact, you're barely 3km from the car park, and you drove here from Glasgow this morning.

The Cairngorms is the UK's largest national park (it's twice the size of the Lake District), centred on a 1000m-high mountain plateau with a subarctic climate that encompasses five of Britain's six highest summits. Its dramatic landscapes are the legacy of the last ice age, when glaciers gouged deep valleys through granite bedrock and hollowed out crag-rimmed corries on the hills' northern slopes.

Scots pine covered much of the Scottish Highlands as the ice retreated, but a combination of climate change and human felling saw the ancient Caledonian forest reduced to a few small remnants, the most extensive of which survive here in the Cairngorms – Abernethy, Rothiemurchus and Glen Tanar. Rare creatures – capercaillies, red squirrels, pine martens, Scottish wildcats – find refuge among trees more than 300 years old.

The savage conditions on the high plateau mean that it has never seen human habitation, but the lower ground has long been used for sheep farming, forestry and deer stalking. The 1960s saw the development of ski areas at Aviemore, Glenshee and the Lecht, and in 2001 a funicular railway was built almost to the top of Cairn Gorm itself. Controversy ensued, with jobs and tourist income pitched against conservation of the natural environment, a debate that continued after the creation of the national park in 2003.

↑ The Cairngorms is among Scotland's best mountain biking destinations. Previous page: Loch an Eilein is one of the park's most beautiful.

500px | Julien David

Toolbox

When to go
Peak periods are December to February (ski season) and July to August (school holidays). April to June is ideal for birdlife (nesting ospreys) and scenery (snow patches on the mountains). Autumn is the best time for seeing red deer.

Getting there
The Cairngorms lie in the centre of the Scottish Highlands, with Aviemore the main gateway (easily reached by car or train, about three hours from Glasgow or Edinburgh). The nearest airport is Inverness (one hour's drive away).

Park in numbers

4528
Area covered (sq km)

1309
Highest point: Ben Macdui (m)

278
Highest recorded wind speed in UK: Cairn Gorm summit (km/h)

Stay here...

Glenmore Campsite
Located near Aviemore, Glenmore Campsite enjoys one of the finest settings in the national park, with tent, caravan and motorhome pitches spread amid clusters of Scots pines beside a lovely sandy beach on the shores of Loch Morlich. The campsite is the starting point for dozens of superb walks and mountain-bike rides in the surrounding hills and forests, and there is canoeing, dinghy sailing and windsurfing on the loch in summer. The site stays open in winter, when it's popular with snow-sports enthusiasts.

The Cross at Kingussie
Housed in a historic weaving mill on the banks of Gynack Burn, The Cross has long had a reputation as the finest restaurant in the Cairngorms. It also offers luxury B&B accommodation in eight cosy bedrooms, one with a balcony overlooking the river.

Auld Kirk
A converted Victorian church in Ballater provides the setting for this seven-bedroom guest house in the heart of Royal Deeside, where you can enjoy a breakfast prepared using fresh local produce in the light from the Gothic arched windows.

Do this!

Hiking
Exploring the high tundra plateaus, pink-granite crags and deep glacial valleys of the Cairngorms is the quintessential park experience. The park contains 43 of Scotland's 282 Munros (mountains over 3000ft high) and offers superb hillwalking, from relatively easy ascents such as Cairn Gorm and Mount Keen to remote and challenging summits like Cairn Toul and Ben Avon. Easier low-level hikes lead you through ancient Caledonian pine forests to sparkling, peat-tinted lochans, with the chance of spotting rare wildlife such as capercaillies, crossbills, red squirrels and pine martens.

Snow sports
CairnGorm Mountain is the biggest snow-sports centre in the UK, with more than 30km of marked runs. In clear conditions you can ski or snowboard with a view over pine woods and lochans, while experienced ski-mountaineers can go touring on the high plateau.

Dog sledding
The Cairngorm Sleddog Centre is the only place in Britain where you can go dog sledding year-round. Even if there's no snow, you can still hurtle around the forest trails on specially designed wheeled sleds hauled by a team of trained huskies.

What to spot...

The heart of Cairngorms National Park is the high plateau, where the climate is subarctic – snow can fall here even in midsummer. The boulder-strewn landscape supports rare alpine flora and hardy bird species including ptarmigan, snow bunting and dotterel. Heather moorland, famous for its August display of purple flowers, covers 40 percent of the park, while remnants of the post–ice age Caledonian pine forest survive among the foothills and are home to capercaillies, crossbills, pine martens and red squirrels.

SCOTTISH WILDCAT
An endangered species (fewer than 400 are left in the wild), the wildcat is recognised by its short, bushy tail with black stripes and black tip. See it up close at Newtonmore's Highland Wildlife Park.

GOLDEN EAGLE
This iconic Scottish species is one of Europe's largest birds of prey, with a 2m wingspan. They're usually seen soaring overhead as they hunt for ptarmigan and mountain hare.

RED DEER
The largest wild mammal in Britain, red deer roam the hills in herds of up to 50. During the rut (October) males grow impressive antlers and fight for dominance and mating rights.

Hike this...

O1 Loch an Eilein
Wander through pine-scented, sun-dappled glades on an easy loop trail around one of the park's prettiest lochs, graced with a ruined island castle.

O2 Meall a'Bhuachaille
Climb to the 810m summit of this shapely hill above Glenmore for stunning views over Loch Morlich and the rugged northern corries of Cairn Gorm.

O3 Lairig Ghru
The park's most challenging low-level walk, this tough 31km hike leads through a wild and intimidating mountain pass strewn with huge granite boulders. For experienced hikers only!

Itineraries

Ride a funicular railway and then hike to the savage subarctic summit of Cairn Gorm, or explore the picturesque villages and castles of scenic Royal Deeside.

◀ Ski-touring is a great way to explore beyond the lifts and get out into Cairngorms backcountry.
➡ Now owned by Clan Farquharson, impressive Braemar Castle was originally built in 1628 by John Erskine, the Earl of Mar.

01
A day

You can explore several of the park's highlights during an easy day trip along Ski Rd, between Aviemore and Cairngorm Mountain. Drive to the Cairngorm Reindeer Centre, arriving by 10.45am (daily year-round), to join a 90-minute guided walk over heather-clad hills to feed the UK's only free-ranging herd of reindeer – the animals are really tame and will feed from your hand! Be sure to take walking boots and wrap up warm.

Continue by car to the ski-area car park, where you can ride the Cairngorm Mountain Railway to the top of the hill and join another guided walk (departs 1.30pm May to October, book in advance) to the snow-patched summit of Cairn Gorm (1245m), Britain's sixth-highest mountain (again, you'll need good boots and warm clothes). Your guide will point out rare alpine flowers amid the granite boulders, and you can search for local wildlife such as ptarmigans and mountain hares – if you're lucky, you might spot a golden eagle or two.

The views south across a wilderness of bare rock to the rounded summits of Ben Macdui, Beinn a'Bhuird and Ben Avon are well worth the trip.

After a late lunch in the Ptarmigan Restaurant – the highest in the UK – return down the mountain and drive back to Loch Morlich for an early-evening stroll (1½ hours on an all-abilities trail) or bike ride (45 minutes) around the loch. Keep an eye out for red squirrels among the pine trees and ospreys circling over the loch.

02
Two days

The southern approach to the park, along the A93, passes through ever wilder scenery as it follows the route of an 18th-century military road. After you crest the hill at Glenshee Ski Centre the view opens out as you descend towards Braemar. Perched astride Cluny Water, the village merits a stroll before a visit to imposing Braemar Castle (open April to October).

Drive west for 6 miles to the Linn of Dee, where one of Scotland's most famous salmon rivers squeezes through a narrow rocky gorge – there's a lovely woodland walk along the banks. Return to Braemar and motor along the scenic valley of the Dee River eastwards to Balmoral Castle (open April to July), the holiday home of the British royal family. You can explore the formal gardens and visit the stone cottage where Queen Victoria used to write her diary.

Overnight in the picturesque town of Ballater before driving north along the A939, one of the highest, steepest and twistiest roads in the UK, to the pretty Highland village of Tomintoul. Here you can loop north for a few miles to visit the famous Glenlivet distillery (open March to November), where you can fill your own bottle of whisky straight from the cask, or go mountain biking at nearby Bike Glenlivet.

Continue to Aviemore via the minor B970 road and stop off at Loch Garten nature reserve to see the nesting ospreys (April to August).

11

UKRAINE

Carpathian National Nature Park

Clipping Ukraine's southwest, the Carpathian Mountains are one of Eastern Europe's last true wildernesses, home to the colourful Hutsul people and Ukraine's most diverse fauna and flora.

Ukraine may be a troubled land these days, but on a hike deep in the Carpathian forest, travelling by country bus in the fading light of a summer evening or surrounded by hearty Hutsuls in a cosy tavern as the snow falls silently outside, you'd never know it. The Carpathians feel a continent away from the post-Soviet badlands of Eastern Ukraine (over 1000km distant), this wedge of subalpine Europe having preserved its upland traditions while now also catering for the needs of modern-day visitors.

These ancient hills are all about the forest, thick, impenetrable and mysterious, marching up the valley walls in regiments of pine, beech and spruce. Humans have traditionally eked out a living in the long, fertile valleys, their villages stretched along rivers in an elongated jumble of timber dwellings. Above the tree line is the polonyna – the alpine meadows where the Hutsuls herd sheep in summer and produce the creamiest of fresh cheeses in tiny

huts. Paying a call on Carpathian shepherds is the essence of any visit to the region.

The remoteness of the Carpathians is the main reason visitors can still enjoy this pristine swathe of nature. Ukraine's forests were decimated in the 18th and 19th centuries, but it was deemed too expensive to fell trees in the inaccessible Carpathians – so the forests survived. Oddly enough, it was the Soviet authorities who did much to protect the environment here, banning logging and declaring the region a national nature park in 1980.

Most come here to enjoy the great outdoors – hiking, skiing and mountain biking are the most popular activities. However, these valleys also have a human story: the Hutsul people and their multi-ethnic highland culture are an unmissable feature of this enigmatic mountainscape.

⬆ Carpathian National Park protects a swathe of ancient forests, including stands of primeval beech forest.

Toolbox

When to go
The park fills with holidaying Ukrainians between June and August and during the winter skiing season (in places). May can still be chilly, but Septembers are mild and bursting with autumnal colour.

Getting there
The park lies in Ukraine's southwestern corner, around 160km as the crow flies from the regional capital, Lviv. Trains link Lviv with several Carpathian towns, but services are threadbare. Most locals rely on frequent buses to get around. Driving isn't recommended.

Park in numbers

515
Area covered (sq km)

2061
Highest point: Mount Hoverla (m)

1980
Year established

Getty Images | standret; stock_colors

Hike this...

01 Mount Hoverla
A very popular hike leads to the top of Ukraine's highest peak. It's almost an act of pilgrimage for Ukrainians and the trail gets busy in summer.

02 Dovbush Trail
This easily accessible 4km walk starts in the park capital, Yaremche, and heads up into the surrounding uplands and forests. The theme is Oleksa Dovbush, 'the Robin Hood of the Carpathians'.

03 Ridge Trail
This 281km trail leads serious hikers from Rakhiv in the south to Volovets in the north, taking in almost all of the park's highest peaks. Allow 14 days to complete the route.

Stay here...

🏠 **On the Corner Bed & Breakfast**
Often celebrated as 'the best place to stay in Ukraine', this family-run guesthouse is a real treat. Mum lays on gourmet-style Ukrainian meals while guests plan their next foray into the Carpathians with assorted relatives. It's in the town of Kolomiya within striking distance of the hills.

🏠 **Smerekova Hata**
The pine-fragrant, Hutsul-inspired rooms at this long-established Rakhiv guesthouse have been a hiker favourite since the region opened up in the 1990s. The knowledgeable owner is a local activist who promotes the region's attractions and budding slow-food movement.

Do this!

🎿 **Skiing**
The Carpathians are one of Eastern Europe's skiing hot spots, with several slopes dotted around the region. The biggest, best-equipped resort is Bukovel, but for a wilder experience try Slavske, Pylypets or Dragobrat. Cross-country skiing has always been popular and trail marking is improving.

🪓 **Experiencing Hutsul culture**
Ukraine's section of the Carpathians has traditionally been home to the Hutsuls, a mountain people whose traditions have largely survived. The best place for visitors to get a taste of their idiosyncratic customs is at the Hutsul folk-art museum in Kolomiya.

What to spot...

The park is home to deer, squirrels, boars, spotted salamanders and (though they're rarely seen) golden eagles and brown bears. The rivers attract otters, trout, storks and herons.

CARPATHIAN SQUIRREL Inhabiting the deep subalpine forests and surviving on the abundant supply of nuts and berries that grow there, this red squirrel has distinctively spiked ears, and fur that changes colour to a winter white.

Itinerary

This comprehensive itinerary takes in the best the Carpathian National Nature Park has to offer.

01
One week

A week is just enough to see the best of the region, and the following itinerary could be attempted by local bus in that time frame – with a little patience. Start in Kolomiya, just outside the Carpathians, acclimatising and getting acquainted with the local Hutsul culture at the town's superb museum. If you are staying at the On the Corner B&B, you'll soon be inspired by your hosts to head for those hills. After two days of exploring it's a short hop to Yaremche, the most touristy of the Carpathian towns but also home to the park headquarters and visitor centre. One of the best places to pick up guides and information, it's also a great base from which to launch flits into the wild. Day four could involve an ascent of Mount Hoverla, Ukraine's highest peak. From there slowly make your way down the valley to Rakhiv, another Hutsul outpost, where there's some great accommodation as well as the chance to explore the southernmost reaches of the Carpathians.

12

Cinque Terre National Park

Is there a more crazily beautiful landscape than Italy's Cinque Terre National Park? Vertiginous vineyards stripe the sea cliffs, and coastal villages make your heart flip at their Battenberg-cake loveliness.

Lonely Planet | Justin Foulkes

Poppies, blossom, jasmine and violets line the Unesco-listed Cinque Terre's not-for-the-faint-hearted coastal path. The stony track skirts the cliffs above a peacock-blue sea, which morphs into a china-blue sky along a soft, melting horizon. Looking up, rows of sinuous-stepped terraces pinstripe the muscular slopes. They look almost tropically lush, sewn together with vines and supported by nearly 7000km of ancient drystone walls, all painstakingly built by hand. Lemons polka-dot coastal orchards. A distant farmer works in the field. Bees buzz and butterflies flutter.

The name Cinque Terre (Five Lands) refers to the village areas along the coast, and dates from the 15th century. The cubist-looking medieval villages with their sunset-hued, green-shuttered houses seem to defy gravity, balanced as they are along this heart-rendingly beautiful stretch of Ligurian coast. They were built on steep hillsides as a defence against pirates, and the narrow streets within twist and turn, the better to outsmart invaders. There have been settlements here since ancient times; inhabited since the Bronze Age, this area has been home to Romans, Saracens and local tribes.

The narrow terraces that stripe the hills have turned the sea cliffs into unlikely agricultural land, producing crisp, dry white wine – sup it for overtones of citrus, green apples and sea air – from ancient vineyards. Work on the terraces and their dividing, supporting drystone walls began around 1000 years ago.

It was only in the 1970s that tourists began to trickle in, but this has over the decades become a flood, so much so that it's now necessary to buy a ticket to visit.

In 2011, storms battered the region, leading to cataclysmic rivers of mud pouring down the hillsides and devastating Monterosso and Vernazza. The damage to the park terraces and towns has been repaired, but parts of the coastal path remain closed – however, there are alternative routes.

↑ The crumbling remnants of Castella Doria sits above the fishing village of Vernazza. Previous page: the view over Corniglia (foreground) and Manarola from the Sentiero Azzurro.

Lonely Planet | Justin Foulkes

Toolbox

When to go
The trails should only be walked in good weather. Ablaze with wild flowers in spring, the park is at its finest from April to May. June to August is crowded and hot. September is still warm, and less busy.

Getting there
Cinque Terre is on the Ligurian coast. The best way to access the park is by boat or train from La Spezia, which is only an hour by train from Pisa (there are also trains to/from Milan and Turin).

Park in numbers

39
Area covered (sq km)

120
Length of the paths (km)

6700
Length of the drystone walls (km)

Stay here...

Torretta Lodge Manarola
In the inconceivably lovely Manarola, this hotel is housed in a 17th-century tower with views of the peach-and-ochre medieval village buildings and vineyard terraces rippling over the hills. The fabulously stylish rooms are all different, but all have lots of attention to detail, charm and antiques. Terraces proffer swoon-worthy views and you can eat breakfast overlooking the sea. There's a nightly *aperitivo* on the terrace, and a hot tub.

La Sosta di Ottone III
Outside the park near La Spezia, this is a wonderful 16th-century country villa set amid luscious countryside with sea views. There are four lovely rooms, exquisitely yet simply decorated in chalky, rich colours, and featuring a mix of antiques and beautifully upholstered furniture.

Hotel Zorza
In the rambling 17th-century house of a former winegrower, this hotel has nine simple but comfortable rooms, some with original beamed ceilings and artfully exposed sections of the stone walls. It's in a great location in Riomaggiore, the first of the Cinque Terre villages.

Do this!

Hiking
As well as the classic narrow, twisting Sentiero Azzurro trail along the coast, there are around 30 other walks criss-crossing the park. Each village has a walk up to its local sanctuary, and there are also mountain trails across the hills. You'll pass through vineyards and olive groves, and past lemon orchards and meadows scented by jasmine and rosemary, opening onto life-affirming panoramas. Paths are easy to follow but often steep, stepped and narrow. You can choose many ways to walk between the villages, particularly if a section is closed.

Mountain biking
Mountain biking along the park's paths, where it's permitted, is a glorious challenge through maquis and vine-covered hills overlooking periwinkle seas. For superlative cyclists, the Granfondo route through the park is a 151km roller-coaster ride.

Diving
The area off the coast is a protected marine zone. Local diving outfits offer the opportunity to explore the rich, gin-clear waters, where you'll spot stingrays, lobsters, eels and scuttling crabs, as well as deep underwater canyons and hidden caves.

What to spot...

The maquis tangling the coastline includes sea fennel, wild capers, rosemary, thyme and lavender. Other common flora are myrtle, juniper and Indian fig. Herring gulls, peregrine falcons and ravens are familiar sights wheeling overhead, while burrowing inland are dormice, weasels, moles, beech martens, badgers, foxes and wild boar, as well as snakes and salamanders. Offshore, keep a keen eye out for whales and dolphins frolicking in the surf.

BADGER
These distinctive, nattily black-and-white-striped creatures are nocturnal and, unusually, in Italy feed on olives, as well as their more usual diet of earthworms.

PEREGRINE FALCON
The world's fastest birds (they can dive at 320km/h) may be spotted from the Cinque Terre. They're seen around the cliffs, preying on smaller birds and catching them in mid-air.

WILD BOAR
Boar roam free in the park, feeding on roots and berries, mainly at night, and are not the most popular creatures locally because of the damage they do to crops. You're most likely to spot them in wooded areas.

Hike this...

O1 Sentiero Azzurro (Blue Path; No 2)

This gorgeous coastal path connecting all five villages is the park's most popular route and requires a ticket. The section from Riomaggiore to Corniglia is closed, but an alternative route is open.

O2 Sentierro Rosso (Red Path; No 1)

This 38km trail from Porto Venere to Levanto is a nine- to 12-hour walk on flat paths through dramatically beautiful countryside.

O3 Trail No 9

One of the area's sanctuary walks – each village has a trail to the local sanctuary – this starts in Monterosso and leads to Santuario della Madonna di Soviore.

Lonely Planet | Justin Foulkes, Shutterstock | Lukasz Janyst, Getty Images | AlessandroColle

Itineraries

See views to make your heart soar, eat fresh-from-the-sea fish at mind-bendingly picturesque restaurants, climb up to hidden sanctuaries, and spot whales and dolphins frolicking offshore.

◄ There's no sand, but Riomaggiore's cobblestone beach – lapped by the turquoise waters of the Ligurian Sea – has its own charm.
► The beautiful seaside train station at the tiny village of Corniglia.

01
A day

The first two sections of the 13km Sentiero Azzurro, which start at Riomaggiore and go to Corniglia via Manarola, were closed after the 2011 storms. However, there's an alternative, slightly more difficult route, which is a little further inland but still has sea views. Check locally for details – the walk takes around three hours. Beyond Corniglia, the route rapidly and strenuously gains height, but you'll be rewarded by views that linger long in the mind. Wild asparagus, wild garlic, figs, prickly pears and shady olive groves line the track. There are few thrills to match reaching the village of Vernazza, 4km away, curled around its natural harbour. This was one of the places most afflicted by the floods of 2011, but it's been restored to its former citrus-hued splendour.

Stop here at 1960s-founded trattoria Gianni Franzi to explore the narrow, winding streets and lunch on fresh-from-the-sea fish on the square overlooking the ocean. From here it's another 3km to the final village of Monterosso, fronted by a white-sand beach.

This is one of the most challenging but most rewarding parts of the trail, a steep, stony path that sometimes clings to the cliff, so that if you meet someone going the opposite way you'll have to carefully squeeze past one another. The views are stupendous at every turn, with the rich vegetation and ancient terraces creating an almost surreally beautiful landscape that plummets to an astoundingly blue sea. Walk, or take a water taxi or train, to return.

02
Four days

With more time to play with, you can explore the coast and inland. Decide on a base: all the villages are fairly close together, so you won't need to move each night.

On the first day, you could walk the section of trail No 2 from Monterosso to Vernazza, starting on a high as you round the corner to look down on Vernazza's fantastical peach-and-rose medieval cluster, which seems almost to lean into the sea. On day two, walk one of the five village sanctuary trails – the most wonderful is from Manarola to Santuario della Madonna delle Salute, which passes through ancient, deep-green vines and ends in tiny Volastra.

After a few laid-back days exploring the coast and sanctuary trails, you could explore a section (or more) of the more challenging Sentiero Rosso (trail No 1). You'll see far fewer people on this inland trail, which is harder than the coastal path but repeatedly thrills with glorious sea glimpses. The first stretch starts from Porto Venere, outside the park to the south, with a humbug-striped church.

The 8km walk takes you through pine, oak and chestnut forest before ending this section at the Telegrafo (513m). If you've packed a picnic, unwrap it here, overlooking the tangle of fragrant maquis. You'll have glorious views down over the Cinque Terre and its vineyards, and out to sea – on a clear day you can spy the rugged spine of Corsica.

13

Connemara National Park

Ireland's signature cliffs and rainy greens crescendo in Connemara, the westerly realm of County Galway that's preyed upon by the Atlantic's wild, unpredictable mood.

There's Ireland, and then there's Connemara – everything a visitor expects from the Emerald Isle, but with the volume cranked all the way up to ten. The mountain passes are more dramatic, the coastal vistas are even more breathtaking, and the grass is, quite literally, greener. The region of Connemara, located in the far western reaches of County Galway, has no official boundary, though it largely occupies the realm of jagged peninsulas and lonely loughs (lakes and inlets) west of the Maumturk mountains. Its name comes from an ancient clan that once ruled the area, though today Connemara is more widely known for being the largest Gaeltacht (Irish-speaking region) in the nation. For visitors, the region is Ireland's best offering when it comes to cottage country – especially along the loop known appropriately as Sky Rd.

Within the greater Connemara area lies Connemara National Park, though it is merely a sliver of land that has come under the jurisdiction of the Irish government – the area around it feels very much a part of the experience, and a trip to the preserve would be woefully incomplete without experiencing the surroundings. Protected within the park's official borders are the skyscraping Twelve Bens, a series of undulating mountains that offer stunning views from the top on a clear day. Diamond Hill, accessible from the visitor centre in Letterfrack, is the national park's most popular climb, promising similar vistas to the more difficult Twelve Bens. Mix and match your hiking with visits to solemn Kylemore Abbey, opulent Ashford Castle and charming Clifden village, and you've got yourself a perfect little parcel of Irish superlatives all within a manageable circle off Rte N59.

Toolbox

When to go
County Galway often sees the least rain and the highest temperatures in May, making early summer the ideal time for hikers. High hills and the rugged, western-facing shoreline mean the weather can be furious and unpredictable throughout the year.

Getting there
The park protects a portion of land within a greater district of the same name (the borders of which are ill defined) in western County Galway. The park's visitor centre can be found in Letterfrack.

Park in numbers

29.6
Area covered (sq km)

729
Highest point: Benbaun, part of the Twelve Bens mountain chain (m)

1919
Year of the first transatlantic flight, which landed in Clifden

Stay here...

Ashford Castle
East of the national park, in the village of Cong (famously known as the setting for the Oscar-winning film *The Quiet Man*), lies one of the most opulent stays in the Republic. The rambling fortress dates back to 1228, and guests can easily spot the embellishments and expansions in the stone over the years. Today, 83 lavish rooms are tucked inside, blending royal motifs – ornate wallpaper, gilded frames – with modern touches like fresh-faced marble bathrooms. More than 120 hectares of grounds, including a stunning lake, will tempt you to stick around longer.

Quay House
Clifden is a great Connemara base, and Quay House offers all the personalised charm you could ever hope for in a B&B-style property. The delightful hosts take good care of their eclectically decorated rooms, some of which have water views.

Hillside Lodge
Another Clifden charmer along the stunning Sky Rd beyond the village, Hillside's delights include an interesting vintage-music collection (the owner has had a lengthy career in the industry), a hearty Irish breakfast, welcoming pets, and genuine hospitality from the owners.

Do this!

Trying falconry
One of world's top centres for training birds of prey is located on the grounds of Ashford Castle, just beyond the park's official borders. Ireland's School of Falconry offers guests private, hour-long 'hawk walks'. A trained falconer accompanies you, feeding the large predatory birds snacks as they swoop from tree to tree hunting small creatures before returning to rest on the comfort of your arm.

Visiting Kylemore Abbey
Home to a coterie of Benedictine nuns, Kylemore looks more like a lonely castle on a fjord than it does a place of contemplation. Visitors are welcome to explore the property.

Riding Connemara ponies
Brought to Ireland by the Vikings and interbred with Andalucían horses from warring Spanish galleons, the famous Connemara ponies are compact but elegant beasts and the pride of local equestrian culture. Riding is available throughout the region at several farms and estates.

← Swept by the Atlantic Ocean winds, Moyrus Beach is a lovely spot for a stroll.
Previous page: Derryclare Lough.

What to spot...

Only 26 mammals are native to Ireland – this relatively small number is due to its geographical separation from the British Isles and Continental Europe over 15,000 years ago. Conversely, more than 400 bird species have been spotted on the island by ornithologists. The somewhat amorphous nature of the park boundaries within the greater region also known as Connemara means that wildlife is generally spotted throughout, with rarer creatures like hares and red deer usually more concentrated within the preserve itself.

STOAT
Usually spotted at night, stoats (short-tailed weasels) are as prevalent within the park's borders as they are in more urban areas.

MOUNTAIN HARE
Sometimes called the Irish hare, the species is well adapted to colder climates and can manipulate its diet based on available nutrients. In western Ireland the hares consume mostly grass.

SUNDEW
The strange, insect-eating sundew looks more like an alien dotted with pink antennae than it does the more conventional carnivorous Venus flytrap.

Hike this...

O1 Diamond Hill trail
Connemara's signature trek starts near the visitor bureau and moves 7km up Diamond Hill, showcasing 360-degree mountain and ocean views.

O2 Sky Road
Aptly named for the beautiful vistas it affords, the Sky Rd loops through Clifden, taking in the sheer verticality of the peninsula it explores.

O3 Omey Island
This tidal island is accessible on foot for only a portion of the day, when the tides have receded. A 6km loop roughly follows the circumference of the granite isle.

Itineraries

The sliver of the Connemara region that belongs to the national park is but a part of a larger system of mountain ridges, lonely peninsulas, farmland and hushed villages.

◀ Protected by a headland from the Atlantic Ocean, Dog's Bay beach is the perfect spot for a summer dip.
▶ Stunning Kylemore Abbey was founded in 1920 for Benedictine nuns fleeing Belgium during WWI.

01

A day

A day in the Connemara area, perhaps begun by travelling up from the nearby city of Galway, is best spent doing a driving circuit that takes in a few of the region's best natural and human-made wonders. Follow Rte N59 from Galway, making a right turn onto Rte R344, a smaller road, which trundles through the legendary Inagh Valley, with views of the quiet Lough Inagh and the towering Twelve Bens on the left.

The end of the road is a different portion of Rte N59, and once you reach the intersection you'll make a left towards Letterfrack. Before you reach the village and the Connemara National Park visitor centre, stop for a few hours at Kylemore Abbey. The stunning estate has several easy walking trails and beautiful Victorian gardens, and the stone mansion itself (while only mildly interesting on the inside) occupies an incredible vantage point over a lake, offering some of the choicest photo opportunities in all the Irish Republic.

Continue down Rte N59 towards Clifden for one last walk along the famous Sky Rd – a paved circuit that both starts and finishes in Clifden, servicing a peninsula of private cottages with the best views in the Connemara region. Follow Rte N59 back to Galway afterwards for some fresh seafood at Oscars in the city centre, or check into one of the delightful inns, like Quay House or Hillside Lodge, for the evening and sneak in a few extra hours of walking to fully appreciate the Sky Rd's moniker.

02

Three days

A long weekend allows visitors to explore the greater Connemara region and not just focus on the fraction of land given the national-park designation. Stunning hiking trails amble beyond the park's headquarters and the Twelve Bens, revealing some of the incredibly scenic cottage country around Clifden – a worthy village in which to hang your hat and explore the appealing shops and pubs. Follow the perfect loop of the Sky Rd just beyond the town centre either by bike or on foot, then swoop down into the park proper at Letterfrack for a short walk around Diamond Hill. Try exploring one of the many beaches in Connemara – be it Ballyconneely or Claddaghduff – on horseback to experience the unique gait of the area's stout-but-athletic ponies.

Tuck your hiking shoes away when you arrive at Ashford Castle, Ireland's premier accommodation option. Set in the village of Cong, the rambling castle guards more than 120 hectares of geometric English gardens and wild forest. The interiors, while thoroughly updated, have retained much of the royal charm one would hope for in castle accommodation. Be sure to enjoy a drink in the wood-panelled bar and have dinner in the George V dining room. Ireland's first school of falconry is located in the grounds, and here travellers can learn about the surprisingly complex work of a falconer and the delicate predator-prey ecosystem endemic to the estate and national park next door.

Connemara National Park

14

LITHUANIA

Curonian Spit National Park

Imagine the desolation of the Sahara, but in Lithuania – you've just pictured the signature curl of orange sand that blankets one of the planet's strangest outcrops.

When you think of the Baltic, images of frigid winters and bleak Soviet power tend to come to mind, but what if we told you that there was a large expanse in Lithuania covered in wild, windswept sand dunes and bearing a striking resemblance to the Sahara – would you believe us? Hard as it may be to fathom, the Curonian Spit – thin like an errant amber hair – shoots across almost 100km of the Baltic Sea promising just that: desolate slopes on which you half expect a Bedouin to invite you into their tent for mint tea.

While odd orange dunes are clearly the main attraction for visitors from far away, the national park itself is actually 70 percent pine forest and protects a compelling assortment of mammals, diverse plant life and a huge collection of nesting birds that seek the lagoon waters created along the spit's boundary. The highest point in the park rises a staggering 60m, making it a great place for explorers in any physical condition. Cycling and bird-watching round out the two most popular pastimes within the Curonian Spit's confines, though you'll also find small clusters of adorable summer cottages, and crowds relaxing where the dunes meet the sea to create accidental beaches.

Formed in the third millennium BC, the spit is a geological anomaly where sea currents and wind in just the right ratio deposit sand along an ancient glacial moraine. According to local legend, a giantess created the outcrop as she played along the seashore; the spit has also been long revered in pagan lore as a place of great importance. Protected as a Unesco World Heritage Site, the park depends on surrounding development remaining minimal, lest the land and weather change, forever destroying this fragile and exotic place.

⬇ The Curonian Spit's curious dunes are caused by a geological anomaly.

Toolbox

When to go
June and July are by far the best months for exploring the spit, when the weather hovers around 20°C. August and the autumn months tend to be the wettest, making spring a better bet for low-season visits.

Getting there
Lithuania's third-largest city, Klaipeda, is the gateway to the sandy spit. For those with the right paperwork, it's possible to continue along the strip of dunes into Kaliningrad, across the Russian border.

Park in numbers

98

Length of the dune-ridden spit – 52 of which is in Lithuania (km)

400

Thinnest point of the sandy land bridge (m)

5500

Approximate age of the land formation, bolstered by a glacial moraine (years)

See this...

01 Vecekrugas Dune
The king of sandy slaloms rises over 60m above sea level, epitomising the barren nature of the spit's signature dunes while providing killer views over the quiet realm.

02 Curonian Lagoon
Go one better than taking in the view and sail across the body of water between the sand and the mainland on a *kurenas* (traditional fishing troller).

03 Klaipeda's sculptures
Providing a cultural component to the neighbouring expanse of protected wilderness, big-city Klaipeda's public artwork details the city's turbulent history under several different flags.

Stay here...

Misko Namas
Base yourself in Nida, at the southern end of the national park, for the perfect mix of holiday relaxation and nature exploration. This guesthouse embodies all the qualities of a classic Nida stay: a prim garden, and blue-and-white gingerbread trim. Visitors have access to bike rentals and a communal kitchen.

Radisson Blu Hotel
A hallmark of quality in the Baltic, Radisson Blu may bear a chain name, but the property promises top-notch service and easy access to Klaipeda's Old Town. It's a worthy choice for travellers seeking to blend bustling city life and desolate dunes.

Do this!

Biking
The Baltic's generally flat landscape lends itself well to the desires of tourists on two wheels, with the 30km stretch from Nida to Juodkrante being one of the most scenic rambles in the entire region. The path meanders through four holiday townships collectively known as Neringa, with their cottage accommodation bedecked in quaint Cape Cod–style detail. The designated bike trail follows the shores of the lagoon around Nida, then veers towards the Baltic side after Pervalka, when the orange dunes morph into sky-scraping pines.

What to spot...

The park protects several adjacent ecosystems, including a pine forest holding dozens of mammals, a sweeping lagoon with flora and birds, and the desolate dunes.

WILD BOAR The most conspicuous animal in the park wiggles out from the shade of the conifers to rummage through rubbish bins. Take special note of its hooves, which look like dainty black stilettos.

Itinerary

Whether you're exploring on foot or by bike, the Curonian's dune-punctuated desert never ceases to amaze.

01

A weekend

A holiday retreat for wealthy Lithuanians, the Curonian Spit is made for slow-paced exploration. Base yourself in Nida at the end of the preserve, with its teeny-tiny chequerboard of quaint vacation homes all styled like fairy-tale cottages. Explore the 30km up to the pine-studded village of Juodkrante by bicycle, a feat easily managed as the path is remarkably flat. Marvel at the small sandy desert between the eponymous lagoon and the roaring Baltic Sea before it turns into a proper northern forest. The area around Juodkrante embodies a more classic version of what a visitor may envision when they think of the term 'national park', with a plethora of birdlife – don't miss the heron- and cormorant-viewing platform – and woodland. Visit the visitor centre in Smiltyne and enjoy the remainder of your time along one of the adjacent beaches, or try your hand at kitesurfing, a popular pastime along the entirety of the Baltic coastline.

Lonely Planet | Justin Foulkes

15

Dartmoor National Park

You can see why legends have grown up about this brooding sweep of moorland in England, which looms above the Devon countryside and is crowned by eerie granite outcrops.

There's always been something supernatural about Dartmoor. Perhaps it's the tortured granite tors, casting spooky silhouettes against the brooding sky. Or it might be the rumours of links to the occult or the intrigue conjured up by Arthur Conan Doyle in *The Hound of the Baskervilles*. Or it could just be the scale of the landscape, cracked open to the sky and painted in a primal palette of blood and earth tones by Mother Nature. If pagan gods did come to Earth, this would be their playground.

Despite the tidy infrastructure and waymarked walking trails, Dartmoor has an unmistakable atmosphere of being 'other' to the territory around it: a short drive in any direction will take you to sleepy fishing ports and villages replete with cafes selling Devon cream teas. Dartmoor's shield of granite moorland was thrust upwards as a pluton of volcanic magma some time in the Carboniferous period, at about the same time as the first amphibians were crawling out of prehistoric seas.

With the passing aeons, tectonic forces pushed the land upwards, while erosion carved downwards, leaving the tough granite of the moors standing proud of the surrounding terrain. The tors on every raised hummock are just the most obvious signs of the vast mass of granite underfoot. Early humans soon realised that there was something special about these dark highlands, leaving a huge collection of stone circles, tombs and primitive settlements scattered across the moors.

Fast forward a few hundred thousand years and humans are still captivated by Dartmoor, though these days the main appeal is the opportunity to hike, scramble, mountain bike, kayak, horse ride or climb

over this vast natural adventure playground. Don't underestimate the terrain, though – the British Army has been using Dartmoor as a survival training ground since at least the 1800s.

⬆ A hiker astride Hound Tor; Dartmoor's weathered granite tors, such as Black Tor (previous page), are popular with hikers and climbers alike.

Getty Images | Rich Legg

Toolbox

⚙ **When to go**
Spring brings lambs and wild flowers to Dartmoor, while summer is prime season for camping, picnics and getting into the great outdoors – and for crowds. It's quieter in autumn, when heather paints the hillsides purple, and winter, when snow airbrushes the higher ground.

🧭 **Getting there**
The park boundaries are in Devon, but you can visit just as easily from Cornwall. Exeter, Devon's county town, has the nearest airport; trains run to Exeter, Plymouth and Newton Abbot.

Park in numbers

954
Area covered (sq km)

621
Highest point: High Willhays Tor (m)

3.1
Length of the world's longest row of standing stones, at Upper Erme (km)

Stay here...

🏠 Bovey Castle

The pick of the grand country hotels on Dartmoor, Bovey Castle is set in landscaped gardens in a lush green valley near North Bovey. The seemingly Elizabethan manor is actually a late Victorian fake, but the interiors have enough period furniture and damask wallpaper for even the most discerning stately-home enthusiast. Befitting the regal setting, there's a lavish spa, an 18-hole golf course, and even sloe-gin-making workshops. OK, you're insulated slightly from the national park, but when the best rooms have private balconies looking out over the hills, you probably won't mind.

🏠 Tor Royal

Lovely Tor Royal B&B occupies an almost absurdly picturesque country farmhouse, with a bell tower looking out over the moors. Spot the fleur-de-lys marks left by the original owner, Sir Thomas Tyrwhitt, personal secretary to the Prince of Wales, later George IV.

🏠 YHA Dartmoor

The Postbridge YHA scores extra points for being located bang in the middle of the moors. Set in a stone Victorian building, this is the classic YHA experience: no frills, clean sheets and the great outdoors starting right on the front step.

Do this!

🥾 Walking the moors

With dozens of signposted walking routes criss-crossing the moorlands, Dartmoor is a three-dimensional Ordnance Survey map for hikers, though you may experience a lingering fear of hearing a monstrous hound baying behind you... There are gentle strolls from car park to tor and challenging multi-day walks weaving right across the national park, but be cautious heading out onto the moors in late autumn and winter – exposure is a risk if the weather deteriorates, and you don't want to wander onto the Ministry of Defence firing range during artillery tests!

🧗 Tor climbing

Victorians were obsessed with Dartmoor's tors as objects of curiosity, but modern gentlemen and gentlewomen are more interested in climbing them, with rock climbs on most of the main outcrops. Routes are short but challenging, with lots of off-width cracks and difficult exits.

🚴 Mountain biking

With mile after mile of tracks and bridleways, Dartmoor is a natural velodrome. Take your pick from rugged mountain-bike trails like the Princetown and Burrator track or calf-tightening road routes through the heart of the moors.

What to spot...

Dartmoor National Park provides a haven for everything from Dartmoor ponies and otters to, if rumours are to be believed, big cats and escaped marsupials. The moorlands and swamps attract abundant birdlife, including signature species such as buzzards, snipe and curlews, as well as Britain's only poisonous snake, the adder, which survives on a diet of frogs and toads. Spring's carpet of wild flowers attracts myriad butterflies and the enigmatic bee fly, which looks exactly as you would expect.

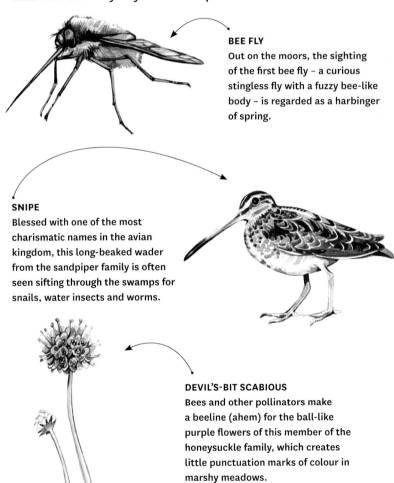

BEE FLY
Out on the moors, the sighting of the first bee fly – a curious stingless fly with a fuzzy bee-like body – is regarded as a harbinger of spring.

SNIPE
Blessed with one of the most charismatic names in the avian kingdom, this long-beaked wader from the sandpiper family is often seen sifting through the swamps for snails, water insects and worms.

DEVIL'S-BIT SCABIOUS
Bees and other pollinators make a beeline (ahem) for the ball-like purple flowers of this member of the honeysuckle family, which creates little punctuation marks of colour in marshy meadows.

Hike this...

O1 West Devon Way
This 59.5km hike through
the western reaches of
Dartmoor National Park
passes tors, Norman
castles and medieval
churches perched on
granite outcrops.

**O2 Haytor Rocks and
Hound Tor**
Following the route of the
Victorian tramway once
used to haul stone from the
moors, this 12.2km day hike
visits two of the park's most
dramatic granite outcrops.

**O3 Wistman's Wood and
Longaford Tor**
This 7.4km ramble takes
in the eerie bower of
Wistman's Wood, one of
Britain's last prehistoric
oak forests, where the
devil is said to keep his
satanic hounds.

Itineraries

Climb a tor, hike over a hillside or wander a woodland – wherever you go, the moors will cast their spell, sometimes serene, sometimes sombre, sometimes spooky, but always affecting.

◄ Postbridge's ancient clapper bridge was built in the 13th century.
➡ The dark, grim facade of Dartmoor Prison, once the holding place for the UK's most violent prisoners.

01

A day

On a day trip from the coast, it makes sense to head straight for the tors. Hound Tor, creating a sinister silhouette on the skyline between Bovey Tracey and Widecombe-in-the-Moor, was allegedly the inspiration for *The Hound of the Baskervilles*, and looking at the tormented shapes of the granite outcrops, it's easy to see why.

The tor backs onto a ruined medieval village, adding to the sense of desolation. Rope-only climbing routes ascend the outcrops, but you can scramble to the top of many of the boulders for sweeping views of clouds skittering over the vast expanse of the moors.

For a longer leg stretch, you can walk on from Hound Tor to Haytor, or make a long loop via Saddle Tor, Top Tor and Bell Tor. The only caveat: it gets crowded here, so come on a rainy day or start early to beat the rush. After an exhilarating walk/climb/scramble, you can wet your whistle at the Rock Inn, a half-hour tramp east of Haytor.

02

Two days

With two days, you can take on the higher ground. The North Moor rises above the town of Okehampton on the northern fringes of the national park, providing direct access to the highest reaches of moorland.

On day one, rent a bicycle and follow the Granite Way west from Okehampton, via a string of granite works, viaducts and other relics from Dartmoor's quarrying days. From Meldon Quarry you can detour onto the blasted heath of the high moors to High Willhays (621m), the highest point in Dartmoor. Use day two for some cultural activity: in Princetown, the Dartmoor Prison Museum tells the story of the jail that once housed Britain's most notorious criminals (stand up, Acid Bath Haigh and the Mad Axeman!).

End with a ramble northeast through a chain of tiny villages: Postbridge, with its 700-year-old bridge; Chagford, with its thatched village square; and Castle Drogo, with the last castle built in England, to plans drawn up by Edward Lutyens.

03

A week

A week will let you get under the skin of the moors. Base yourself in Widecombe-in-the-Moor and make forays in all directions. To experience Dartmoor's rumoured diabolic links, spend the night – if you dare – in moss-cloaked Wistman's Wood, where Dewer (the Devil) is said to ride out with his wisht hounds, searching for lost souls to drive over the rocks of Dewerstone. From here, it's an easy hop to Princetown's Prison Museum, and north to Castle Drogo. Allow one day to explore the Teign Gorge from Castle Drogo, passing woodlands, trickling brooks and the tidy white village of Drewsteignton. There'll be time to cycle the Granite Way across the North Moor and climb Hound Tor and Haytor, or at least scramble over the easier crags. Also make time for the towns around the rim of the national park: Tavistock, home to Buckland Abbey (the one genuinely Elizabethan country house on the moors); Okehampton, with its ruined castle; and Plymouth, for gin-sampling tours and boat trips around Plymouth Sound.

Doñana National Park

Where Spain's mighty Guadalquivir River empties into the sea, Doñana National Park is a fabulous outpost of sand dunes, rare Mediterranean forests and stunning biodiversity.

Doñana National Park is one of those places where you'll spend most of your visit on the edge of your seat. As you follow ancient byways through the dense undergrowth of cork, oak and pine, deer appear suddenly in the distance, isolated by a shaft of sunlight, or without warning a colourful pheasant runs into view. As thrilling as these sightings are, it's the bewhiskered face of the Iberian lynx, the world's most endangered species of wild cat, or the vast wingspan of the equally imperilled imperial eagle soaring high on the thermals, that will provide you with some of Europe's most memorable wildlife-watching experiences. That's because Doñana is a relic of the past, a refuge for ancient species that once roamed all across the Iberian Peninsula.

How this came to be owes much to the park's history. Eight centuries ago, at a time when the Muslims of Al-Andalus ruled much of Spain's south, the Christian king Alfonso X seized Doñana and turned it into a royal hunting estate. In the centuries that followed, while burgeoning populations and warring armies stripped Spain of its forests and hunted its wild animals to extinction, the occasional royal plaything of Doñana remained intact, an island in a sea of shrinking biodiversity.

Doñana may not be Spain's largest protected area, but it spans an extraordinary range of habitats, of which its famous forests form only a part. Beyond the forests lie open plains shared by lynx and birds of prey, wild boars and genets, badgers and mongooses. These plains in turn yield to vast wetlands, where flamingos and herds of semi-wild horses step through shallows that stretch to a horizon of low sand dunes and then the sea.

Toolbox

When to go
Doñana is accessible year round, but avoid Pentecost, when more than a million pilgrims descend on the gateway town of El Rocio. At this time accommodation is scarce and wildlife elusive.

Getting there
Doñana is in Spain's extreme southwest, close to the border with Portugal. It is adjacent to El Rocio, which in turn is south of Almonte, off the Huelva–Sevilla motorway.

Park in numbers

543
Area covered (sq km)

76
Number of Iberian lynx (in 2015)

360
Bird species recorded

A rancher rounds up semi-wild horses from the marshes of Doñana to sell in the nearby town of Almonte.

Stay here...

Hotel La Malvasia
Staying in El Rocio makes the most sense, allowing you to get an early start and stay inside the park until sunset. The pick of the places is Hotel La Malvasia, trim in its terracotta and whitewash and surrounded by palm trees like an Andalucían postcard. Overlooking the marshes, this truly magisterial building has rooms brimful of character, including rustic tiled floors, vintage photos of the town and iron bedsteads in floral designs.

Hotel Toruño
An attractive villa overlooking the *marismas* (marshes), Toruño has 30 well-appointed rooms. Some have marsh views, so you can see the spoonbills breakfasting when you wake. The restaurant dishes up generous portions.

Hospedería El Cazadero Real
In the heart of El Rocio, this attractive old inn has decent rooms. Those upstairs have views out over the wetlands and the ornate Ermita de El Rocio, the town's celebrated church.

Do this!

Driving
The only way to explore Doñana is in a vehicle with an accredited guide. There are numerous operators in El Rocio that organise two- to three-hour driving safaris through the national park. These follow set routes and you'll usually share the vehicle with eight to 10 other paying customers. It's also possible to arrange private forays. Guides know the best places to see lynx and are experts in bird identification.

Walking
The national park is bordered on the north side by a *parque natural*, a more accessible protected zone where you may walk around on your own. Ask for directions from El Rocio, then walk along the sandy trails in search of lynx.

Exploring El Rocio
There's nowhere quite like El Rocio, Doñana's gateway village, and it's an essential element in the Doñana experience. Streets here are unpaved, horses are everywhere and it feels like the Wild West but with numerous Spanish twists.

Drive this...

O1 Coto del Rey
This northern area of Mediterranean forest is home to the planet's highest density of Iberian lynx. Beautiful stands of trees and quiet driving tracks make this the place to be late in the day.

O2 La Viciosa and around
A combination of dense foliage and open country in the heart of the park makes La Viciosa another lynx hot spot, with many sightings close to sunset or sunrise.

O3 Marismas
These wetlands are a twitcher's paradise, and their far southern reaches are generally home to flamingos at any time of the day.

What to spot...

Doñana's wildlife is most active during the two hours after sunrise and the last couple of hours before sunset. The lynx is most commonly seen in the north, where there is sufficient cover. Other mammals, including foxes and hedgehogs, are best seen in the same forests or in the plains on the forests' southern fringe. Birds of prey are common throughout the park, but the southern and coastal wetlands are home to the largest number of species, especially water birds.

IBERIAN LYNX
The Iberian lynx is a medium-sized cat with ear tufts, an unusual beard and a spotted coat. It is a highly selective feeder, with rabbits making up almost 80 percent of its diet.

SPANISH IMPERIAL EAGLE
This large brown eagle has a 2m wingspan. Numbers fell to 30 pairs in the 1960s, but there are now more than 300 in Spain, thanks to intensive conservation programmes.

COMMON GENET
The cat-like genet, which is mostly nocturnal, is a small mammal with leopard spots along its flanks, a dark stripe along its spine, and a fox-like face. It's an excellent climber.

Getty Images | Lola L. Falantes; jesus david carballo prieto : Walter Bibikow

Itineraries

Doñana National Park is at its best in the morning and late afternoon, leaving the rest of the day clear for exploring El Rocio, one of Spain's most unusual villages.

 Catholic pilgrims come from far and wide to pay homage to a small carved statue called the Virgin of El Rocio at the Ermita de El Rocio.

If you're lucky, you might catch a glimpse of one of Doñana's elusive Iberian lynx.

The colourful former ice factory that now operates as the park's visitor centre.

01

A day

Though you may worry that this won't be enough time, a single day exploring Doñana National Park can be perfect, provided you plan ahead and make an early start. Early-morning and late-afternoon nature drives will ensure you see the park at its best and give you a fighting chance of spotting its signature wildlife. Make sure one of your drives includes a visit to the former royal hunting pavilion, a lovely, quintessentially Andalucían structure where kings and queens stayed while on excursion in the park. Don't forget to scan the nearby trees for nesting storks. In between drives, spend your day in El Rocio, a singular place with sandy streets, horse corrals and a remarkable church, the Ermita de El Rocio, the epicentre of a powerful annual pilgrimage; on Sunday, expect crowds dressed in traditional Spanish finery. Local restaurants serving Andalucían specialities are worth lingering in, with the widest selection of places in the thoroughfares around the hermitage.

02

Two days

After the full first day, take a morning or afternoon to walk east of El Rocio into the Coto del Rey section of forest just outside the park. From the main track – where, if you're lucky, you'll see some of El Rocio's many horse-drawn carts heading to and from the town – you can see through the fence into the national park; sightings of lynx along here are reasonably common. Alternatively, venture into the forest to the north to see if you spy a lynx there. In the afternoon, drive for two or more hours around to Sanlúcar de Barrameda. This pretty Andalucían sherry town looks across the mouth of the Guadalquivir River (which Columbus sailed down en route to the Americas) towards Doñana and has a national park visitor centre with interesting displays. At the centre, arrange a guided boat-and-4WD excursion into the park. Such visits focus on the park's coastal scenery and birdlife – seeing a lynx down here is near impossible – and nicely round out your experience with its many charms.

17

Durmitor National Park

A glorious kingdom of sky-scraping peaks, jade-green glacial lakes, ancient black pines, mossy forests and plunging river canyons, Montenegro's Durmitor National Park is pure perfection.

Lonely Planet | Julian Love

No matter from which side you approach Durmitor National Park, you will be in awe – the glorious mountain peaks are rugged, smooth, sloping and jagged, all at the same time. The ancient pine trees dot the mountainsides with perfect cones, some reaching 50m high. And amid all this are the 18 glacial lakes that range in colour from frosty blues to deep navy and turquoise, like precious beads scattered on the massif. Durmitor has 48 peaks above 2000m in altitude, with the highest, Bobotov Kuk, measuring 2523m, making the park the perfect place for hiking, especially in the warmer months. There are spectacular karst or forest trails, and stunning views that stretch hundreds of kilometres.

The park's flora is dominated by forests of pine, birch, juniper, fir and beech, and, notably, Durmitor boasts one of Europe's last virgin black-pine forests. The vast range of fauna includes clouds of breathtaking butterflies, 163 species of bird and some 50 types of mammal, among them the grey wolf, brown bear and European wildcat. And beneath the surface of the park's rich waters hides the endangered Danube salmon.

Inscribed on the Unesco World Heritage List since 1980, Durmitor National Park also includes Europe's deepest river canyon, which is a stunning 1.3km from top to bottom. Cradling the Tara River, it makes rafting down the majestic torrent an even more unforgettable experience.

The park was founded in 1952, though its conservation history dates back to 1907, when Black Lake was declared a protected area. Today, just under 2000 people live in Durmitor, most of them shepherds – the region's heights and remoteness have always been a deterrent to settlers.

Toolbox

When to go
December to March is ski season, with spring, summer and autumn best for hiking and rafting. The mountains are cool even on the hottest days, though spring and autumn are particularly divine for their wild flowers and turning leaves, respectively.

Getting there
Durmitor sits in northwestern Montenegro, edged by three river canyons: Tara to the north, Piva to the west and Komarnica in the south. The nearest airports are Dubrovnik (Croatia) and Podgorica, at least three hours' drive away.

Park in numbers

390
Area covered (sq km)

2523
Highest point: Bobotov Kuk (m)

1.3
Depth of Tara River Canyon (km)

Stay here...

 Family Farm Apartments
Wooden cottages are Durmitor's signature buildings and this place is typical, with its combination of wood and stone, topped by brightly coloured roofs set against the mountainside. Three wonderful cottages have wood heating, open staircases and traditional furnishings for ultimate cosiness, and the location – a short walk from Black Lake and the start of most hiking trails – is perfect. There's a garden with wooden tables and chairs for summer days, when breakfast and dinner can be had with the fantastic views of the plateau unfolding before you.

 Hotel Soa
This modern take on Durmitor's traditional mountain-lodge structure, surrounded by pines and other conifers, has contemporary city-style bedrooms, and the sauna and Turkish bath are ideal after a hard day's hiking. It's an easy walk from here to Black Lake.

 Camp Mlinski Potok
Sitting in an alpine meadow with views of mountain peaks all around, this campground is perfect for summer and autumn visits; if it's chilly, there are wooden huts to stay in. The night views of the open skies are unbeatable.

Do this!

 Rafting
The deepest canyon in Europe, Tara River Canyon is unmissable. It's 80km long and 1.3km deep, and it's best seen from within, so rafting it is the natural choice. The water is potable, so fill your bottle as you rush down the 25km of foaming river bends. Tours start in the morning; watch the light change as the day progresses, and observe the plant and animal life on the canyon walls. You'll be mesmerised.

Mountain summiting
Hike to Bobotov Kuk (2523m), Lokvice (1800m) or Planinica (2300m), each offering spectacular karst or forest trails, and unbeatable views from the top that stretch hundreds of kilometres. Depending on the time of year, wear sunscreen or wrap up.

Lake gazing
Durmitor is full of dramatic beauty, but its 18 glacial lakes are gentle, blue drops amid black-pine forests. Also known as 'forest eyes', they reflect the mountain peaks and woods around them and are an idyllic place to swim in high summer.

Durmitor National Park is Montenegro's most spectacular hiking destination. Previous page: the park has been on the Unesco World Heritage List since 1980.

What to spot...

Durmitor National Park sits in the Dinaric Alps, and its wide range of altitudes gives it both Mediterranean and alpine microclimates. There are 163 bird species, including the peregrine falcon and the golden eagle, which soar over 400-year-old black-pine trees. The rich underwater fauna includes the endangered Danube salmon. But the real sign of Durmitor's extraordinary ecological preservation is the presence of big predators such as wolves and brown bears.

EUROPEAN WILDCAT
The great-grandparent of the domestic cat, the wildcat, with its long, thick, brown-striped coat, looks a lot like a tabby cat. It inhabits thick forests and is largely nocturnal.

GREY WOLF
This most mythical of animals has mottled grey fur and can travel great distances (up to 700km) from its pack in search of prey, averaging around 35km per day.

DANUBE SALMON
This endemic species, with its copper back and crescent-shaped freckles, is threatened by overfishing. It can reach an incredible 1.5m in length and can weigh more than 50kg.

Hike this...

O1 Bobotov Kuk trails

There are two approaches to Bobotov Kuk: the rocky and exposed southern landscape (three hours) and the classic, pine-dense northern trail (five to eight hours).

O2 Zeleni Vir lake trail

Zeleni Vir is Durmitor's highest lake and one of its smallest. Sitting in a glacial basin, it's enveloped by spectacular peaks. The trail is a three-hour hike.

O3 Planinica trail

The six-hour hike weaves through rich forests and the glacial Alisnica Valley. It takes in a summit atop the plateau that offers views of peaks and Tara River Canyon.

500px | Canipel, Getty Images | Walter Bibikow; Marko Radovanovic

Itineraries

Hike up to rugged mountaintops through ancient forests, dip into glacial lakes and go rafting in plunging river canyons – Durmitor is the ultimate immersion in dramatic beauty.

← The Piva river, which eventually meets the Tara river and the two become the Drina.
→ Ice stalagtites and stalagmites in Ledena Pecina (Ice Cave).

01
Two days

Pack in rafting and hiking to get the best out of Durmitor. Rafting starts nice and early, and it takes most of the day to get through the 25km length of Tara River Canyon; it's an adrenaline-pumping experience on the rushing torrent that slices through the imposing rock towering around you. If you have time, a three-day rafting trip is available that can take you through the total 100km of the canyon and involves camping in the wild. Look out for the mix of flora and fauna, much of it residing on the cliff walls. A well-deserved lunch is eaten beside the water in the idyllic landscape.

On day two, head up to Lokvice (1800m) from Black Lake through a dreamy conifer forest that eventually turns into a beech wood; be sure to check out the variety of berries and mushrooms along the way. The Lokvice Valley has shepherds' houses and grazing flocks in the warm months, and you will navigate through a stark landscape, stunning in its range of rock formations. Keep an eye out for the eagles that soar in the skies above. The five hours of hiking can be interrupted by a visit to Ledena Pecina (Ice Cave) – the route to the cave forks off about halfway along the path to Lokvice. Inside the cave, you can see ice stalactites and stalagmites, which remain intact year-round. Take warm clothes for the cave, since the temperature hovers constantly just a few degrees above zero. Enjoy the afternoon on the shingle shores of Black Lake; you can hire a rowing boat for a spin on the lake itself.

02
Four days

A longer stay needs to include a hike up to Bobotov Kuk, which can take up to eight hours in total. Take the classic route from Black Lake and start early by making your way up through lush forests of ancient conifers and mossy undergrowth, feeling as if you're on the set of *The Lord of the Rings*. Gaze up at the 50m-high pine trees, many of which can be up to 400 years old, and expect to see grazing herds on alpine meadows. Spot maples and beech trees and admire the karstic rock formations that surround you. Have lunch on the summit, enjoying the views of the massif stretching out all around, and then return to Black Lake; in high summer, reward yourself with a dip and a rest on the shingle beach.

Day four should be spent exploring the glacial lakes on light walks; from Black Lake, walk on for an hour and a half to Jablan Lake under the imposing cliffs of Crvena Greda. Nearby is Zminje Lake, cupped by centennial fir and juniper forests, and Barno Lake, shrouded by conifer trees. If you're visiting in springtime, Škrčka Lakes should still be snowy. Unpack your lunch on the grass by any one of the lakes. Listening to birdsong in the shade here has to be one of the most heavenly experiences that life can bring.

Getty Images | HAUSER Patrice/hemis.fr

18

Écrins National Park

Watch as dawn illuminates the pearly summit of Barre des Écrins, and hike to rocky ledges and along shepherds' trails worn smooth over the centuries.

Écrins National Park

Imagine the frostbite, racing pulses and top-of-the-world exhilaration English climbers Edward Whymper, Horace Walker and AW Moore must have experienced as they scrambled up scree-driven slopes, braving whatever the elements threw at them and hacking out steps in the rock, to finally crest the 4102m summit of Barre des Écrins on 25 June 1864. Since then the mighty peak has been the stuff of mountaineering legend. One glimpse of its gnarled, arrow-shaped summit and Glacier Blanc spilling down its flanks tells you everything you need to know about Écrins. These mountains are not gentle. They are great, dark, forbidding monsters of gneiss and ice, rearing above valleys and meadows like shark's fins. Like the climbers who tackle them, they are hardcore.

Edward Whymper and co might have been the first peak-baggers, but they were by no means the first to discover Écrins. Bronze Age remnants point to a long history of settlement, as do footpaths pounded into shape by shepherds and smugglers over centuries. In the 19th century, intrepid mountaineers and guides came to find their thrill in this mountainous region, tucked in southeastern France and nudging the Italian border.

It is this raw wilderness coupled with the park's off-the-radar remoteness that gives Écrins a peace rarely found in the French Alps. Go today and you'll have trails – all 700km of them – virtually to yourself. There's one with your name on it, whether you fancy a gentle amble to a looking-glass lake, a half-day hike to a high mountain refuge or a multi-day expedition into the backcountry, where fang-like peaks reveal snarling tongues of glaciers. And when you tire of walking, you can pit yourself against four-thousanders, pedal Tour de France-style to Alpe d'Huez, canyon, ski, ice climb – or simply revel in scenery that makes you feel glad to be alive.

🔼 Écrins National Park has many spectacular places to pitch a tent. Previous page: La Meije (3983m) looms over the village of La Grave.

Toolbox

⚙️ **When to go**
Écrins is high-Alpine terrain with sharply defined seasons. Summer is best for hiking, and the park rarely feels crowded even in peak months. Dry, mild weather often sweeps up from neighbouring Provence. Winter brings hefty snowfalls, with skiing and boarding at resorts fringing the park. Golden days and forests define autumn.

🧭 **Getting there**
The park stretches between Bourg d'Oisans, Briançon and Gap. The closest airport is in Grenoble, 92km from the western gateway village of Bourg d'Oisans.

Park in numbers

918
Area covered (sq km)

4102
Highest point: Barre des Écrins (m)

800,000
Approximate number of visitors annually

Stay here...

Hôtel les Vallois
With front-row views of glaciated mountains, this chalet in Vallouise is brilliantly positioned for hiking and skiing at nearby Puy-St-Vincent. The rooms are kitted out with pine furnishings and downy bedding, and many have mountain-facing balconies. Besides the heartfelt *bienvenue* (welcome), it's the little touches that appeal: staff can advise on activities, there's a pool and the restaurant is top-notch.

Hotel de la Chaussée
The Bonnaffoux family has run this chalet for five generations – since 1892, in fact.

Close to Briançon's walled old town, it fulfils every Alpine fantasy, with wood-clad rooms and fabrics in Christmassy reds and greens. The restaurant does a brisk trade in cheese-laden classics, from *tartiflette* (cheese, potato and onion tart) to raclette.

Ferme Noémie
This family-run affair near Bourg d'Oisans is a cracking base for exploring the national park – it's particularly popular with road and mountain bikers. Pitch a tent from April to October or stay in a barn-style apartment (available year round).

Do this!

Mountain biking
If you've ever watched the Tour de France and pictured yourself tearing up a mountain pass in a blaze of sweat, adrenaline and Lycra, now's your chance to live the dream. Bourg d'Oisans is the trailhead for the notorious 14km road that swings around 21 hairpins to the mountain resort of Alpe d'Huez (1860m) – a heart-pumping ascent of 1100m. After the gruelling climb, naturally, comes the spirit-lifting descent.

Snowshoeing and cross-country skiing
Gliding through snowy forests in quiet exhilaration on cross-country

skis or padding up to mountain ridges in snowshoes, with a crisp blue sky overhead, is nothing short of magical. Vallouise and Puy-St-Vincent are fine bases, with marked, well-groomed trails. Hire gear at local shops.

Adventure sports
Fancy upping the adventure a notch? Major park resorts and villages, Briançon and Bourg d'Oisans included, have *bureaux des guides* that are one-stop activity shops, offering everything from gorge canyoning to *vie ferrate* (fixed-rope trails), mountain climbing, ice climbing and off-piste skiing.

What to spot...

Écrins is rippled with 150 peaks over 3000m, their summits eternally ice capped. Dark, serrated mountains and glacier fields drop to meadows speckled with gentians, buttercups, edelweiss and saxifrage, and woodlands of spruce, Swiss pine, beech, alder and juniper. The park's remoteness attracts abundant wildlife: chamois and ibex on rocky slopes, marmots and snow hares in pastures, black grouse and willow ptarmigan in woods, and griffon vultures, golden eagles and pygmy owls in the skies.

GOLDEN EAGLE
The park shelters France's largest population of golden eagles (37 pairs). These agile predators soar on thermal currents and eye up prey from rocky ledges. They are true lovebirds and pairs stay together for life.

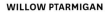

WILLOW PTARMIGAN
A member of the grouse family, the ground-dwelling willow ptarmigan struts around the park's forests. It changes its feathers from brown to white in winter. Listen for its gurgling cackle of a call.

MARMOT
These podgy, burrow-dwelling rodents, found around 2000m, are related to the squirrel and native to the Alps. They are sociable and live in colonies. Like meerkats, they regularly post sentries, who whistle once for an air predator and twice for a ground predator.

Hike this...

O1 GR54

Among France's most fabled *grandes randonnées* (long-distance hikes), this 198km, eight- to 10-day circuit begins in Bourg d'Oisans, plunges into the park's glacier-capped wilds and involves some steep ascents and scrambling.

O2 Refuge du Pelvoux

This challenging 14.3km, seven-hour round hike starts in Ailefroide and clambers past rocky ledges and grassy slopes to a *refuge* with stirring views of ice-frosted mountains.

O3 Pigeon Loft Loop, Gioberney

With exhilarating views of the Rouies glaciers (3589m), Gioberney is often dubbed the 'French Himalayas'. This 9.9km, medium-level loop involves an ascent to eyrie-like Refuge du Pigeonnier (2423m).

Itineraries

Feel your mood soar as high as the snow-crusted peaks around you as you hike the magnificent GR54, marvel at Vauban's star-shaped citadel in Briançon and scramble up to the Pigeon Loft.

◀ Hikers will find stunning views and lung-busting trails in Gioberney, a glacial cirque at the heart of Écrins National Park.
▶ Climbing the park's eponymous peak, Barres des Écrins (4102m), is popular with mountaineers.

01

A weekend

Touch base in pretty Bourg d'Oisans, the national park's western gateway. Get the inside scoop on hiking and a decent map from the Maison du Parc, then nip into the village's museum. From here, strike out on one of the outstanding hiking trails – you could attempt a section of the wild GR54 – or slip into a mountain-bike saddle to tackle the 21 switchbacks up to Alpe d'Huez, capped by the summit of Piz Blanc. Straddling slopes that reach from 1250m to 3330m, this sunny bowl of an Alpine resort is one of the finest bases in the French Alps for outdoor activities. Back in Bourg d'Oisans, go for pizza at La Falaise before bedding down for the night at Ferme Noémie.

Rise early on day two to see first light playing on colossal mountain faces. Now it's time for a distractingly scenic drive east along the northern fringes of the park to Briançon, past thundering falls, sheer cliffs and jagged peaks topped by glaciers and skirted with larch forests. But you'll need your wits about you – the local attitude to overtaking on hairpin bends is *pas de problème*.

Close to the Italian border, Briançon opens up more fabulous hiking country and is the jumping-off point for pulse-racing activities from canyoning to ski touring, depending on the season. Devote at least a couple of hours, too, to exploring the Vauban fortifications of its World Heritage–listed walled old town perched high on a hill. Dinner is at bistro Au Plaisir Ambré, where dishes like wild snail and monkfish fricassee are served.

02

Four days

Tag on an extra couple of days in the national park and you won't be sorry. On day three, penetrate the park further by driving on to Vallouise, which looks like a village straight out of a snow globe, with its cute stone-and-timber chalets, Romanesque church and staggering mountain backdrop. Some of Écrins' finest hiking begins right here and in neighbouring Ailefroide. You could dive into truly mountainous terrain on the 14.3km circuit up to the Refuge du Pelvoux (and stay the night if you wish). The GR54 also passes by here, as do myriad other hiking trails. When the flakes begin to fall, excellent cross-country skiing and snowshoeing allow you to tiptoe into the silent hinterland. Dinner is an Alpine feast of glorious cheese – raclette, *tartiflette* or fondue – at La Table de Nany, before a peaceful night's kip at Hôtel les Vallois.

On your final day, end on a high – quite literally – by delving right into the heart of the park to Gioberney, where a striking round walk to the Pigeon Loft begins. You'll be totally immersed in stark Alpine country: over millennia, glaciers have bulldozed out this landscape of ice, scree and cirques. Stay the night at 2423m Refuge du Pigeonnier or return before the light begins to fade.

19

Parco dell'Etna

In Italy's Parco dell'Etna, walk with lava and legends on Europe's tallest and most tempestuous volcano, where unspoilt nature endures amid the ash and cinders.

Getty Images | Jeremy Woodhouse

The farmers of Sicily have always known that the fertile soils under their feet were forged by volcanoes, so the brooding cone-shaped peak of Mount Etna could be considered the ultimate elephant in the room. This looming mass of basalt lava is both Europe's highest volcano and its most active, belching ash and fire into the skies over Catania and Taormina with alarming regularity. This hasn't stopped farmers and winemakers from making extensive use of the lower slopes, but locals have avoided living too close to the crater-scarred summit, creating a de facto conservation area long before the Parco dell'Etna was founded in 1987.

The ancient Greeks believed that Etna was the home of the cyclops Polyphemus, the fearsome one-eyed monster who captured Odysseus, but even older legends link Etna to the Gigantes, giants who challenged the gods of Olympus for control of the cosmos. The Romans upgraded Etna in their mythology to become the workshop of the tempestuous god Vulcan, lord of metalworkers and the forge – and seeing Etna spitting plumes of molten lava into the night sky, it's easy to see where they got the idea!

But that's ancient history. Etna today is a place to get close to elemental forces – particularly if the volcano is putting on one of its famous strombolic light shows – and, conversely, to appreciate the surreal peace and quiet around those cones that are still slumbering, within sight of the built-up bustle of Catania and Taormina. This is prime walking country, and even prime skiing country in winter, but many visitors are content to drift around the vineyards on the fringes of Parco dell'Etna,

sampling local vintages with the sombre summit of the volcano rising imposingly against the horizon.

⬆ Hikers climb to the ash-covered summit of Mt Etna (3350m). Previous page: the volcano shadows the town of Cesarò.

500px | Henry Wolde Godfrey

Toolbox

When to go
Come from June to August for prime walking conditions on the upper slopes, but expect plenty of day trippers from Catania and Taormina. December to March is ski season in Nicolosi and Linguaglossa.

Getting there
Catania is the closest gateway to Etna, served by flights from Europe and ferries from the Italian mainland and Malta. Buses run daily from Catania to the cable-car station at Rifugio Sapienza.

Park in numbers

581
Area covered (sq km)

3350
Highest point (m)

475
(BC) First recorded eruption of the Etna volcano

Stay here...

Rifugio Sapienza
If you like being close to the action, bed down just metres from the lower cable-car station at this mountain refuge, the main departure point for the smoking summit. The refuge has a hint of ski lodge, but the plumes of steam from the summit create a surreal backdrop. The hotel has a fine restaurant, serving some of the produce raised on Etna's fertile slopes, though the wood-fired pizza oven may be too vivid a reminder of the lava bubbling below.

Agriturismo San Marco
On Etna's less-visited northern slopes, this family-run *agriturismo* is agreeably rustic, right down to the hearty, homestyle Sicilian meals prepared in the farm kitchen by Mrs Rosaria. The owners run a host of excursions, including eco-walks around the volcano.

Hotel Villa Dorata
Set in the former home of Duke Giovan Battista Paternò Castello di Roccaromana, this antique-filled heritage property basks in front of stunning views over the coastal plain, just 1.5km from the nearest crater. For outdoorsy types, the forest starts right outside the front door.

Do this!

Climbing into a crater
The main attraction at Mount Etna is fairly obvious – everyone wants to get up on top of the volcano to peer into the steaming crater. In fact, there are four primary cones – Bocca di Nord-Est, Voragine, Bocca Nuova and Cratere di Sud-Est. Which you can get close to will depend on how active the volcano is feeling on any given day (bear in mind that this is Europe's most active volcano). Voragine has been belching fire with particular regularity in recent years, including some stunning strombolic eruptions.

Skiing a volcano
As Sicily's highest point, Etna makes for a surprisingly good ski destination. From December to March, the upper slopes are dusted with snow and eight pistes offer lifts and other ski essentials, accessible from either Nicolosi or Linguaglossa.

Sampling the local plonk
Etna's volcanic soils are rich and fertile, and winemakers crowd the lower slopes. Many wineries are open for tastings of the delicious local Etna DOC vintages. Expect plenty of fruit, strong alcohol and, some claim, hints of mineral smokiness.

What to spot...

The richness of wildlife in Parco dell'Etna is perhaps unexpected considering the unstable environment, but the volcano is home to martens, Sicilian foxes, European wildcats, peregrine falcons, golden eagles and even porcupines. Of course, they couldn't survive here without the mice, voles and other small rodents who scurry between the lava flows. In fact, the volcano isn't all sand and clinker; the lower slopes are cloaked in vineyards and oak and pine forests that give shelter to abundant birds and butterflies.

SICILIAN FOX Hunted to the brink of extinction, Sicily's largest predator is making a comeback on Etna, where its red coat provides excellent camouflage in the russet volcanic sands.

MARTEN These robust mustelids – in the same family as otters and weasels – were once as common as rabbits, but farmers grew tired of their poultry-pinching ways, leading to a big decline in their numbers.

PORCUPINE Certainly Etna's most exotic resident, the crested porcupine clings on in warmer areas below 1300m. Despite superficial similarities, this prickly customer is more closely related to the hare than the hedgehog.

Hike this...

01 Rifugio Sapienza to the summit

It's a 5km scramble to reach the tormented landscape around the summit craters, but the approach offers spectacular views over vineyards to Catania.

02 Climbing Monte Zoccolaro

When activity builds up to dangerous levels in the main craters, the best vantage point is the peak of Monte Zoccolaro, reached by a 2km hike from Zafferana Etnea.

03 Zafferana Etnea to the Valle del Bove

This rewarding 10km tramp goes into the dragon's den of the Valle del Bove, moving from peaceful rural countryside to black lava and fuming vents.

Itineraries

Come face to face with nature's fury on the slopes of Sicily's tallest mountain; if you're lucky, the volcano may even put on the full lava show for your benefit.

◄ While the lower slopes of Mt Etna are famed for their fertility, towards the summit little grows but cushions of soapwort (*Saponaria sicula*).
➔ Mt Etna is an excellent and, occasionally, dramatic ski destination.

01

A day

With only a day to appreciate the Parco dell'Etna, it pays to get straight up into cinder country. Nicolosi is the gateway to the southern slopes of Etna, and buses rumble daily to Rifugio Sapienza, on the edge of the desert of ash and clinker that surrounds the active cones at the summit. Even in summer, the approach can be chilly and exposed – you are above 3000m, after all – but this only adds to the drama as you crunch over the cinders spewed out by past eruptions. For our

money, it's best to approach the summit on foot to connect with the spirit of the volcano – save the jeep and cable-car ride for the journey downhill, when you'll have earned the right to take the easy way down. Needless to say, the views are pretty special from the 500m ascent on the Funivia dell'Etna cableway. If you do brave the 5km climb from Rifugio Sapienza to the summit under your own steam, you'll tramp through a landscape painted in a diabolical palette of colours – hellish reds, ash greys,

burnt umbers – before finally reaching the ominous cones at the tip of the mountain. Each of the four craters has its own brooding character, but if any of the cones is delivering the full sound-and-fury package, it's best to view the lava fountains from a safe distance. You'll be able to get closer to one of the other cones for a glimpse into Vulcan's furnace.

02

Four days

With several days at Etna, there's no need to charge headlong to crater-town. Prime yourself for the volcanic encounter by exploring the handsome, stone-cut streets of Catania, which narrowly escaped a fiery death in 1669, when flumes of lava reached the city walls.

On day two, swing by Piazza Duomo and pay your respects to the lava-cut elephant that is Catania's official symbol, then head to Linguaglossa, on the northern flanks of Etna, and roll out to the Gambino

Vini vineyard to sample the lip-smacking combination of traditional grape varietals, Sicilian sunshine and volcanic Etna terroir.

On day three, perform a ritual circuit around the base of the mountain on the Ferrovia Circumetnea train, basking in front of classic Etna views around the lava-stone village of Randazzo. Make time for a gentle amble through the serene forests around the Rifugio Ragabo before you settle down in the pretty hill town of Nicolosi for the night.

Day four is summit time, so follow the craggy trail from Rifugio Sapienza, with the dry crunch of cinders ringing in your ears. As well as the active craters, make sure that you admire the views over the Valle del Bove, the fuming depression created by the collapse of an ancient lava cone. Finish off by winding your way back to Nicolosi, to sample volcano-grown farm-fresh produce at Antico Orto dei Limono, in the rustic setting of a vintage olive-oil and wine press.

20

— LATVIA —

Gauja National Park

Latvia's Gauja National Park is a realm of infinite pines spiced with millennia of wartime scars, from ancient tribal rites and medieval strongholds to bizarre Soviet geometry.

Dense layers of coniferous forest cast soothing shade on the snaking Gauja River as it wends its way across Vidzeme, Latvia's eastern region. The vast realm – bright green in the summer months and blanketed in white, unsullied snow in winter – became the Baltic nation's first official national park in 1973, protecting sandstone cliffs, natural springs, dozens of lakes and a truly incredible amount of biodiversity almost two full decades before the country reinstated its independence from Mother Russia.

But Gauja National Park offers much more than a diverse ecosystem of migratory birds and mammals; it also fosters a swathe of land that has, for thousands of years, been a tree-filled nexus of trade and turmoil. Tribes bearing names not too dissimilar from *Game of Thrones* characters fought vicious battles in the Gauja, staking land claims by creating large earthen mounds. Medieval warfare was etched into the ground with imposing turrets of stone – the castles at Turaida and Cēsis remain even today as poignant reminders that control of the park's namesake river was always a bloody undertaking.

Relics from modern history scar the terrain in equal measure. The dominant Soviet presence after WWII had little regard for natural preservation, adding Communist-style tenement blocks throughout the landscape. Many have been torn down, others have been transformed to suit modern use, but a few of the structures are well worth exploring in greater detail. The Soviet Olympic bobsled team, for example, trained within the park's confines along a track that looks like some kind of apocalyptic concrete confetti, and deeper within the sky-scraping evergreens is a giant nuclear-fallout shelter encased in iron and situated many metres below the earth.

Toolbox

When to go
July and August are best for exploring, when the weather's warm and live music wafts through the castle ruins – celebrate the solstice with all-night pagan rituals. Winter pairs park skiing with a steam in a local *pirts* (sauna).

Getting there
The Gauja is an hour from Rīga, Latvia's capital, and can be accessed by suburban train, bus or private vehicle. The park features two towns: the century-old leisure village of Sigulda and the medieval stronghold of Cēsis.

Park in numbers

917.5
Area covered (sq km)

1214
Year construction began on Turaida Stone Castle

1200
Length of Soviet luge and bobsled track (m)

With tales of star-crossed lovers and an outlook over the slow bends of the Gauja River, Turaida has everything you could possibly want in a castle and more.

Stay here...

 Ungurmuiža Manor
A vestige of Latvia's infamous feudal times when wealthy German merchants co-opted the land and employed locals as their serfs, this stunning wooden mansion is the only Baroque-era manor left standing in the whole of the country. Grand portraits, porcelain furnaces and restored wooden beams transport visitors back to the lap of luxury in the 1700s. Two of the manor's rooms are available for overnight guests; there are additional accommodations in the old schoolhouse next door.

Hotel Ezeri
Loaded with all the mod cons you could desire, Ezeri bills itself as a spa resort, but the real drawcard is its lakeside cedar 'country sauna' that's only available for those in the know.

Hotel Bergs
If you're planning to base yourself in Rīga then be sure to consider a stay at boutique Hotel Bergs. Set on one of the grand boulevards of the city centre, the hotel blends traditional manor-house decor with sleek glass embellishments.

Do this!

Visiting Līgatne bunker
Hidden deep in the forests of the Gauja is a crumbling convalescent home, its perpendicular Bauhaus-esque edges starkly contrasting with the rambling natural landscape. While still in use as a rehabilitation centre, the structure had another purpose, which wasn't generally known until the mid-2000s: underneath it lay a massive secret Soviet bunker, the fallout shelter for Russian officials should there be a nuclear attack. Tours are readily available.

Bobsledding
Once the training ground of the Soviet bobsled team, Sigulda still boasts its original concrete practice track. Visitors can give it a whirl with a proper retro luge in the winter months, or test drive the summer bob.

Touring Cēsis Castle
Have all your medieval fantasies come true at the perfectly preserved Cēsis Castle. Candlelit lanterns will guide your way through a thousand years of history, not to mention a rather gruesome dungeon.

See this...

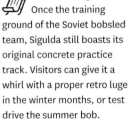

01 Araiši Lake Castle
From this authentic replica of a 9th-century settlement, take in the classic lakefront views for which Latvia is known throughout the region.

02 Turaida Stone Castle
Latvia's fabled tale of Turaida involves star-crossed lovers and a soaring brick tower. Climb to the top of the turret for sweeping views of the serpentine Gauja River.

03 Cable car
Zip across the grotto-speckled gorge on the park's short cable-car service. (If you really want a thrill, you can bungee jump from the cable car at 43m as it crosses the river!)

What to spot...

Seasons in the Gauja are very pronounced, with a long, frosty winter – as though Santa owned the acreage – and steamy summer nights that thrum to the sound of excited crickets. Famed for its towering pines and quiet lakes, the land can be shady and swampy at times, with hidden caves and crumbling ruins strewn about here and there. Keep an eye out for the park's 900 species of plant and 150 types of bird.

ELK (MOOSE)
Elk are plentiful throughout the park and the rest of the country, and are often hunted for sport and game meat.

RACCOON DOG
Originally from East Asia, the raccoon dog was introduced to the Baltics as a fur-bearing animal and has managed to fully integrate into the predator-prey ecosystem.

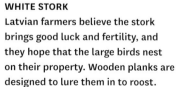

WHITE STORK
Latvian farmers believe the stork brings good luck and fertility, and they hope that the large birds nest on their property. Wooden planks are designed to lure them in to roost.

Getty Images | nikonaft

Itineraries

Swing through crumbling fortresses between the pines à la Robin Hood, then practise your best Bond-villain accent in the depths of a nuclear bunker.

◀ Medieval Cēsis Castle and its dungeon can be toured by candlelight.

▲ Communication equipment inside the Soviet-era Līgatne bunker, a top-secret fallout shelter for the Soviet elite.

▲ Gauja River cuts its way through the heart of the park.

01
A day

To make the most efficient use of your day away from the capital, it's best to navigate the park by private vehicle. Start in Sigulda, around 60km from Rīga, which was purpose-built as the leisure gateway to the forested expanse. Here you can try out the retro-cool bobsled track constructed for the Soviet Olympic team. Career down the concrete track at speeds of up to 125km/h as you breathe in the Gauja's thick scent of pine.

Stick with the Russian theme at the hidden bunker in Līgatne, just a dozen kilometres up the road, and get a lesson in Soviet propaganda. If you time your visit over lunch you can dine in the dank galley amid plastic flowers that haven't left the room since they finished the bunker at the height of the Cold War.

Follow the road up to Cēsis to take a giant leap further back in time as you wander through the medieval ruins of one of northern Europe's most picturesque castles by candlelight.

02
A weekend

Take the train out to Sigulda for an eventful weekend. Start by getting the blood rushing on a visit to a local *pirts* (Latvian sauna). There are several private *pirts* to choose from in the area, and all of them offer the same thing: sweating it out in your birthday suit at baking temperatures while mixing in swigs of beer (or shots of vodka) and invigorating splashes in a neighbouring lake or pond.

Crank the adrenaline up one more notch in the heart of the Sigulda township, where you have the choice of bungee jumping from the cross-river cable car, bobsledding down an old Soviet track, and trying out other novelty pursuits such as the Aerodium vertical wind tunnel, or Vells, the highest climbing tower in Eastern Europe.

The warmer months lend themselves well to cycling – a worthy pursuit for your second day. Bike between Līgatne and Cēsis while uncovering nature trails that follow the ancient warpaths of the tribal Livonians.

21

Parco Nazionale del Golfo di Orosei e del Gennargentu

Strike out into near-vertical ravines, puzzle over prehistory and tick off pearl-white bays like rosary beads in Sardinia's biggest national park, where limestone mountains razor above celestial-blue sea.

The SS125 corkscrews over mountaintops cloaked in juniper, holm oak and olive, swinging haphazardly around bends that redefine the word 'hairpin'. You crunch gears, say three Hail Marys, and dodge wild pigs, flocks of fearless sheep and the occasional hell-bent Fiat driver. The views, too, are quite simply distracting. On one side unfolds a broad valley, quilted with lush greens, carved by ravines and buckled with ragged limestone peaks. On the other, cliffs sheer down to the bluest of blue seas. You take the helter-skelter road down to Cala Gonone and there – sweet Jesus! – is the full sweep of the Golfo di Orosei, shimmering like quicksilver as day fades to dusk.

Dipping into the heart of the Parco Nazionale del Golfo di Orosei e del Gennargentu, the drive along the coastal road from Orosei to Baunei is way up there with Italy's best road trips. Here the mountains of the Gennargentu collide abruptly with the sea to form a colossal amphitheatre. And here nature puts on a sensational performance: cliffs are riven with false inlets, pockmarked with caves, stippled with rock arches and pinnacles. In between hide horseshoe-shaped bays that beggar belief, with pebbles so white and water so exquisitely blue they look digitally enhanced.

Who can say what memories you will take away? Perhaps they will be of your kayak paddle slicing through topaz waters to reach castaway bays, or of stumbling across Bronze Age Nuraghic settlements in the silent hinterland, or maybe of watching a full moon hang above the gulf like a stage prop as cicadas strike up their twilight drone. Indeed, whether you are admiring grandstand views of Gola Su Gorropu canyon or the spring beauty of the valleys spread gold with mimosa and broom, the magic of this park will settle over you as gently and clingingly as pollen.

⬆ The glittering white sands of cliff-lined Cala Luna beach.

Toolbox

When to go
Wild flowers daub the landscape in spring, a terrific season for hiking, climbing and cycling. Avoid July and August, when crowds swell, rates skyrocket, temperatures soar and roads get congested. Autumn is often fine, with clear skies and warm days.

Getting there
The closest airport is Olbia, around 1½ hours north. Alghero (to the west) and Cagliari (to the south) are alternatives. The SS125 road forms the backbone of the park.

Park in numbers

730
Area covered (sq km)

1834
Highest peak: Punta La Marmora (m)

1998
Year established

Hike this...

O1 Cala Fuili to Cala Luna
From Cala Fuili, an easy-to-follow, two-hour (4km) clifftop trail teeters through *macchia* and woods to the ravine-backed crescent of Cala Luna, pummelled by turquoise water. Hike or boat it back.

O2 Gola Su Gorropu
Wear sturdy boots for this half-day hike to a boulder-strewn canyon. Climbers spider up a 400m rock face at the narrowest point: Hotel Supramonte. Begin at Genna 'e Silina pass.

O3 Selvaggio Blu
Billed as Italy's toughest, this epic seven-day, 45km beast of a trek takes in the wildest chunk of the Golfo di Orosei.

Stay here...

Lemon House
Peter and Anne run this B&B in Lotzorei. It's a cracking base for outdoorsy breaks – the sports-loving couple can arrange bike hire and pick-ups, give climbing and kayaking tips, and organise the logistics of the Selvaggio Blu. Try the homemade lemon marmalade at breakfast.

Agriturismo Guthiddai
On the Nuoro–Dorgali road, this whitewashed farmstead nestles among fig, olive and fruit trees below the arresting peak of 1463m Monte Corrasi. The family runs the place with love, and the olive oil, fruit, vegetables and Cannonau wine that appear at mealtimes are home produced.

Do this!

Boating the Blue Crescent
If you do just one thing, make it a boat trip along the southern Golfo di Orosei, where each cliff-flanked beachette – Cala Luna, Cala Sisine, Cala Biriola, Cala Mariolu – is more gorgeous than the last, their waters fading from aquamarine to sapphire to deep purple.

Visiting the Grotta di Ispinigoli
Imagine the surprise of the shepherd who stumbled across this whopper of a cave in 1950. Just north of Dorgali, descend 60m into the grotto's giant well to glimpse a forest of petrified pinnacles and the world's second-tallest stalagmite (38m).

What to spot...

Fragrant macchia (Mediterranean scrub) fringes the coast, holm oak, juniper and pine the interior. Park residents include Sardinian wildcats, foxes, hares, mouflon, griffon vultures, golden eagles and peregrine falcons.

GREATER WHITE-TOOTHED SHREW
This mouse-like shrew loves Sardinia's Mediterranean climate and hides out in grassland and woodland. It's pretty vocal, using high-pitched echolocation to find its way.

Itinerary

Hike vertiginous trails, detour to Bronze Age wonders and lap up the gulf's coastal beauty.

01
One week

Begin with a head-spinning drive on the SS125, starting in Orosei – once a Pisan port, now notable for its historic core and beaches. Push south, detouring into farmland to eye Bronze Age Nuraghic sites like Serra Orrios and *tombe dei giganti* ('giants' tombs'; mass graves) like S'Ena 'e Thomes. The road becomes increasingly spectacular as you approach Dorgali, with its backdrop of limestone peaks and the Grotta di Ispinigoli, where the world's second-biggest stalagmite sprouts. Prettily arranged around a bay, Cala Gonone is a terrific base for hiking, climbing and water sports. From here, visit Cala Fuili, Cala Luna and other gasp-eliciting bays, putter along the Blue Crescent by boat, or hike to the wild Gola Su Gorropu canyon and Tiscali, an enigmatic archaeological site in a collapsed cave. The final, spectacular drive south takes you to Baunei, where old mule trails wriggle down from the other-worldly Golgo plateau to knockout Cala Goloritzè.

Hardangervidda National Park

Norway's wild, high-altitude heartland, Hardangervidda ranks among northern Europe's most accessible wilderness areas, with Arctic foxes, wild reindeer and trails across the tundra three highlights among many.

The high plateau of Hardangervidda that dominates Norway's largest national park has for centuries held Norwegians and other travellers in its thrall. Once an ancient trade route that connected eastern and western Norway, Hardangervidda is now best known for providing a spectacular backdrop to the peerless Oslo–Bergen railway. It is a prelude to the fjords, with impossibly steep cycling and hiking trails, and the Flåmsbana railway line dropping down into the surrounding abyss. At Geilo, high on Hardangervidda, you can almost step off the train and straight onto a ski lift. This version of Hardangervidda's story tells of a land between two worlds, a place to admire as you cross it on your way elsewhere.

But Hardangervidda is also a destination in its own right, an expansive tableau of sweeping alpine beauty and horizons that never seem to end. This is big-sky territory, a largely treeless high country of rolling moorlands cast in green or white depending on the season. Summer hiking and cross-country skiing in winter reward those who devote time to exploring its intriguing topography – its other-worldly remnants of mountains and hills worn inexorably down by glaciers during the last ice age.

Fauna is also essential to the Hardangervidda story. The region's high-altitude climate has created an unlikely Arctic outpost: the Arctic fox is a charismatic presence. The fox's snowy-white pelage makes it almost invisible in winter, but it's far less elusive in its brown-black summer coat. You'll also find Norway's largest herd of wild reindeer, and to see them grazing is to return to an older time when great herds of wildlife roamed free all across Norway.

Toolbox

When to go
Hardangervidda's weather can be wild and unpredictable, though you can cross by train year-round. Hike in July and August; cross-country skiing is possible during the rest of the year.

Getting there
Hardangervidda inhabits the central Norwegian interior between Oslo and Bergen, close to the nearby fjords; Eidfjord and Flåm are accessible gateway towns. Geilo and Myrdal are important stops along the Oslo–Bergen railway.

Park in numbers

3430
Area covered (sq km)

1721
Highest point: Sandfloegga (m)

7000
Number of wild reindeer

⬆ The Myrdal to Flåm train traverses spectacular mountain scenery.

Stay here...

🏠 Fossli Hotel

The Fossli is set just back from the precipice of the stunning, 182m-high Vøringfoss, where Hardangervidda begins. The views are stunning and the rooms are a little faded but have character. Owner Erik, whose great-grandfather built the hotel in the 1890s, is an engaging host with a treasure trove of Hardangervidda stories. The in-house restaurant serves excellent Norwegian dishes, and there's a waffle cafe.

🏠 Finse 1222

The exceptionally pleasant Finse 1222, right by the train station and partly built out of old trains, has modern rooms, some with outrageous views over lake and glacier. It's also the starting point for many Hardangervidda activities and has a great restaurant.

🏠 Finsehytta

Most budget travellers stay at the staffed DNT hikers' hut, Finsehytta, which has decent dorms, some of which sleep only two or three people, making it great for couples and families. Set three-course meals are also available.

Do this!

🥾 Hiking

Hardangervidda has outstanding hiking, but such are its altitude and wild weather that you'll have to be quick – hiking is only possible in July and August. Hikes range from day trips to three-day crossings of the plateau, and it's on the latter that you'll best escape the crowds and increase your chances of spotting wildlife. Guided seven-hour glacier walks also take you onto the edge of the ice sheet, an exhilarating world of crevasses and ice caves.

🎿 Cross-country skiing

Ski trails criss-cross the Hardangervidda area. Those around Geilo or Finse are best for those with little experience, while the longer trails out onto Hardangervidda are for experienced skiers only, as conditions change quickly.

🪧 Traversing by train

For those unable to hike, much of the best scenery can be enjoyed from the window of your train as it crosses the plateau between Oslo and Bergen. Break up the journey with a steep detour down the Flåmsbana branch line to Flåm.

Hike this...

01 Hardangerjøkulen

The popular four-hour, 13.7km trek from Finse to the Blåisen glacier tip of Hardangerjøkulen is a stunning walk. Scenes from the planet Hof in *The Empire Strikes Back* were filmed around the glacier.

02 Vøringfoss to Kinsarvik via Harteigen

This three-day hike visits the picturesque mountain of Harteigen and then descends the Monk's Stairway to Kinsarvik.

03 Halne to Dyranut via Rauhelleren

Trails lead south off the Rv7 and away from the crowds on this two-day hike. It's one of the best trails for spotting reindeer herds in summer.

What to spot...

Hardangervidda is wonderful wildlife country. Most reindeer are domesticated, so the wild herds here are quite exceptional; Arctic foxes and snowy owls further mark the region out as a refuge for wildlife found this far south nowhere else in Norway. Wooded until perhaps 5000 years ago, Hardangervidda is now eerily treeless. In the east, wild grasses, fungi, lichens and mosses are all that really survive the alpine climate, although Hardangervidda's west can boast a few hardy species of alpine flower.

REINDEER Feeding on lichens, Hardangervidda's reindeer migrate from winter grazing grounds in the east to western breeding grounds in summer. The population is now stable after having blown out to nearly 19,000 in 1998.

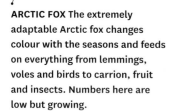

ARCTIC FOX The extremely adaptable Arctic fox changes colour with the seasons and feeds on everything from lemmings, voles and birds to carrion, fruit and insects. Numbers here are low but growing.

SNOWY OWL This large, handsome owl nests on the ground and hunts small rodents such as lemmings. Males are almost completely white, while females have grey-flecked feathers.

FINSE 1222

Itineraries

Such is Hardangervidda's scale and beauty that you can only do it justice by combining a train (or car) crossing with some hiking.

◄ Hotel Finse 1222 is handily placed next to the train station.

↑ Huts provide shelter for hikers from the often harsh weather on Hardangervidda plateau.

↑ Norway's most dramatic waterfall, Vøringfossen, is a major tourist attraction.

01
A day

There can be few more pleasurable travel experiences than journeying between Bergen and Oslo by train, and the high point, literally, of this trip is the hours spent crossing Hardangervidda. So vast is this, Europe's largest mountain plateau, that there's no better way to see it in a short time frame than by train – in considerable comfort. It's also most likely the only way you'll be able to visit in winter. All the way you'll be glued to your window (be sure to reserve a window seat...) as the train climbs onto the plateau and follows the contours of this bare and beautiful land. Numerous trains pass by every day, meaning that it's easy enough to get out in Finse, Geilo or Myrdal, even if it's only to breathe the fresh mountain air. If you make the journey in your own vehicle, that's better still: you'll be able to pull over and enjoy the view whenever you like. Staying at Fossli, on the western side of Hardangervidda, next to Vøringfoss, is a wonderful way to end a glorious day.

02
Two days

With an extra day, you can break up the journey by staying overnight, preferably at Finse, and add an activity or two to the big-picture impressions you enjoyed on day one. The long summer days mean that there will come a time after the day trippers leave when the silence of Hardangervidda takes hold – always a magical moment. Although you may be tempted by the call of multiday hikes, most visitors find the trip to Hardangerjøkulen to be a memorable sampling of the plateau's beauties, combining a lovely hike with the drama of the permanent ice sheet. Another option is to organise a glacier walk, a vertigo-inspiring experience on many travellers' bucket lists. Still another alternative is to take the Flåmsbana railway from Myrdal down to Flåm and back up onto the plateau – an extraordinary window on two very different, very pretty worlds that will put Hardangervidda in an altogether different context – before you continue on your way.

23

Hohe Tauern National Park

Experience the Austrian Alps at their most elemental in this giant of a national park, with top-of-the-beanstalk views from the Grossglockner Rd that runs through its spectacular heart.

Getty Images | Westend61

As you crest a rise on the Pinzgauer Spaziergang, suddenly the view cracks open and there, lining the horizon, is Hohe Tauern's hit parade of three-thousanders, their summits frosted with glaciers. It's hard to tear away your gaze, but you trudge on, past tarns that glint like gemstones and through moors flecked with silky cotton grass that bends in the summer breeze. The ever-narrowing path navigates slopes streaked with the moraine of a thousand avalanches, skims glass-clear streams and wriggles up to a saddle where an ibex surveys you from its rocky outpost. As day slips into dusk, shadows creep across the mountains, sharpening contours into relief. Beyond, the summit of Grossglockner, Austria's highest peak, glows in the fading light. *Alpenglühen*, it's called.

After the last ice age, Hohe Tauern was but a rock-and-scree wasteland. Then animals arrived from the steppes of Central Asia, the Arctic and the Siberian tundra as temperatures rose and glaciers retreated. Ten millennia later, the Romans made it the dividing line between their southern territories and northern conquests. A trade route for pack animals ran along the pass at the end of the Tauern Valley. But people were mistrustful of settling in this raw wilderness – tales of malevolent ice spirits were rife.

If Mother Nature surpassed herself in the Alps, Hohe Tauern is her magnum opus. Every bend on the Grossglockner Rd offers thrilling new perspectives: glaciers spilling down wrinkled mountainsides, meadows gilded with arnica and crowfoot, Heiligenblut pilgrimage church lifted above a valley as though cupped in celestial

hands. This is scenery that makes you want to yodel aloud – or at the very least grab your boots, jump in a saddle or climb to an above-the-clouds crag where you feel, if only for an instant, like a speck on the face of the planet.

⬆ The awe-inspiring Krimml Falls is Europe's highest waterfall, dropping 380m.
Previous page: mountain biking lives up to its name in stunning Hohe Tauern.

Getty Images | hsvrs

Toolbox

When to go
Wild flowers start appearing in late spring. Summer is best for climbing, hiking and cycling, with snow-free trails and the hut season in full swing. Autumn brings cool days, stag rutting and golden larches. There's heavy snow in winter.

Getting there
The park straddles Tyrol, Salzburgerland and Carinthia. A good gateway is Zell am See, roughly an hour's drive or train ride south of Salzburg. To limit traffic, many roads have toll sections and some close in winter.

Park in numbers

1856
Area covered – largest national park in the Alps (sq km)

3798
Austria's highest peak: Grossglockner (m)

300
Number of peaks above 3000m

Stay here...

Matreier Tauernhaus Mountaineers ready to climb Grossvenediger, hikers eager to hit the trail and nature-seeking families all love this hut at 1512m. Right in the park's heart, it has large, comfy, pine-clad rooms, plus climbing wall, petting zoo and rustic inn where you can dig into house specials like trout and *Kasnocken* (cheese dumplings). It also has history: it was founded by the Archbishop of Salzburg in 1207 and is on the old trade route over the Felbertauern pass.

Pension Hubertus Beate and Berndt extend a warm welcome at their chalet in Zell am See, where you'll find sunny, pine-clad rooms and fabulous hiking right on the doorstep. Organic produce and fair-trade coffee feature at breakfast.

Chalet Hotel Senger Fitting the storybook bill nicely, this Alpine chalet in Heiligenblut nuzzles up to forested slopes and has phenomenal views of Grossglockner. The Senger family make you feel instantly at home in the chalet's woodsy nooks and fire-warmed crannies. Breakfasts and dinners are generous, and there's also a flowery garden, a sauna and a hammam.

Do this!

Road-tripping With 36 hairpin bends and an average gradient of 9 percent, gear-crunching Grossglockner Rd is Hohe Tauern's showpiece and one of Europe's greatest drives. Roll down the window to breathe in the Alpine air and listen for whistling marmots as you cruise to the highest lookout, 2571m Edelweiss Spitze. The drive climaxes at Kaiser-Franz-Josefs-Höhe with close-ups of the glaciated hump of Grossglockner and the deeply crevassed Pasterze glacier.

Cycling the Tauern Trail Rolling through Austria's most spectacular Alpine scenery on the fringes of the national park, this 310km trail is not technically difficult but requires stamina. Beginning in Krimml, it heads downstream to Salzburg and Passau. Even cycling a short section of it is unforgettable.

Climbing Grossglockner For mountaineers, the ascent of Grossglockner is once-in-a-lifetime stuff. Anyone with experience can climb it via the 'normal' path, a two-hour route that begins at Erzog-Johann-Hütte, traverses rock and ice, and then follows a steel cable up a snowy ridge. Guides are available in Heiligenblut.

What to spot...

Hohe Tauern National Park is high-Alpine country, with heavy snowfalls in winter. Forests of pine, spruce and larch fringe meadows dappled with gentians, arnica, Alpine rhododendrons and edelweiss. These rise to moors riddled with marmot holes and in turn to bald, glacier-encrusted peaks of granite. Dawn and dusk are best for sighting chamois and ibex, while birds of prey such as bearded and griffon vultures, falcons and golden eagles can often be seen wheeling in the skies overhead.

GRIFFON VULTURE Hohe Tauern offers the best chance in the Alps of spotting these sociable, white-headed vultures. Up to 50 flock here between May and September, resting at the same roosts each year.

SAXIFRAGA RUDOLPHIANA These five-petalled, pink-purple blooms cling to mossy beds in the half-shade of rocks and gorges. They are well adapted to the Alpine ecosystem, preferring cold or even glacial habitats up to 3000m.

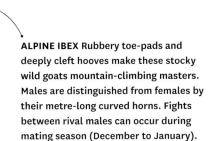

ALPINE IBEX Rubbery toe-pads and deeply cleft hooves make these stocky wild goats mountain-climbing masters. Males are distinguished from females by their metre-long curved horns. Fights between rival males can occur during mating season (December to January).

Hike this...

O1 Pinzgauer Spaziergang

Starting above Zell am See, this 19km high-ridge trail weaves through tarn-splashed meadows and moraine-streaked mountains, taking in the full sweep of the eternally ice-capped Kitzbühel and Hohe Tauern Alps.

O2 Glocknerrunde

This challenging 93.2km, week-long, hut-to-hut circuit of the mighty Grossglockner starts and ends in Kaprun. A head for heights, surefootedness and some Alpine experience are necessary.

O3 Glacier trail

Hike this easy but mind-blowing four-hour-return trail for close-ups of the swirling, fissured ice of the Eastern Alps' longest glacier, the 9km Pasterze. Begin at Glockner House (2121m).

Itineraries

Get high on the hairpins of the Grossglockner Rd, at the rainbow-laced Krimml Falls and on trails that send spirits soaring from peak to wondrous glacier-topped peak.

 Male Alpine ibex battle it out during mating season.
 Tourists gather at the head of spectacular Krimml Falls.

01

A day

Get an early start and hit Grossglockner Rd before everyone else does. Allow an entire day to do justice to this mood-lifting drive, which swings giddily around switchbacks and plunges into the national park's wild Alpine heartland.

It's all uphill from Bruck to Hochmais, where glaciated peaks including 3564m Grosses Wiesbachhorn crowd the horizon. The road zigzags up to Haus Alpine Naturschau, which brings local flora and fauna up close. Detour on a side road up to the highest lookout,

Edelweiss Spitze (2571m), for an arresting 360-degree view of 3000m peaks.

Refuel over coffee and strudel at the Edelweisshütte before driving on to gem-hued Fuscher Lake. Look for podgy marmots standing sentinel above their burrows as you cruise through high meadows, branching west to flag-dotted Kaiser-Franz-Josefs-Höhe (2369m), where views of highest-of-the-high Grossglockner and the Pasterze glacier unfold. Time permitting, hike the glacier trail before easing out the day in Heiligenblut.

02

Three days

Follow the day itinerary and devote extra time to Heiligenblut. One of Hohe Tauern's most striking sights is the needle of its 15th-century pilgrimage church framed by Grossglockner's snowy hump. Inside is a tabernacle that purportedly contains a tiny phial of Christ's blood, hence the name Heiligenblut ('Holy Blood'). Mountaineers use this postcard-pretty village as a base for bagging peaks in the national park.

Back in Zell am See, walk or cycle the mountain-

facing promenade, hire a pedalo or go for a skin-tingling dip in the lake itself, peering up at Grossglockner and co. As the sun dips behind the mountaintops, head to Steinerwirt for a gutsy goulash with dumplings.

You'll be itching to get out and stride in those mountains by your third day and Zell is a terrific base, with walks ranging from gentle ambles through Alpine pastures tinkling with cowbells to high-altitude day hikes like the Pinzgauer Spaziergang.

03

A week

With a week on your hands, you can take a walk on the park's wild side by hooking onto one of the guided ranger hikes (July to September), stretching from glacier treks to wildlife-spotting walks. If climbing is more your bag, scramble up Grossglockner from Heiligenblut or the perennially ice-capped Grossvenediger (3674m) from Matreier Tauernhaus.

Hiking and climbing are, however, just tip-of-the-iceberg stuff. Outdoor activities abound in Hohe Tauern, with Zell am See

a central base. Besides glacier skiing 10 months of the year atop Kitzsteinhorn, you could up the adventure quotient with white-water rafting, canyoning, waterskiing, wakeboarding or tandem paragliding.

Factor in a day trip, too, to the thunderous Krimml Falls. Europe's highest waterfall at 380m, it crashes over three tiers in billowing clouds of mist and is arched by a rainbow when sunlight rakes through the mixed forest that skirts it. A trail shimmies up to viewpoints jutting out over the falls.

24

Hortobágy National Park

Galloping cowboys, vivid sunsets, buffalo roaming across wind-sliced plains – Hungary's eastern prairies are the pastoral soul of this central European nation.

A lone cowboy tips his hat. He spurs his steed into a brisk canter across wide open plains. These vast prairies carry more than a whisper of the wild, wild West. But the *puszta* – the flat grasslands and marshes of Hortobágy National Park – stir the Hungarian soul. They are the bedrock of this country's agrarian history.

The national park is part of the Great Hungarian Plain, which rolls across the eastern half of the country. This was once the homeland of *csikósok*, skilled herdsmen who thundered across the prairies. Pastoral lifestyles of lapsed centuries are frozen in time in Hortobágy: traditional sweep-pole wells dot its meadows, while herdsmen's inns retain their original character. And while the *csikós'* lifestyle has faded away, his descendants remain, many of them still learning horse-riding arts.

These plains hold remainders of *kurgans* (burial mounds), suggesting that nomads passed through as long ago as 2000 BC. More established settlements came to Hortobágy from the 9th century, although a more tangible history dates to Hortobágy's cowboy heyday, in particular its 18th- and 19th-century stone bridges and travellers' lodgings.

At first glance, Hortobágy's patchwork of alkaline pastures, meadows and wetlands has a mesmerising uniformity. And somewhere between tramping through meadows and watching cranes alight by lagoons, the *puszta* works its magic. These prairies extend towards a dusty horizon where conditions are ripe for Fata Morgana mirages: optical illusions that distort and invert distant images. So, as the sun begins to dip, washing the fields of ryegrass in gold, don't be surprised if you seem to spot an 18th-century horseman out of the corner of your eye…

⬆ Endangered Przewalski's horses.

➡ Bearded reedling.

Toolbox

When to go
The season for safaris and family-friendly activities is April to October. Outside these months, museums close, though the visitor centre stays open. Wildlife watchers should visit during crane-migration season (late September and October).

Getting there
Hortobágy village is a natural starting point. It's 40km west of Debrecen, Hungary's elegant second city, and easily accessible by bus or car via Rte 33. Debrecen's airport has links to numerous European destinations. From Budapest, Hortobágy is an 180km drive east.

Park in numbers

820
Area covered (sq km)

135,000
Peak annual population of migrating cranes

300
Age of Hungary's cowboy hub, the Máta Stud Farm (years)

See this...

O1 Hortobágy Bird Park
See injured avians and orphan chicks being nursed back to health at this bird hospital before they return to the Hortobágy wilds.

O2 Nine-Hole Bridge
Legends say an outlaw was able to flee when his nine lovers linked hands, forming a bridge. An elegant stone span stands testament to this feat of polyamorous cooperation.

O3 Tisza Lake
Twitchers should prime their telephoto lenses for Tisza Lake, west of the park, where you can spot more than 160 species of bird, from nesting geese to migratory cranes.

Stay here...

Thermal Hotel Balmaz
Budapest isn't Hungary's only hot-water retreat. Reward a day of windswept walks by slipping into a steamy soak at this spa hotel on the park's eastern edge. Thermal waters are tinged the colour of tea, thanks to a reputedly muscle-soothing cocktail of minerals.

Ökotúra Camping
With this pleasant campground as your base, you can sleep under starry skies, awaken to the sound of whistling great bustards and attach yourself to plenty of guided excursions into the park. There's a simple guesthouse if canvas isn't your thing.

Do this!

Going on a *puszta* safari
The most enriching way to explore the bare heart of the *puszta* is with a knowledgeable guide aboard a Land Rover safari tour. You can access breathtaking views and spy on star residents like white-tailed eagles and wild horses.

Stargazing
Light restrictions and a low population ensure heavenly conditions for budding astronomers in Hortobágy, which has been recognised with silver-tier Dark Sky status. Sign up for a stargazing walk organised by park authorities or simply bring a telescope and dream of galaxies far away.

What to spot...

Farm animals like long-horned grey cattle and Goldilocks-tressed Mangalica pigs are Hortobágy icons. Przewalski's horses kick up dust, and 300 bird species can be spotted.

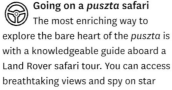

GREAT BUSTARD Recognisable by its pale-grey head and stripy russet feathers, the bustard is one of the world's heaviest flying birds. We mean it as a compliment: the heftiest one recorded tipped the scales at 21kg.

Itinerary

Summon your inner cowboy for a weekend of buffalo spotting and roaming wide open plains.

01

A weekend

Steep yourself in the lore of the wild east at Hortobágy Herdsmen Museum, before nourishing yourself like a true *csikós* at 300-year-old Hortobágy Big Inn nearby. From here, trundle by horse-drawn carriage to Máta Stud Farm to eye up Hungary's distinctive woolly pigs and shaggy Racka sheep before witnessing an astonishing display of traditional horsemanship by *csikósok* descendants. Horsemen can command their steeds to lie perfectly flat – once an essential defence from livestock rustlers – and some have mastered the 'puzsta five', where a single horseman stands astride five galloping horses.

On day two, start with a safari across the sweeping plains; bring binoculars for a close look at buffalo and prancing Przewalski's horses. Spend the afternoon exploring on foot: if you're travelling with kids, they'll adore the narrow-gauge railway to Hortobágy Fishponds, a teeming wetland threaded with footpaths.

25

Jostedalsbreen National Park

Built around mainland Europe's largest glacier, Norway's drama-filled Jostedalsbreen National Park combines sheer rock walls and groaning rivers of ice within sight of the fjords.

Jostedalsbreen National Park

One moment you're following a sinuous, fjord-hugging road that snakes across Norway's west, the next you round a corner and find yourself face to face with one of the most extraordinary sights anywhere in Europe. Mighty Jostedalsbreen is the glacier you always dreamed of – vast in scale, magical in its ice-blue beauty, and seemingly alive as it groans and inches its way like a scythe through high mountain valleys and down to the water.

The massive ice sheet feeds numerous glacier tongues that descend to the water's edge, shaping this vertiginous world as they ebb and flow, advance and retreat. For years, Jostedalsbreen bucked the worldwide trend and actually grew in size, but sadly even this contrarian glacier has been pulled back into shape by the vagaries of global warming, and recent years have seen the glaciers here shrink markedly. With an area of more than 800 sq km and an ice sheet up to 600m thick, though, Jostedalsbreen and its offshoots remain a remarkable, compelling, irresistible force of nature. To see what we mean, watch for the remnants of farms destroyed by the glaciers' march in 1750.

Wildlife is less of a feature in this park than elsewhere in Norway, not so much because it's not there but rather because much of the park is inaccessible to ordinary visitors; brown bear, elk and red deer inhabit the few areas of the park not covered in ice. But it's the glaciers themselves – Nigardsbreen, Briksdalsbreen, Bødalsbreen, Bøyabreen and Supphellebreen are among those that are considered part of the wider Jostedalsbreen ice sheet and fall partly within the park's boundaries – that are the most impressive elements of this magnificent place.

Toolbox

When to go
While the roads of the region usually remain open year-round, most operators that offer glacier experiences close from October to April. The best time to visit is from mid-June to late August.

Getting there
Jostedalsbreen is in the heart of the fjord country of central Norway, close to the towns of Fjærland and Stryn, and around halfway between the most popular fjords of Geiranger and Sognefjorden.

Park in numbers

1310
Area covered (sq km)

2083
Highest point: Lodalskåpa (m)

400,000
Rock eroded by glacier annually (tonnes)

Stay here...

Hotel Mundalx
Retaining much of its period furniture and run by the same family ever since it was built in 1891, Hotel Mundal in Fjærland, a main gateway town to Jostedalsbreen, features a welcoming lounge and a lovely round tower. You can even sleep the night in the tower's one room with wraparound views – as did US ex-president Walter Mondale, whose family came from Mundal. The restaurant serves truly wonderful traditional Norwegian dinners.

Jostedal Hotel
In the Jostedal Valley near Nigardsbreen, this friendly place has been run by the same family for three generations; much of what appears on the restaurant menu comes from their farm. In addition to standard rooms, there's a handful of five-person family rooms.

Jostedal Camping
This trim, well-kept campground sits right beside the Jostedal River. It has hiking information, the owners are friendly, facilities are impeccable and there's a lovely riverside terrace. Britain's Prince William once stayed here on a university field trip.

Do this!

Glacier walking
There's a real cachet about walking atop a glacier, and numerous operators in the area surrounding Jostedalsbreen run expertly guided explorations onto the ice sheet. The shortest walks spend an hour on the ice, but up to five hours is also possible. This is not your usual stroll – expect crampons and ropes and plenty of time spent staring into a bottomless abyss. Standard hikes are also available

Kayaking
Many of the glacier tongues end their descent at the water's edge, so the easiest way to get close is out on the water. Kayaking up to the more isolated spots is a soulful experience – outfitter Ice Troll is the pick when it comes to escaping crowds and motorboats.

Rafting
Moving at an anything-but-glacial pace, the Jostedal River, fed by the high glaciers of Jostedalsbreen, is for those looking for an adrenaline rush to go with their quiet contemplation of the ice sheet.

◄ Dramatic Nigardsbreen glacier is an arm of the greater Jostedalsbreen glacier.
Previous page: Briksdalsbreen glacier, popular with hikers.

What to spot...

You may not come here for the wildlife, but the park shelters some pretty impressive creatures, among them brown bears, elk, red deer, foxes, hares and squirrels. The area also has the highest density of bird species in western Norway, with the most variety in summer, when migratory species return from Africa.
Stands of alder, birch and pine increasingly carpet the open ground close to the water's edge, with heathers, ferns, mosses and flowering plants moving in as glaciers retreat.

EURASIAN BROWN BEAR Spot a brown bear in Jostedalsbreen and you've hit the jackpot. Norway's bears can weigh up to 300kg; although they were once primarily carnivores, meat now makes up as little as 10 percent of their diet.

ELK (MOOSE) The elk (*elg* in Norwegian) is common in Norway and the largest extant species of deer. Fully grown males have extravagant antlers.

RED DEER Another large deer species, red deer can be seen in big groups led by a single male; when another male seeks to take over the group, the clash of antlers can be heard from kilometres away.

Hike this...

01 Nigardsbreen

A boat trip across Nigardsvatnet lake takes you to the trailhead for this glacier, where one- to five-hour guided glacier walks are possible.

02 Kjenndalsbreen and Bødalsbreen

Less a single hike than a whole valley of possibilities, the little-visited Kjenndalsbreen glacier tongue is good for five-hour glacier hikes or valley walks in adjacent Bødalsbreen.

03 Briksdalsbreen

This glacier was popular for glacier hikes until splintering made it unsafe, but that may change. On dry land, it's a lovely, if steep, 5km-return hike up to the glacier face from where the road ends.

Itineraries

Exploring Jostedalsbreen means finding a base or two from which to launch daily forays into the park, although there is one overnight option for the adventurous.

 Ice-axes and crampons are mandatory for glacier walks on Nigardsbreen.
 The Breheimsenteret Glacier Centre at Nigardsbreen.

01
A day

A day spent in the vicinity of Jostedalsbreen goes something like this. Base yourself in Fjærland (which is accessible from Sognefjorden and other towns of the western fjords by regular ferry services) and browse the bookshops of this world-famous book town. Then learn everything there is to learn at the town's excellent Norwegian Glacier Museum. Thoughtfully conceived exhibits explain how fjords are formed (by glaciers, of course), let you touch 1000-year-old ice, and take you on a terrific video journey through the world of glaciers. Follow this up with a trip to the glacier tongue of Supphellebreen, where you can walk right up and touch the ice; ice blocks from here were used as podiums at the 1994 Winter Olympics in Lillehammer. At blue, creaking, more-spectacular Bøyabreen over the hill, you might happen upon glacial calving as a hunk tumbles into the meltwater lagoon beneath the glacier tongue. If you've left enough time, organise a short glacier walk with one of the numerous operators in the area.

02
Two days

You could continue on from where you left off on day one by taking a longer glacier walk (up to five hours' duration is possible, depending on the glacier) and in the process take in some of the other glaciers in the area. Nigardsbreen is accessible, spectacular and perfect for a different slant on glacier life, although it can get busy at the height of summer. You could even take a guided kayaking trip out onto the fjord and into the shadow of the glacier where it meets the water. For something truly unforgettable, consider Ice Troll's overnight kayak-and-hike expedition – you'll kayak to a shoreline within sight of a glacier and, with the crowds far away, hike along the shore and up onto the glacier under expert guidance. A beautiful campground – is there any other kind in Norway? – is the ideal vantage point for a memorable escape from the world and its noise, with the night-time groans of calving ice a soundtrack you'll never forget, before you kayak back to Fjærland next morning.

03
Three days

Fjords are very much a part of the Jostedalsbreen experience – it was, after all, glacial ice in vast quantities, down through the ages, that carved the fjords – and Stryn, north of Jostedalsbreen, is a fabulous base for both glaciers and the western fjords; Geirangerfjord in particular is not far away. Wherever you slept on the night of day one, spend your second night in Stryn, an appealing little town in its own right. To complete your set of Jostedalsbreen glaciers and glacier tongues, add Kjenndalsbreen and its near neighbour Bødalsbreen to your day-three explorations, and don't miss Briksdalsbreen. It might be one of the most popular glacier day trips, but Briksdalsbreen has an extra attraction: cute little carts or steep trails lead you to the ice, while inflatable dinghies provide another novelty-rich way to approach the glacier. However, your excitement over the mode of transport will not so much wear off as disappear from your mind as you gaze in awe at a glacier so beautiful that it casts everything else into shadow.

26

Jotunheimen National Park

Crowning Norway's high country like the ramparts of a lost mountain kingdom, Jotunheimen is a stirring wilderness of jagged peaks, sinuous hiking trails and abundant wildlife.

Getty Images | kiszon pascal

The steep, serpentine roads that climb from the fjords to this high mountain realm have the quality of a revelation. The blue of the fjords yields to quiet summer valleys of green, before the drama of ice, snow and rock takes hold. It can be an abrupt change, this journey into and across the roof of Scandinavia – as you crest a rise along one of only a handful of access routes into the park, the sudden panorama of summits is known to prompt in first-time visitors equally sudden exclamations of awe and joy.

Not for nothing is Jotunheimen known as Norway's 'Home of the Giants' – more than 275 of the mountains inside the park rise above 2000m. To put it another way, Jotunheimen is home to every peak in Norway to rise above 2300m. Some of them bear names that evoke the mysteries of Scandinavian sagas, among them Galdhøpiggen (the highest peak in northern Europe), Glittertind and Store Skagastølstind. From the heights, glaciers and countless waterfalls empty into deep ravines and ice-blue lakes far below, deep in mountain shadow.

The park has long provided inspiration to Norway's storytellers – it was along one of Jotunheimen's high ridges that Henrik Ibsen's Peer Gynt famously rode a wild reindeer. But humankind's desire to traverse the park has an altogether more prosaic back story. A perilous supply route crossed the area from the 15th century. Much later, the paved road that crosses the park – the extraordinary Sognefjellet Rd (Rv55) that rises to 1434m and is the highest mountain road in northern Europe – was built in 1939 by Norway's unemployed youth. Connecting Lustrafjorden with Lom, and reliably open only from sometime in May until September,

this is one of the most beautiful roads through one of the most beautiful national parks anywhere in Europe.

⬆ Lom's 12th-century stave church.
➡ The 275m Vettisfossen, Norway's biggest single-drop waterfall.
Previous page: the wondrous landscape.

Getty Images | Tinieder, Michele D'Amico supersky77

Toolbox

When to go
Unless you're an experienced cross-country skier, the park is only accessible from when the road can be cleared of snow sometime in May until late August or September. Most of Jotunheimen's hiking trails open from mid-June until late August.

Getting there
Jotunheimen is in central Norway, roughly equidistant from Bergen to the southwest and Trondheim to the northeast. Access to the park and its trailheads is by car, with road access from the western fjords region.

Park in numbers

1151

Area covered (sq miles)

2469

Highest point: Galdhøpiggen (m)

>60

Number of glaciers

A ski tourer stops to survey the view over 'the roof of Norway', Jotunheimen National Park.

Stay here...

 Elvesæter Hotell
This gorgeous hotel has pretty rooms and lovely architecture, and sits adjacent to the Sagasøyla, a 32m-high carved wooden pillar tracing Norwegian history from unification in 872 to the 1814 constitution. The hotel is in Bøverdalen, on the northern approach into the park. The restaurant serves up excellent meals. Open May to September.

 Turtagrø Hotel Lodge
This friendly base for exploring Jotunheimen has wonderful views and supremely comfortable rooms, but there are also dorm beds, camping and cheaper rooms in the annexe. The hotel conducts guided day trips and there's a great bar full of historic photos.

 Jotunheimen Fjellstue
From the outside this modern mountain lodge is overshadowed by its majestic surrounds, but inside are light and airy rooms that represent some of the best-value accommodation in Jotunheimen. There's a busy in-house restaurant and cafe.

Do this!

Hiking
Jotunheimen National Park is one of northern Europe's premier hiking destinations. Its short, intense summer season from June to August is the ideal time to visit and see what the park has to offer, with many of the hiking possibilities following the high ridgelines, offering views that are unrivalled anywhere else in Norway.

With so much to offer, trails can be crowded – an estimated 30,000 hikers walk the glorious Besseggen route every summer – but the park has many quieter trails that immerse you in the wilderness and open up myriad wildlife-watching possibilities.

Summer skiing
In the shadow of Galdhøpiggen, Jotunheimen's summer ski station sits at an altitude of 1850m, which is the highest point reachable by road in Norway. The skiing is relatively easy, save for the dangers inherent in taking your eyes off the slopes as you admire the view...

 Driving through
Even if you can't hike, large swathes of Jotunheimen are accessible by road. The Sognefjellet Rd from Lom to Lustrafjorden is one of Europe's most scenic drives, but don't forsake the quieter side roads of Turtagrø to Øvre Årdal or Jotunheimvegen.

What to spot...

Much of Jotunheimen lies above the tree line, but mountain birch, mountain pine, black alder, elm and hazel flourish in Bøverdalen and Utladalen. Watch also for ice-age relics such as alpine rock cress, hairy stonecrop and alpine catchfly. With so many visitors in summer, spotting wildlife can be a challenge. Even so, keep an eye out for wild reindeer, elk, foxes, martens, wolverines, Eurasian lynx and roe deer. The park's 75 bird species include the icterine warbler, woodpecker, gyrfalcon and golden eagle.

WOLVERINE Long and lithe, fierce and solitary, the wolverine is a strangely bear-like member of the weasel family and, though elusive, is one of Jotunheimen's peak carnivore species.

GLACIER BUTTERCUP A real mountain specialist, the glacier buttercup is a pretty white-and-yellow flower and the king of Norway's alpine slopes, growing close to the summit of Glittertind (2465m), more than 1km above the tree line.

GYRFALCON The largest of the falcon family, the handsome gyrfalcon has a predominantly white coat with black flecks and is best seen soaring high on the thermals watching for prey.

Hike this...

01 Galdhøpiggen
With dramatic cirques, arêtes and glaciers, this challenging six- to eight-hour, 6.2km day hike begins at Spiterstulen where the toll road starts and climbs 1470m to the summit of Norway.

02 Besseggen
Norway's most popular hike, this spectacular trail along the Besseggen ridge takes six to eight hours and covers 22.9km, with fabulous views all the way. A boat takes you back.

03 Øvre Årdal
From Øvre Årdal, head 12km northeast up the Utladalen valley to the farm Vetti, from where hiking tracks lead to Vettisfossen (275m), Norway's highest free-falling waterfall.

← The drive of a lifetime? Spectacular glacier views greet visitors to the 'Home of the Giants'.

Itineraries

Whether you're on foot or exploring the park on four wheels, the joys of Jotunheimen rank among Norway's most accessible (and unforgettable) mountain experiences.

▶ Reindeer are a common sight in Jotunheimen National Park.

01
A day

You could easily drive across the park in three hours, but so many viewpoints will call you to pull over that much pleasurable time will pass before you realise that evening is approaching. Begin in Lom, a lovely fjord-side village with a glorious stave church, then climb through Bøverdalen, a deceptively gradual ascent alongside the Bøvra River, past pretty lakes, glacial streams, grass-roofed huts, wooden farm buildings and stands of pine forest. As the road climbs, offering glimpses of ice-bound peaks, there is everywhere a suggestion of big mountains up ahead. In time, glorious panoramas begin to open up and there's no finer place to stop for lunch than Sognefjell, the summit of the Sognefjellet Rd. Long summer days mean you can continue on at your leisure, past the lodge at Turtagrø (stop in here for a beer and to surround yourself with mountaineering memorabilia), and then take the final stretch of road, with fine views and numerous switchbacks en route, all the way down to Lustrafjorden.

02
Two days

Two days is a much more sensible amount of time to dedicate to the park, and is the minimum time needed to complete one of the hikes. The route here is broadly the same as for the one-day itinerary but allows for detours and an overnight stay. Quite early on your ascent through Bøverdalen, take the turn-off to Spiterstulen, park the car at the toll point, and set off on foot for the summit of Galdhøpiggen – a six- to eight-hour return hike. Head back to the main Rv55 and stay overnight in one of Bøverdalen's many lodges and hotels. The next morning, take the turn-off to Juvasshytta, a lodge set in utterly spectacular country close to Galdhøpiggen's summer ski station. If you've bought your ticket online in advance, visit the Mímisbrunnr Klimapark and Istunnel, a 70m-long ice tunnel with an exhibition on the region's natural history and climate change. Return back down to the main Rv55, turn left and continue up and over Sognefjell, then onwards down to Lustrafjorden.

03
Four days

By adding a day or more you can do everything that you've done on the first two days but factor in all the additional detours you'd like. One favourite is Jotunheimvegen, a quiet and magnificent mountain road running 45km from Bygdin to Skåbu. Another is the shorter detour up to the toll point at Øvre Årdal; if you take this road early in the season, you may find yourself driving between deep, deep towers of cleared roadside snow. And then there's the turn-off to Leirvassbu, a remote mountain lodge with wild streams, bare hillsides and gneiss rock formations at every turn. Stop here for your picnic lunch to admire the superlative views.

If you've time, factor in more day hikes – the iconic, ridge-top Besseggen trail is popular for good reason, but don't miss the marvellous Hurrungane massif that rises darkly above the westernmost end of the park; it's accessible from the hotel at Turtagrø. For hikes that link some of these trails on one or more unforgettable loops, ask for directions at your hotel or lodge.

Getty Images | Nicolas Kipourax Paquet

— IRELAND —

Killarney National Park

A wild expanse of ancient woodland, gushing waterfalls, slate-grey lakes and rugged peaks protects rare wildlife and historic sites in Ireland's oldest park.

Killarney National Park

Deep-russet hillsides dotted with swathes of yellow gorse and whole slopes of purple heather sweep down to the lake shores in Killarney. Behind them rise the brooding Macgillycuddy's Reeks, Ireland's highest mountains, in a dramatic lakeland landscape that has an undeniably romantic allure. In the ancient, twisted forests that surround the lakes, a thick, velvety carpet of moss covers the ground and drips from the trees, giving these woods a mysterious, enchanted air.

It's the kind of place a hobbit or a hermit might well appear and, indeed, human history is an intrinsic part of the park, with the devout, the outcast, the artistic and the wealthy all leaving their mark here. Bronze Age copper miners were the first to arrive, followed in the 7th century by St Finian, who founded a leper colony and monastery on Innisfallen Island, where the monks lived for 850 years and reputedly educated the high kings of Ireland. If you're lucky, you'll spot Ireland's only herd of native red deer swimming to the island to graze among the ancient ruins.

The impressive landscapes lured the nobility, too, with the imposing bulk of medieval Ross Castle lording over Lough Leane and defiantly asserting its position across the lake from elaborate Muckross House, a Tudor-style mansion that played host to Queen Victoria in 1861. The house and its vast estate, which forms the core of the park, was presented to the state in 1932.

Since then the park has become one of the most popular, and commercialised, in the country, and in midsummer you'd do well to escape the shamrock-festooned souvenirs and well-trodden paths and retreat instead into the hills, to escape

the crowds and enjoy the expansive views that attracted all those ancient saints and scholars in the first place.

⬆ The verdant cascades of Torc Waterfall are a local landmark. Previous page: the park's emerald expanse sparkles in the sunlight.

Getty Images | Nicolas Kipourax Paquet

Toolbox

☼ **When to go**
Late spring and early autumn are best, as the park's less crowded. Muckross House gardens and the invasive but beautiful rhododendrons are most colourful from April to June; the deer rut dramatically in October and November.

🧭 **Getting there**
The park sits on the edge of Killarney town in southwestern Ireland; the nearest airport is 16km north at Farranfore. The N71 cuts the park roughly in half, with bike, boat, and horse and carriage access to quieter areas.

Park in numbers

102
Area covered (sq km)

839
Highest point: Mangerton Mountain (m)

4500
Years that humans have been active in the park area

Stay here...

🏡 **Muckross Park Hotel** Originally part of Muckross estate, this grande dame of Killarney hotels has been welcoming guests since 1795. Over the course of its history it has hosted the most prominent visitors to the park, including Queen Victoria, George Bernard Shaw and Daniel O'Connell. Bag a room in the original house if possible and enjoy its old-world charm, antique furniture, crystal chandeliers and heavy drapes. Service is impeccable, and in autumn the hotel is one of the best places in the park to watch and hear stags roaring and rutting.

🏡 **Carriglea House** A sweeping tree-lined avenue leads up to this Victorian manor house in large, tranquil grounds with lakeside walks and stunning mountain views. The spacious rooms are decorated in period style and offer a taste of Irish country living. Open April to November.

⛺ **Grove Lane Glamping** Enjoy starry nights and the sounds of nature in a luxurious bell tent set in a private orchard. Plush duvets, a solid-fuel stove, a fire pit and riverside walks make it a great spot for couples or families. Open mid-March to October.

Do this!

🛶 **Sunset kayaking** As the sun sets, hop in a kayak and paddle silently into the inky depths of the Killarney lakes. About a quarter of the park is covered by water, and as night begins to fall over the woods you'll see swans bedding down for the evening, and possibly spot red deer swimming across the lakes or brown trout jumping from the water. Then kayak back towards Ross Castle in the dwindling light, its magnificent silhouette looming against the darkening sky.

〰️ **Visiting Canyon Torc Gorge** Escape the crowds and slip, slide and splash your way down a deep mountain gorge above Torc Waterfall. Abseil down a cascade into Gollum's Pool, slide along rapids, jump over rocks and float in tranquil pools below a moss-draped forest canopy.

⚙️ **Taking a jaunting-car ride** The quintessential Killarney experience, these pony-and-trap rides are the traditional way to tour the National Park and, despite the paddywhackery, offer an excellent insight into local folklore and customs thanks to drivers whose well-honed wit and storytelling have sustained their families for decades.

What to spot...

Most famous for its ancient oak and yew woods, Killarney National Park covers a wide range of habitats, with blanket bog ablaze with heather and gorse on the upper slopes, and sessile oak and yew sweeping down to the steely lakes. The Gulf Stream offers a blanket of warmth, allowing plants and animals from southern Europe to thrive here. You'll see sika deer as well as native red deer, and a wealth of birdlife including the reintroduced white-tailed eagle.

RED DEER Ireland's largest deer are found in the wild only in this park. They have a deep red colour in summer, and the males' large antlers are put to dramatic use during the autumn rut.

ARBUTUS More typically seen around the Mediterranean, the arbutus (strawberry tree) has distinctive clusters of red or yellow spiky fruit and masses of white flowers that bloom in November and December.

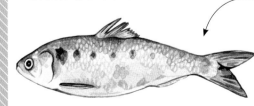

KILLARNEY SHAD A critically endangered species endemic to Lough Leane, this member of the herring family, known locally as the goureen, was trapped in the lake about 16,000 years ago.

Hike this...

O1 Muckross Lake Loop
Explore the lakeside woods and parklands on this flat 15km trail around Muckross Lake, discovering rocky coves and the ancient yews of Reenadinna Wood.

O2 Torc Mountain
A relatively easy 6km hill walk on maintained trails, Torc Mountain offers stunning views over the Killarney Valley, Mangerton and the Macgillycuddy's Reeks.

O3 Mangerton Mountain
Make your way to the top of the park's highest peak on this challenging 10km hike on open hillsides. Ascending about 1000m, it offers spectacular views of the Devil's Punch Bowl and Horses Glen.

Itineraries

Take a leisurely boat trip across some of Ireland's most stunning lakes, discover thundering waterfalls in ancient forests or explore the wild and rugged mountains on foot.

◄ Ross Castle was built in the 15th-century by the O'Donoghue clan.

► A horse-drawn jaunting car takes tourists around Muckross Lake.

01

A day

One of the best options for a day trip around the park is to hire a bike in Killarney town and cycle the 2km to 15th-century Ross Castle on the edge of Lough Leane. After a guided tour, load your bike into an open rowing boat for a 1½-hour guided trip across the park's three lakes, taking in glorious views of the surrounding mountains en route. You'll pass Innisfallen Island and the Meeting of the Waters, where the park's three lakes join, before docking by Lord Brandon's Cottage, where

you can stop for lunch, though a picnic in a tranquil spot is far more rewarding.

Then it's time to get back on your bike to head up the Gap of Dunloe for a 12km cycle along a magnificent glacial valley. Although it is technically outside the park, the Gap is one of the most scenic and famous passes in the area. Rugged and wild, it's a steep climb along the meandering road to the Head of the Gap, but the spectacular views back down over the park from the summit are well worth the effort. From here it's

downhill to Kate Kearney's Cottage to enjoy a well-earned drink or snack and then an easy ride along a new cycle path back into Killarney town. If you'd prefer not to cycle you can take a jaunting car or walk along the Gap and take a coach back to town.

02

Three days

After a day on the lakes and in the Gap of Dunloe, get out on foot or by bike to discover the park's rich history and ancient woodlands on the 15km Muckross Lake Loop. The first stop is the atmospheric ruins of Muckross Abbey, a well-preserved 15th-century friary, and then you can continue on to Muckross House to explore its old-world rooms and discover what life was like for the wealthy Victorian elite. Make your way further along the lake shore, possibly adding in a 4km loop to Torc

Waterfall, a gushing cascade that tumbles over rocks in a magical forest blanketed in moss. Once you're back on the main trail, head for Old Weir Bridge and 200-year-old Dinis Cottage, where early graffiti on the windows was carved by visiting honeymooners.

Then it's time to return along the Muckross peninsula, stopping to walk through Reenadinna Wood, one of only three remaining yew forests in Europe, before coming back to town. On day three, escape the crowds

and retreat into the hills with a hike up Mangerton Mountain. The hike begins along a dry riverbed and as you gradually gain height the lakes are revealed below you in spectacular fashion. You'll pass the beautiful Devil's Punch Bowl, a gorgeous glacial lake, and then head along a precipitous ridge to the summit, where the park and the neighbouring Macgillycuddy's Reeks stretch out before you, offering a sense of real wilderness in what can feel like a very busy park.

28

Kornati Islands National Park

Croatia's 89 jagged Kornati Islands float on the Adriatic like splashes of mercury, their moon-like surfaces covered with low ochre grasses and silvery sage.

There's a sense of floating into another world when you first catch sight of the Kornati archipelago. Sailing around the Mediterranean's densest collection of islands is an exercise in silence and bareness; mostly devoid of visible life, the islands' surface is speckled with wild herbs and low scrub. The karst rock, shaped by the elements, takes jagged, unruly forms, with steep cliffs, shadowy caves and arid, sun-drenched flatness. Lizards and butterflies slither and flutter. This stillness of the land has made it possible for the local marine life to remain relatively undisturbed – the waters of the Adriatic hide a thriving ecosystem in their depths. Scuba diving here offers a glimpse of a plenitude of life that was once at least partially matched by that of the islands' terrain.

The archipelago was covered in forest during times of Venetian occupation, when the Zadar aristocracy allowed the peasants of Murter to produce cheese and olive oil on the islands in return for some of the produce. Thus the existing greenery was burned down several times to make pasture for sheep and goats, leaving the island as barren as it is today. The remains of Roman villas on the island of Kornat, and the evidence of archaeological digs, indicate that there was once a vibrant Roman settlement here. In the Middle Ages the islands were used for fishing, stone quarries, and Venetian storage and military supplies. Even though Kornat has around 50 houses, the islanders mostly live in Murter now, moving back only in summer months.

The archipelago has been a national park since 1980, and the relative inaccessibility of the islands has made them a preferred destination of private yacht owners, who are catered to by local fishermen in exclusive cove restaurants.

Toolbox

When to go
The islands are at their best in early and late summer. The high summer season is hot and crowded with tour boats. Sailing with a private yacht is more flexible.

Getting there
The islands are south of Zadar (the nearest airport). Kornat, 35km long and 2km wide, is the main and largest island; Piškera and Žut have yachting marinas. You can visit the park on a boat tour, or rent a yacht (or bring your own).

Park in numbers

320
Sea area covered (sq km)

89
Islands

69
Varieties of butterfly

Do this...

01 Diving
Head underwater to discover the islands' wondrous sea life, such as multicoloured fish, corals, crustaceans and sponges.

02 Exploring underwater cliffs
Dive down to the *krune* (crowns), steep cliffs that descend vertically below sea level. The highest crown within the park is 82m.

03 Birdwatching
Spot some of the archipelago's 79 bird species, among them the Caspian gull, the Eurasian eagle owl, the peregrine falcon, the kestrel and the buzzard.

Stay here...

Fishers' houses
For an authentic insight into life on the islands and a real chance to explore the beauty of the national park, the stone cottages that used to be fishers' houses are a direct route to silence, peace and possibly an island to yourself. You have to enjoy simplicity to stay here, because the facilities are minimal: you get rainwater in a tank for your water supply, solar energy runs your light, and your shower water is heated by the sunshine. It's an absolute treat for lovers of the outdoors.

Do this!

Boat cruises
The best way to get to know the islands is by boat. Renting a boat and skipper means you can decide on your own itinerary and stop where and when you please. You can also go on an all-day cruise with a group.

Diving
Exploring the archipelago's rich marine life is a real treat: you'll be able to see caves, wrecks, red coral, octopuses, crustaceans, sea slugs and brightly coloured fish. Kornat island has agencies that organise dives inside the park.

◄ Boats ply the cerulean waters of Kornati Islands National Park.

What to spot...

The park enjoys a mild climate. Its fauna includes the Dalmatian wall lizard, the brush-footed butterfly and the yellow-legged gull.

DALMATIAN WALL LIZARD
This yellow, orange and white lizard, endemic to the region, enjoys shrubby vegetation, rocky areas and pastureland. It's easily spotted slithering in and out of the karst rocks on hot summer days.

Itinerary

Go sailing around the islands and dive into the clear waters of the Adriatic.

01
A day

The best of Kornati National Park is to be had by hiring a boat and skipper so that you can explore the islands at your own pace; failing that, a day-long boat tour will cover the main islands. Start by seeing the karst rock formations on Kornat, then come ashore for a morning walk around the island (note that the midday heat can make walking quite taxing).

Make arrangements with a diving agency for an afternoon dive here, and in the meantime sail around the archipelago, witnessing some of the tiniest land formations you're likely to see – some of the islands are a mere 0.2 sq km. Swim into remote caves and look at the jagged, whirling rock formations made by water and wind over the past 65 million years. Bathe in the warm, still Adriatic and have lunch on the boat. Head back to Kornat and enjoy a dive or snorkel, taking in the wonderful world below. Don't miss the underwater cliffs.

29

ESTONIA

Lahemaa National Park

Forest paths, bog boardwalks, abandoned beaches and manor-house halls are sprinkled around the 'Land of Bays', the perfect country retreat from Estonia's nearby capital.

A microcosm of Estonia's natural charms, Lahemaa National Park takes in a stretch of deeply indented coast with several peninsulas and bays, plus 475 sq km of pine-fresh hinterland that harbours forest, lakes, rivers and bogs. Sleepy villages are scattered throughout the park, cosying up to woods and stretching along inlets. Wildlife abounds, from hard-to-spot brown bears and lynx to busy beavers setting up home in rivers; more than 200 types of bird also nest here. The landscape is mostly flat or gently rolling, so physical exertion isn't required to get the most out of the park – in fact, cycling is a delightful way to get around, and gentle walks and refreshing swims are high on visitor agendas. Adding to today's ease and accessibility, cosy guest houses, restored manor houses, remote seaside campgrounds and rustic taverns offer R&R and ample refreshment.

Don't go thinking it's all about the great outdoors, though. The counterpoint to the natural charms is found in Lahemaa's cultural life, which preserves the estates of long-gone Baltic-German aristocrats, celebrates sea-captain legends and displays captivating contemporary work from Estonian artists.

Nowadays a main attraction is the water lapping the shores, but from 1945 to 1991 the entire national park's coastline was a military-controlled frontier, with a 2m-high barbed-wire fence ensuring villagers couldn't access the sea. When it was founded in 1971, Lahemaa was the first national park in the Soviet Union. Though protected areas existed before that, authorities believed that the idea of a national park would promote incendiary feelings of nationalism. Canny lobbying (including a reference to an obscure decree signed by Lenin that mentioned national parks as an acceptable form of nature protection) and years of preparation led to eventual permission.

⬆ Lahemaa's beautiful bays are perfect for camping.

Getty Images | Guntars Grebezs; AGrigorjeva

Toolbox

⚙ **When to go**
The bays, beaches and shady trails are magnets in summer (for holidaymakers as well as mosquitoes). Autumn colours glow, especially around the bogs, while in winter Lahemaa is transformed into a wonderland of snowy shores and frozen seas.

🧭 **Getting there**
The park's visitor centre at Palmse is 80km east of Tallinn, accessed by highway E20. Lahemaa is best explored by car or bike, as bus connections are limited (although day tours run from the capital).

Park in numbers

725
Area covered (sq km)

50
Mammal species

115
Highest point (m)

Walk this...

O1 Beaver Trail
Keep your eyes peeled on this beautiful 1km walkway, which passes beaver dams on the Altja River. (Note: you'll be lucky to spy the shy, nocturnal creatures.)

O2 Oandu Old-Growth Forest Nature Trail
On this 4.7km circular trail through virgin forest, boards explain the evidence of animal activity, such as trees scratched by wild boars and bears, and bark chewed by irascible elk.

O3 Viru Bog Nature Trail
A 3.5km boardwalk extends across the Viru Bog, with panels explaining flora and fauna characteristics, and a viewing tower providing a scenic vantage point.

Stay here...

Toomarahva Turismitalu
In the ancient fishing village of Altja, thatch-roofed farmstead buildings sit in a flower-filled garden. Guests can choose from a handful of rooms, or doss down in the hayloft in summer. Visiting the neighbouring tavern is a must.

Sagadi Manor
Waking up in the rarefied confines of Sagadi Manor, with its gracious gardens, is a lovely experience. This is one of the park's major estates, now home to a pink-and-white baroque mansion and museum, and a hostel, hotel and restaurant. The stables have been converted into fresh, comfortable hotel rooms.

Do this!

Cycling
Lahemaa's tree-lined back roads are perfect for cyclists; many accommodation providers have bikes to rent. Cycle between fishing villages, forest paths and manor estates, or head off-road – the best route is the 11.6km Käsmu trail. Starting in idyllic Käsmu (once a village for sea captains, now popular with artists), the trail heads through the forest to the Matsikivi erratic boulder (a large and incongruous rock carried via ancient glacial action), then continues to the tip of the peninsula, down to Lake Käsmu, and pops out back in the village, near the church.

What to spot...

Brown bears, moose, lynx and wolves lurk in the forests here, but alas, you're unlikely to see them without specialist help.

BEAVER Beavers are known for building dams, canals and lodges (homes), and in most of Lahemaa's water bodies you can observe the handiwork of these industrious builders, with dropped or half-chewed trees and lodges aplenty.

Itinerary

Drive or cycle between park highlights, from rocky beaches to elegant estates.

01
Two days

Start at the park visitor centre at Palmse, then tour the showpiece estate, a remnant of the long-vanished Baltic-German aristocracy. Palmse Manor dates from 1720 and is now a museum. From Palmse, swing northeast to Altja for traditional Estonian fare at the uber-rustic Altja Kõrts, then walk it off: first on the 3km circular Altja nature and cultural trail, taking you past fishing shacks and cottages, and then on the forest and beaver trails around Oandu. On day two, the park's peninsulas beckon. Visit pretty Käsmu for its maritime heritage and erratic boulders, and remote Viinistu for its remarkable art museum plus lunch with a sea view. The private art collection here belongs to Jaan Manitski (fun fact: he made his fortune as the business manager for Swedish superstars ABBA). Head back to the highway via the photogenically tumbledown Kolga Manor and make a final leg-stretch at the boardwalk that traverses Viru Bog.

500px | Graham Norton

30

Lake District National Park

Beautiful, dramatic and inescapably English, the Lake District has been Britain's favourite natural playground since Victorian times. Come for hikes, boat trips and poetry in the landscape.

Lake District National Park

OK, we admit it: the Lake District is every bit as picturesque and dramatic as you've been led to believe. This glorious collection of craggy hills, shimmering lakes and limpid pools has always held a special place in the English heart. Authors and poets waxed lyrical about it. Naturalists combed its hills for rare insects and butterflies. Climbers scrambled up its rocky peaks. Adrenaline junkies set speed records on its otherwise tranquil waters. And industrialists turned their backs on it and built dark satanic mills, kilns and quarries surrounded by its natural splendour.

Founded in 1951, this was one of England's first national parks, and it has consistently been the nation's most popular national park ever since. That means crowds, particularly at the height of summer, when the sombre stone villages are repainted in rainbow colours of Gore-Tex, and walkers form orderly queues in front of every lookout and beauty spot. But fear not – this is a landscape that rewards those who go the extra mile, ford the extra river and climb the extra crag to see the national park as it deserves to be seen: spectacular, silent and serene.

The landscape here is defined by the lakes – finger-like slivers of silver left behind by retreating glaciers that gouged out the gullies and rucked up the surrounding landscape into soaring ridges. Wastwater and Windermere, the deepest and longest bodies of water in England, have been the focal points for holidaymakers ever since the Kendal and Windermere Railway line was extended here in 1847. Come in summer and the lakes are a Wordsworth poem made real; come in rain, and the landscape becomes brooding, tormented and elemental. So, poetic in personality as well as appearance.

Toolbox

When to go
Summer brings the whole world to the Lake District, but the balmy days create perfect conditions for walking fells and mucking about in boats. Spring and autumn swap crowds for soggy conditions, peace and quiet. In winter, the region is at its most inhospitable and spectacular.

Getting there
Flights to Manchester provide easy connections to the railway line from Manchester to Oxenholme, Kendal, Penrith, Carlisle and Windermere. Buses pootle around in season, linking Ambleside, Windermere, Coniston and Keswick.

Park in numbers

2292
Area covered (sq km)

978
Highest point: Scafell Pike (m)

15
million
visitors per year

Stay here...

 Gilpin Hotel
You'll struggle to find more luxurious digs than Gilpin, which straddles the line between country house and boutique spa. For the former experience, book one of the six rooms in the Lake House, set in 40 hectares of grounds. For modernism that still respects its surroundings, stay at the hotel itself for spa treatments in cedar-wood lodges and outdoor hot tubs where you can watch the snow fall in winter.

Randy Pike
A bawdy name hides boutique sensibilities at this eccentric B&B, with three designer suites full of found furnishings, designer fabrics and personality. It's stone-skipping distance from Windermere and Ambleside but famously hard to find – all part of the appeal.

Wastwater YHA
A gorgeous country house at a shoestring price, the Wastwater YHA has an enviable setting in Wastwater Hall, a 19th-century manor basking on the shores of the lake. It proudly advertises the lack of wi-fi and mobile-phone signal.

Do this!

Climbing Scafell Pike
England's highest peak may not sound that impressive at 978m, but the summit is an epic vantage point. What appears to be a rounded hill becomes increasingly rocky at the top, and the final stage of the climb is rugged and exposed. The five- to six-hour ascent from Borrowdale is the most popular route, but a map is essential because of the maze of trails and the landmark-obscuring mist that can roll in.

Splashing around on the lakes
Swallows and Amazons author Arthur Ransome etched boating in the lakes into the national consciousness, and Ullswater, Coniston Water, Derwent Water and Windermere are splendid spots for a sail, splash or paddle. Take your pick from rafting, kayaking, waterskiing, sailing, motor-boating, or dry-as-a-bone steamer cruises.

Tackling a crag
Although most of the Gore-Tex-clad legions are bound for Scafell Pike, there are shorter routes to the top of the Lake District – namely straight up, with ropes and harness, on a spectacular collection of buttresses and crags.

◄ Idyllic hiking past Tarn Hows.
Previous page: the pretty Blea Tarn.

What to spot...

With its varied topography, Lake District National Park provides a haven for some of the most threatened species in the British Isles, including Britain's largest surviving population of red squirrels and the critically endangered vendace, Britain's rarest freshwater whitefish. Until recently, the park was also home to England's only golden eagle. Ospreys, red kites and peregrine falcons are doing rather better, as are red deer, migratory ducks and the otters seen slipping into waterways in search of Arctic char.

RED SQUIRREL What's a common old squirrel doing on a list of special species? Well, Britain's indigenous red squirrel is threatened by American interlopers, and it's especially loved in the Lake District because of Beatrix Potter's Squirrel Nutkin.

VENDACE Britain's rarest fish – due to a sadly predictable combination of habitat loss, pollution and foolishly introduced predator species – the vendace now lives only in Bassenthwaite Lake and Derwent Water.

SUNDEW Everyone loves a carnivorous plant! The beads of liquid glistening like dew on the leaves of the sundew are actually a sweet-smelling glue that lures insects close to curling tendrils, where they are enveloped and digested.

Hike this...

O1 Old Man of Coniston
The climb to the summit of this 803m peak is short and sweet at 6km, but it's blessed with the kind of views that inspire hymns.

O2 Helvellyn
A worthy competitor to Scafell Pike, Helvellyn's twin ridges encircle a still and silent tarn. The route via Striding Edge is a challenging 15.4km, with some serious exposure on the rocky upper sections.

O3 Cumbria Path
With 112km to cover, you'll be thankful for the country pubs dotted along this trail linking Ulverston to Carlisle via Coniston, Langdale, Borrowdale and Derwent Water.

Itineraries

In this dramatic natural cauldron, you can take in the views in an hour, or soar high and low on epic multi-day treks via lake, hill and dale.

◀ Poet William Wordsworth described the village of Grasmere as 'the loveliest spot that man hath ever found'.
▶ Yachts moored at the town of Ambleside on lake Windermere.

01

Two days

If you only have two days to take in the splendour, make them count. Stay the night before on the shores of Windermere, so you can make an early start for a potter around the streets of Bowness-on-Windermere, and then board the steamer for Ambleside. En route, you'll pass a series of classic lake vistas – shore-side manor houses, Victorian follies, mist-cloaked ridges, sheep – before rolling into Ambleside in time for a pub lunch, or more interesting vegetarian fare at Fellini's. Digest while you check out the town church, museum and ruined Roman fort, then head back through Bowness to Windermere and pick up the trail opposite the train station for the hour-long climb to Orrest Head, where views spill over to the neighbouring Langdale Pikes and the Troutbeck valley. On day two, head to the southern end of the lake and make the steep climb to Gummer's How, a 321m hummock with a Viking name and an almost uninterrupted view along the full sinuous length of Windermere. Catch your breath with a nostalgic steam-train ride on the Lakeside & Haverthwaite Railway, then detour over to Coniston Water to earn your serious Lake District stripes with the steep 803m scramble up the Old Man of Coniston. From the cairn at the summit, frequented by famously tame sheep, the southern reaches of the national park are laid out before you like a topographic model. By way of reward, finish the day with a pint of local ale in Coniston's award-winning Black Bull Inn.

02

A week

With a week to play with, there's no need to rush the views. Start down at water level at Bowness-on-Windermere, where you can cruise by steamer, paddle under your own steam in a rowing boat or kayak, or go by slow speedboat (thanks to the 10mph speed restriction on the lake). On day two, pick a country house to explore – Blackwell, 2.4km from Bowness, was an aesthetic reaction to the grim functionality of the industrial revolution, built in classic Arts and Crafts style by Mackay Hugh Baillie Scott. Start day three with a bracing walk to one of the Windermere viewpoints, then potter downhill to Dove Cottage, where Wordsworth penned many of his eulogies to the Lake District. Next, strap on your walking boots and head north to Helvellyn to test your head for heights and calf strength on a proper lakes ascent. If you feel really brave, try the vertiginous knife-edge approach along Striding Edge. Reserve day five for Derwent Water and the atmospheric stone circle at Castlerigg, where people have been appreciating the views for nigh on 4000 years. Use days six and seven for more serious Lake District scrambles – take your pick from Scafell Pike, Great Gable or Haystacks, the favourite of Alfred Wainwright, who literally wrote the book on fell-walking in the lakes. Or, for something a bit different, soak up the sea views from Black Combe, the treeless fell that rises above the tiny village of Whicham in the west of the park.

31

Lake Skadar National Park

A paradise of rare birds, rich underwater life and rugged mountains, Lake Skadar, on the Albanian–Montenegran border, is one of Europe's last spots of perfect, untouched nature.

Lonely Planet | Julian Love

The lake holds your gaze with its perfectly still surface, birds and flowers bobbing on the water. If you're a bird lover, Skadar will be your Shangri-La: the lake is home to an estimated 270 bird species, including the rare Dalmatian pelican, and storks, herons, egrets and ibises are commonly seen. In spring, thousands of birds gather here to mate, and the spectacle of their wooing is a treat.

Summer sees the lake covered with white and yellow water lilies, and the rich underwater life includes carp, bleak and around 45 other fish species. Autumn brings majestic preparations for the mass avian migration, with birds gathering strength for the long journey ahead. You won't forget the sight of Lake Skadar dotted with feathered residents, or the dawn chorus of hundreds of species. Around 50,000 birds are thought to winter in the region.

Lake Skadar was part of the ancient Slav kingdom of Zeta, but it came under Ottoman rule following the empire's invasion in the 13th century and remained under Ottoman control for five centuries. Named after the nearby Albanian town of Skadar (Shkodra), the wetlands were a battling ground for dominance between the Slavs and the Ottomans. Following the collapse of the Ottoman Empire, the Montenegrin royal family established holiday residences in Rijeka Crnojevića, on the shores of the lake. Virpazar, to the south, was the site of the first Montenegrin anti-Fascist uprising in WWII. Today, two thirds of Lake Skadar is in Montenegro and the remaining third is in Albania; it is the largest lake in the Balkans. The area has been a protected national park since 1983, and in late 2011 it was formally nominated for Unesco World Heritage status.

Toolbox

When to go
The lake is worth visiting all year. Late spring and early summer are perfect for observing avian love rituals, and autumn is the time of the wondrous mass migrations. High summer is good for diving, and you can birdwatch even in winter.

Getting there
Lake Skadar sits on the border between Albania and Montenegro. The nearest airports are in Dubrovnik (Croatia) and Podgorica (Montenegro), about two hours' drive to the park.

Park in numbers

370-550
Area covered by the lake (sq km)

270
Bird species

48
Fish species

Stay here...

🏠 Villa Miela
A beautiful, elegantly redone traditional stone house, Villa Miela sits on a lush hillside overlooking the green valley and surrounding mountains. The hosts offer a range of activities, from boating to hiking, and they can cater to different needs and abilities. There's the bonus of an outdoor hot tub to relax in at the end of the day. The rooms are simple and stylish, and the grounds are dotted with fig trees. Located in Virpazar, by the shores of the lake, it's a perfect base for exploring the area.

🏠 Virpazar Cave Apartment
A curiosity in the world of accommodation in this area, this little apartment is inside a cave, with exposed cavernous walls, quirky furniture and a spacious communal terrace. It's perfect if you want to add a bit of character to your stay.

🏠 Apartments Jovicevic
Located in lakeside Rijeka Crnojevića, this place is a mix of the traditional – with exposed-stone walls and wooden beams – and the retro. The views of the lake from the wood-encased terrace are wonderful.

Do this!

🔭 Birdwatching
There are few places in Europe that appeal to ornithologists and birdwatchers as much as Lake Skadar. Up to 300 species of bird gather here, attracted by the variety of habitats and the vast marshland. Spring, early summer and autumn are ideal, but come prepared with your best binoculars and boots to catch a glimpse of wintering birds. You will have the chance to spot ibises, squacco herons and the rare Dalmatian pelican, as well as grebes, egrets and terns. Bird spotting is done in a boat or a kayak, depending on your preference.

⛵ Lake boating
A Lake Skadar boat tour offers the ultimate combination of the idyllic and the informative – you get an insight into the lake's geology, its bird and underwater life, and the mountains and hills that surround it.

🛶 Kayaking
Get your hands on some oars and kayak your way – in a guided expedition – around the lake. Paddle up close to pelicans and through fields of water lilies, and get plenty of swimming done, either off the kayak or by a beach.

◀ Lake Skadar is home to the large Dalmatian pelican.
Previous page: kayaking the waters.

What to spot...

Bird lovers will be in heaven amid Lake Skadar's 270 species, including the Dalmatian pelican, the last of its kind in Europe. The variety of herons and the immense range of migrating birds are a marvel to observe. Freshwater life is abundant, including carp, bleak and 34 native fish species. The bamboo that edges the lake is the natural habitat of many birds, and the marshes are rich in white and yellow water lilies.

DALMATIAN PELICAN The largest and heaviest of all pelicans also has the widest recorded wingspan. You can spot it by its curly back feathers, grey legs and silvery-white plumage. Adolescents are grey.

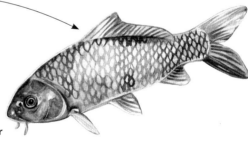

CARP This vulnerable species is red, with a protruding mouth, and can weigh up to 14kg. It feeds on vegetation and crustaceans, and it is known to leap out of the water when frightened.

BLEAK Measuring around 25cm in length, the bleak can be spotted by its shiny silver colour and upturned mouth. It moves in large schools and prefers open waters.

Hike this...

01 Vranjina trail

This one-hour hike ascends Vranjina mountain from the eponymous village, via the 15th-century Vranjina monastery. There are wonderful views of Lake Skadar from the top.

02 Rumija trail

Rocky Rumija mountain (1597m) separates Lake Skadar from the Adriatic coast. This four-hour hike takes you up to the summit, from where there are spectacular views of the sea and the lake.

03 Obod Cave trail

This three-hour circular hike passes a 14th-century printing press and Obod Cave – you can dive into its refreshing rock pools.

Itineraries

Boat or kayak through water lilies to spot a range of rare bird and fish species, and hike up mountains for views that encompass Lake Skadar and the Adriatic Sea.

◀ The spring-fed river Crnojević flows into Lake Skadar.
▶ Villa Miela offers a range of activities to its guests, from boating to hiking – and it has a hot tub.

01

A day

Going on a kayak or boat tour on Lake Skadar is a sure way of getting a taste of all the park's highlights in the shortest possible time – make sure you bring along your binoculars, swimsuit and camera. If you opt for a boat tour, you'll be able to spot a good range of fish and birds (among them the rare and mighty Dalmatian pelican), take in the sight of ancient Orthodox monasteries set atop tiny islands, see Albanian mountains off in the distance and swim in the lake's deep end. Stop at the restored 14th-century Kom Monastery and gaze at its original frescoes. Bring your own lunch for kayaking around the lake, though some operators can arrange for freshly caught fish to be prepared on one of the small islands – a real treat. You'll have the chance to paddle through swathes of white and yellow water lilies or glide down the unbroken surface of the lake, approaching islands that are used as avian resting grounds. The silence of the kayaks affords a closer look at pelicans and other birds, and if you're lucky you might spot a carp leaping out of the water. Swimming in the lake is the ideal way to cool down, so make sure you get a few dips in before you head back to shore. Great beaches on the lake include Murići beach and the secluded Pješačac beach. Catching the sunset while still out on the water is an experience you're unlikely to forget.

02

Two days

Getting an aerial perspective of Lake Skadar National Park is best done on a hike to one of the surrounding mountain tops – but be sure to bring plenty of sunscreen and a hat in the summer, plus good walking shoes. There are several hikes to choose from, but none extend for more than six hours in total, and you can deviate from some of the routes on the way down to get some swimming in. Most hikes start from Rijeka Crnojevića or Virpazar. Choosing from one of the couple of circular trails is a good way to go. One such trail takes you up to Obod Cave, offering a fantastic look at some underground life, including a variety of bats and insects, and a chance to enjoy a divine swim in the rock pools; you'll see a 14th-century printing press, one of the first in the region, on the way. The second circular trail goes over Mount Sutorman to the medieval village of Upper Godinje. On the way down to Virpazar, be sure to have a swim at Pješačac beach. A hike through Walnut Valley is beautifully shady, and there are several natural spring-water pools and waterfalls to swim in along the way; these are also perfect places to stop for a picnic lunch. Possibly the toughest hike takes you up to the summit of Rumija mountain, which sits between Skadar Lake and the Adriatic – the effort of the journey up is repaid with splendid views.

32

FINLAND

Lemmenjoki National Park

A candidate for the continent's biggest expanse of uninhabited nothingness, Finland's Lemmenjoki National Park tucks a startling array of culture into the folds of its forests, bogs and bald fells.

G old in them hills? No, it's in the low, rolling fells of utterly removed Lemmenjoki, Finland's largest national park, fanning above the Arctic Circle up to the border with Norway. This was traditionally a land for rough, tough loners: the odd prospector, or scatterings of the nation's indigenous tribespeople, the Sámi.

The few visitors who venture this far north find a region where gold glistens not solely below the surface. Summer visitors encounter gold above ground in the veins of sharp, perpetual light bathing the river valleys and the marshy, forested fell country behind them, while winter park-goers witness the colour transposed upon the heavens when some of the world's most dazzling northern lights flit phantasmally above.

This is perhaps the continent's greatest tract of roadless wilderness: old-growth forests, bogs and bare hilltops bisected by snaking tributaries. Yet, incredibly, Lemmenjoki's natural beauty might not be its main allure: the human history here is equally compelling. Rare remnants of Finland's ancient past, in the area's reindeer-farming legacy, as well as in the traditional Sámi communities surviving hereabouts mean the cultural clout is mighty indeed.

The most inviting inroad into Lemmenjoki's heart is by water. Voyaging by boat along the Lemmenjoki River ushers you up to the rushing, tumbling park highlight, the Ravadasköngäs waterfall, and beyond, into the core of this area. The trip is dipped in a majesty that the vistas from the trails seldom rival. But even a boatload is a crowd up here. So don your hiking boots you must in order to take to the park's myriad pathways and appreciate the true solitude of this place in the same way the park's other famed loner – Lemmenjoki's emblem, the wolverine – does.

⬆ The spectral sight of the northern lights.

Toolbox

☼ When to go
Snow on the ground eight months of the year means a short window for enjoying everything. For cross-country skiing April is best; for hiking, September, when it's usually snow-free and full of radiant autumn colours.

🧭 Getting there
Ivalo airport, with several daily connections to Helsinki, sits 49km southeast of Inari, which is connected to Finland's northern railway terminus (Rovaniemi) by bus. From Inari, the park entrance at Njurkulahti is a further 47km southwest via Roads 955/9551; there's no public transport.

Park in numbers

2855
Area (sq km)

29
Number of endangered European bird species

70
Length of Lemmenjoki River (km)

Hike this...

O1 Joenkielinen Circle Trail
A must-do 16km introduction to Lemmenjoki, beginning in Njurkulahti and factoring in picturesque Joenkielinen Fell, from where there are spectacular views.

O2 Lake Ravadasjärvi and Ravadasköngäs waterfall
A 26km-return trip, this trail kicks off at Lake Ravadasjärvi, linking an old gold-digging base and Ravadasköngäs waterfall (from where boats run to Njurkulahti). There are several wilderness huts to stay in overnight.

O3 Sallivaara Trail
This 12km out-and-back traipse starts at Repojoki, along the Inari–Kittilä road, and leads you out to the historic Sallivaara reindeer round-up fence.

Stay here...

 Hotel Korpikartano
This is the hotel closest to Lemmenjoki, and while it's hardly high-end, it's a pleasant place to stay: a former schoolhouse with an idyllic setting on the Menesjärvi lakeshore just outside the park boundary. There are a couple of restaurants (one Lappish) and no shortage of saunas and wilderness excursions.

 Lapinpirtti
Just 50m from the banks of the Lemmenjoki River near Njurkulahti, this lovely ruddy-coloured self-catering cabin sleeps just one to six people but comes bedecked in traditional Lappish style – with its own rowing boat for guests' use.

Do this!

Boating
Along the 22km-long Lemmenjoki River Valley, the section between Njurkulahti and Kultasatama, regular boats connect the park entrance with thunderous Ravadasköngäs falls and beyond. For wilder water-based explorations, kayaks can be rented in Njurkulahti. A sublime two- to three-day canoe route runs to Lake Paadarjärvi.

Historic sightseeing
Lapland's most important ancient cultural sights lie within Lemmenjoki. The region was crucial for reindeer herding, and the ancient pitfall traps used to catch the beasts until the 1800s, as well as the Sallivaara round-up site, offer glimpses of this heritage.

What to spot...

Lemmenjoki's contrasting fell-and-forest landscape ensures high avian diversity: 29 of Europe's endangered birds are found here.

WOLVERINE Park emblem the wolverine is a distinctive long-tailed mustelid the size of a medium dog, with long, chestnut fur protecting it from Lemmenjoki's sub-zero temperatures. It's hard to spot but easier to smell: the unpleasant odour it projects gives it the nickname 'skunk-bear'.

Itinerary

Begin with a mesmerising boat trip to waterfalls and historic sites, then hike the park's most picturesque fell.

01

Two days

Overnight at the most well-appointed accommodation hereabouts, Hotel Korpikartano in Menesjärvi. Fill up on hearty Lappish food, sweat in the sauna and soak in the hot tub before driving the 15km to the park entrance, Njurkulahti, next morning. Stock up on picnic supplies, then take the boat out to the Ravadasköngäs falls. The largest of the Lemmenjoki River tributaries flurries into a tumult, plummeting 10m down a rocky gorge, and there are tranquil spots for picnicking as well as several hiking trails. Continue to the end of the boating route at Kultasatama, where riveting insights into the region's gold-digging history await.

The next day, try the park's classic leg-stretcher, starting in Njurkulahti and clambering to one of Lemmenjoki's iconic fells, Joenkielinen. The views from here show off some of the most splendid parts of the park just 9km from the entrance and, on the return route, track a particularly gorgeous swathe of the Lemmenjoki River.

33

Loch Lomond and The Trossachs National Park

Woods and water, hills and heather, highlands and islands – the bonnie banks and braes of Loch Lomond epitomise the best of Scottish scenery.

Loch Lomond and The Trossachs National Park

The only sound is the gentle splash of your paddle as it slices the water, propelling your canoe the last few metres before the bow crunches ashore on the island's gravel beach. There's time for a spot of fishing off the nearby rocks before you prepare lunch on the campfire and then settle back to soak up the grand view of Ben Lomond rising above the loch's wooded shores.

Scotland's oldest national park is centred on 39km-long, island-studded Loch Lomond, the largest lake in mainland Britain, famed in song and story. Just to its east lie the Trossachs (from the Gaelic *Na Trosaichean*, meaning 'rough terrain'), a scenic mix of lakes, forests and rocky hills first popularised by Sir Walter Scott's romantic poem *The Lady of the Lake* in the 19th century. The park straddles the border between lowland and highland Scotland, encompassing a wide range of scenery.

The region is rich in history, most famously as the stamping ground of legendary outlaw Robert Roy MacGregor (1671–1734), whose exploits were the subject of the 1995 movie *Rob Roy*. In the 1800s, Scott's poetry inspired a flood of visitors – and the birth of Scotland's tourist industry – as the Victorians romanticised mountain scenery and all things Scottish, and newfangled trains and steamboats made inroads into the wilderness.

Despite the region's close proximity to Glasgow (Scotland's largest city), difficulty of access meant that the islands of Loch Lomond and the roadless hill country to its east remained an unspoilt haven for native woodland and wildlife. Generations of hikers, cyclists and canoeists have sought refuge from the urban hurly-burly amid its peaceful lochs and mountains, and the region was finally protected as Scotland's first national park in 2002.

⬆ Autumn in the Falls of Falloch.
Previous page: the SS *Sir Walter Scott* journeys across Loch Katrine.

When to go
May sees the lakeside woods at their loveliest, with carpets of colourful bluebells amid the trees, while October offers a riot of autumn colours, reflected in the sparkling waters of the lochs. July and August are the busiest times and the worst for midges.

Getting there
The park is in the southwestern part of the Scottish Highlands, less than an hour's drive (or train journey) from Glasgow (two hours from Edinburgh). The nearest airport is at Glasgow.

Park in numbers

1865
Area covered (sq km)

1174
Highest point:
Ben More (m)

22
Number of lochs (lakes) in the park

Stay here...

Monachyle Mhor
Set on an 18th-century farm, this rural retreat in Balquhidder combines the luxury and design of a boutique hotel with the relaxed informality of a B&B, while its restaurant is famed for fresh Scottish produce. Its stunning location is the perfect starting point for hikes in the hills or fishing trips on the local lochs, while kids will love exploring the farmyard and meeting the hotel's own dogs, ducks and sheep.

Rowardennan Lodge Youth Hostel
A former hunting lodge on the eastern side of Loch Lomond with elegant lawns stretching down to the shore, Rowardennan is a cut above your average hostel. The communal lounge enjoys grand views across the loch, and the West Highland Way passes close by.

Culag Lochside Guest House
You'd be hard-pressed to get any closer to Loch Lomond without hiring a boat. Located in Luss, Culag's comfortable and good-value accommodation is set in courtyards around a smart Victorian villa, with a huge loch-side garden and its own private beach.

Do this!

Hiking
The park is criss-crossed with hiking routes, from easy walks through bluebell woods and scenic paths along the loch shore to rough mountain trails leading to the park's highest summits. Scotland's first official long-distance hiking trail, the West Highland Way, passes through the heart of the park on its way from Glasgow to Fort William, while the Rob Roy Way links Drymen with Killin; sections of these trails provide good day or half-day expeditions.

Boating
Whether you take a cruise on a historic steamboat or rent a canoe and paddle it yourself, exploring the park's waterways and islands by boat is a must. The Loch Lomond Waterbus offers a network of passenger ferries that link up with hiking trails.

Fishing
With so much water around, it's no surprise that the park offers some of Scotland's finest angling. You can fish for salmon and brown trout in dozens of rivers and lochs, while the Lake of Menteith is a famous rainbow-trout fishery. Loch Lomond itself is known for its monster-sized pike and perch.

What to spot...

Woods and water are the key habitats in the park, with lochs and rivers rich in brown trout and salmon, otter and water vole, dragonflies and damselflies. Large areas of native birch and oak woods support mosses, lichens, and wild flowers such as primrose, bluebell and red campion, while the higher hills are home to mountain hare, red grouse and ptarmigan. One oddity is a group of Australian wallabies, introduced by a landowner in the 1940s, that roam wild on a Loch Lomond island.

OSPREY Several pairs of this rare but beautiful bird of prey nest in the national park; good places to see them include Loch Venachar, Loch Lomond, Loch Eck and the Lake of Menteith.

PINE MARTEN Most commonly seen around dusk and dawn, the elusive pine marten is a member of the weasel family. The best location for spotting them is the feeding station near the park's David Marshall Lodge.

RED SQUIRREL Increasingly under threat from the invasive grey squirrel, native red squirrels are a common sight in the park, especially in autumn as they busy themselves storing nuts for the winter.

Hike this...

O1 Balmaha

This attractive village offers plenty of walks, from woodland strolls along the loch to an easy climb up Conic Hill, with great views over Loch Lomond.

O2 Ben A'an

This miniature mountain is one of the park's most popular hikes, a three-hour-return trip to a rocky viewpoint with a breathtaking vista along Loch Katrine.

O3 Ben Lomond

As you tramp to the 990m summit of the park's most famous peak, views open up in all directions, including north to Ben Nevis (65km away).

Itineraries

Explore the woods and wildlife of Loch Lomond's lovely islands, take a cruise on a vintage Victorian steamship and say hello to a golden eagle.

◀ The Falls of Dochart at the village of Killin.
▶ Sheep graze fields high above Loch Lomond.

01

Half-day

Even without a car, you can sample the park's main attractions on a day trip from Glasgow. Take the train to Balloch, whose railway station dates from the days of steamer trips on Loch Lomond. A short walk along a riverside path leads to the loch itself, with a glorious view of Ben Lomond. Moored nearby is the *Maid of the Loch* (open weekends and holidays), a 19th-century paddle steamer that is being restored. A stroll around the bay takes you to Loch Lomond Shores, where you can learn about local landscapes and wildlife at the National Park Gateway Centre, and get up close and personal with a golden eagle at the Birds of Prey Centre. Enjoy lunch at one of the nearby restaurant terraces with views of the loch before returning to the station for the train back to Glasgow (every 30 minutes).

02

A day

Set out along the A809 Glasgow–Drymen road, pausing at the Queens View to soak up the fine vista of Loch Lomond and Ben Lomond up ahead. Take the B837 to Balmaha and arrive around 10am to catch the ferry to Inchcailloch. Allow an hour to explore this thickly wooded island nature reserve that's rich with birdlife.

Back on shore, walk to the Oak Tree Inn for lunch, then drive north through Aberfoyle and over the Duke's Pass – the viewpoint at the top is worth a photo stop – and down into the Trossachs. At Trossachs Pier, board a vintage Victorian steamship, the *Sir Walter Scott* (departs 2.30pm daily), for a one-hour scenic cruise along Loch Katrine. The 18km-long loch has been Glasgow's main water supply since 1859, but it's also one of Scotland's most beautiful lakes, dotted with wooded islands at its eastern end. Afterwards, drive east along the shores of Loch Venachar to the town of Callander for fish and chips before returning to Glasgow.

03

Two days

Head north from Glasgow on the A82 and arrive at the village of Luss in time for the Capercaillie Cruise (departs 10am Easter to October). The boat will take you on a tour around the islands of Loch Lomond, gliding through the picturesque narrows between Inchtavannach and Inchconnachan, and then crossing over to the nature reserve of Inchcailloch, where you might spot an osprey. Back in Luss, stroll around this pretty loch-side village before enjoying lunch in one of its tearooms.

As you continue driving north along Loch Lomond the loch gets narrower and the mountains higher as you enter the Highlands proper. Stretch your legs with a short walk to the Falls of Falloch, then soak up more glorious scenery as you drive on to Killin for an overnight stop. Next day is an extravaganza of scenery, from the lovely Falls of Dochart at Killin to the viewpoint at the top of Glen Ogle and down to Balquhidder, where you can visit Rob Roy's grave. Round off the trip with a cruise on Loch Katrine aboard the SS *Sir Walter Scott*.

Loch Lomond and The Trossachs National Park

34

GREECE

National Marine Park of Alonissos Northern Sporades

Explore a cluster of ancient Greek islands surrounded by aquamarine seas, home to the rare Mediterranean monk seal and vestiges of human habitation since the Stone Age.

B oating away from Alonissos island into the heart of the marine park, you'll see dolphins leaping and spot dozens of bird species as you approach protected caves and islands. Fish will surround you as you snorkel the azure waters and, diving deeper below the surface, you'll discover ancient shipwrecks.

Greece's first marine park and Europe's largest marine protected area safeguards six islands and 22 uninhabited islets emanating from the one inhabited island of Alonissos. In Paleolithic times the islands were joined in a sheet of land with the other Sporades islands and mainland Thessaly. By the Middle Stone Age, humans had found a home at Kokkinokastro on Alonissos. The remains of a settlement here are perhaps the oldest in all of the Aegean. The story goes that the islands were later settled by the Minoans, who travelled from Crete in the 16th century BC, and it was they who introduced the vineyards and olive groves you still see today. Successive rulers

included Mycenaeans (Achilles' father is said to be buried here), Athenians, Romans, Venetians, Crusaders and Turks. Always a strategic spot along Mediterranean shipping routes, Alonissos weathered the many changes, and today you'll find a bustling harbour at Patitiri.

While humans were going through centuries of drama, the local sea life, birds and animals continued to thrive. The park was established to protect more than 300 species of fish and about 80 species of bird. *Gioura* (wild goats) are endemic to an island of the same name, and dolphins and whales cavort in these waters as well. But the reluctant star of the show is the terribly endangered Mediterranean monk seal (*Monachus monachus*). With only about 600 left worldwide, half of this rarest of seals are found in Greece, and the park's Piperi island is a main breeding ground.

⬆ The dreamy vista of Kyra Panagia beach on Karpathos.

Toolbox

⚙ **When to go**
Avoid crowds but dive freely into warm, aqua seas by visiting in June, September or October. July and August are packed with visitors.

🧭 **Getting there**
Alonissos Marine Park encompasses a string of islands in the Sporades in the northwestern Aegean. The park lies off the coast of the mainland Pelion Peninsula, with ports at Volos or further south at Agios Konstantinos. The nearest airport is on Skiathos island, from where boats serve the park's main island of Alonissos.

Park in numbers

2260
Area covered (sq km)

80
Species of bird

10,200
Years that humans have been active in the park area

Hike this...

01 Palia (Old) Alonissos to Patitiri
Descend this 2.5km cobblestone trail from Alonissos' old capital to waterside Patitiri. The fortified houses were built to protect against pirates.

02 Kalovoulos Mountain
Climb the eastern side of this 325m mountain, dense with olive groves and pine forests, in time to arrive for sunset views over its steep western side.

03 Kyra Panagia Monastery
Boat to Kyra Panagia island, then walk up to this ancient monastery on an east-facing cliff. From AD 963 the island was a source of thyme honey, olives and wheat for the Mount Athos monasteries.

Stay here...

Liadromia Hotel
Patitiri's first hotel remains one of its finest. This welcoming and impeccably maintained place overlooks the harbour and has lashings of character. The gracious owner, Maria, takes pride in making it all work: from hand-embroidered curtains to rich buffet breakfasts.

Paradise Hotel
This neat-as-a-pin hotel lives up to its name with its gorgeous setting above a private swimming cove. Rooms have rustic stone floors and balconies, but the real standouts are the large pool area with sweeping sunset views, and the pathway leading to the water's edge.

Do this!

Boating
Zipping along the clear waters of the marine park is the highlight of any visit. Only authorised companies are allowed into the park's protected areas – head out with them to cruise azure coves, dive off the boat decks and picnic on white-sand beaches, or find ancient monasteries.

Diving
With waters plied by sailing ships since ancient times, the marine park offers the rare opportunity to play amateur underwater archaeologist. Dive deep, searching for over 300 species of fish as you seek Byzantine shipwrecks or jettisoned ancient amphorae.

What to spot...

Alonissos has a mild Mediterranean climate. Maquis and pine and cedar forests dot the land. Rare species include Eleonora's falcons, wild goats and Mediterranean monk seals.

MEDITERRANEAN MONK SEAL These shy, endangered seals were depicted on ancient Greek coins and mentioned in Homer's poems. Today, fewer than 600 remain in the world, and they hide in partially submerged caves to breed.

Itinerary

Zip around azure seas in search of rare seals, falcons and wild goats. Dive in, too.

01
A day

Set out early by boat from Patitiri on Alonissos to take advantage of the cool morning temperatures and the best of the daylight hours. While the boat's captain will pick your route, a typical day would include cruising between the islands in the most protected areas of the park. You'll stop in azure bays to dive into the crisp water and search for Mediterranean monk seals. If you're patient, you stand a great chance of seeing dolphins, even if the seals elude you. Or become a twitcher for the day: look for species like Audouin's gulls, shags and the mighty Eleonora's falcon, hunting on high. When you approach Gioura island, try to spot the wild goats of the same name as they scramble up cliff faces. At Kyra Panagia island, anchor in one of the sheltered bays and walk up the wind-buffeted eastern side to its 16th-century monastery. End the day back in the harbour at Patitiri sipping ouzo and snacking on *mezedhes* (small-appetiser plates).

35

NORWAY

Nordvest-Spitsbergen National Park

As far north as you can go in Europe and still be on land, Norway's Nordvest-Spitsbergen is stunningly beautiful and one of the continent's last great wilderness areas.

Nordvest-Spitsbergen National Park

The far northwest of the Svalbard archipelago is an extraordinary place - deliciously inaccessible, home to far more polar bears and walruses than people, and filled with landscapes that evoke the Arctic North of childhood imaginings. And although it belongs officially to Norway, you're actually much closer here to the North Pole than you are to Oslo.

This is a mythic landscape, with so many echoes of Arctic exploration and hardship, a land of such serene and silent beauty that you'll wonder if you've wandered into an Arctic fairytale. Here you'll find so many signposts to the human presence in the Arctic, forgotten outposts telling a story of humankind's desire to master the frozen north. There are, for example, the forlorn remains of 17th-century whaling stations littering the beaches like so much driftwood. There are the remnants of nobler expeditions to reach the North Pole, among them at Virgohamna on Danes Island from where the Swedish engineer Salomon August Andrée launched a failed attempt in 1897 to reach the Pole in a hydrogen balloon. And the gateway into the park, tiny Ny Ålesund, is now a research station for scientists studying the impact of global warming on the Arctic environment, not to mention one of the most remote settlements on earth.

But it is nature that has the final say out here, from the ethereal beauty of Kongsfjorden and Magdalenefjord to walrus-rich Moffen Island. At every turn, jagged peaks stab at the sky and deep, ice-filled valleys cut great scars into the interior. Such is nature's dominance that this is no place for the casual visitor and

coming here must be part of a well-equipped expedition by land or sea. But the rewards are enough scenes of sheer magnificence to last many lifetimes.

⬆ Sea kayaking is one of the best ways of getting up close and personal with Svalbard's remarkable wildlife.
Previous page: the glacial landscape.

Budget Travel | Kuhalizzi

Toolbox

When to go
The ocean surrounding Nordvest-Spitsbergen National Park is ice-bound for much of the year. Although long-haul winter snowmobiling expeditions from Longyearbyen may be possible, most people arrive by boat in July and August.

Getting there
Nordvest-Spitsbergen National Park occupies the far northwestern tip of the Svalbard archipelago (and indeed the far northwestern tip of Europe), with most of it on the main island of Spitsbergen (as the whole archipelago was once known)

Park in numbers

3583
Land area covered (sq km)

623
Marine area covered (sq km)

3500
Estimated number of polar bears in Spitsbergen

Stay here...

On board a ship

If, like most visitors, you've arrived in the park on board a ship, whether cruise or icebreaker or both, you'll appreciate retreating back to your cabin at the end of the day; even in summer, temperatures can be bitterly cold. Not that you'll be sure when day begins and ends: in summer, daylight never ends. Meals are taken on board, while inflatable Zodiacs transport you to land. Cabin accommodation ranges from the comfortable to the semi-luxurious.

Ny Ålesund

Scientists don't inhabit the world's most comfortable digs, but if you end up staying here overnight (they sometimes have rooms available for visiting expeditions) you'll have the essentials – somewhere warm and polar-bear proof to rest your head for the night.

Camping

If you've arrived by land, you've probably come in winter on a snowmobiling expedition. Which means that you'll be well accustomed by now to keeping watch for polar bears, carrying a gun in case one turns up, and setting up camp in the 24-hour-long night...

Do this!

Visit Magdalenefjord

The landscapes of Nordvest-Spitsbergen National Park lend themselves easily to hyperbole but it is impossible to exaggerate the sublime beauty of Magdalenefjord, one of the most splendid Arctic landscapes on earth. The lovely blue-green bay, flanked by towering peaks and intimidating tidewater glaciers, is the most popular anchorage along Spitsbergen's western coast. In the 17th century, this area saw heavy Dutch whaling; at Graveneset, near the mouth of the fjord, you can still see the remains of two stoves used to boil the blubber.

Watch wildlife

The park's waters are home to numerous marine mammals – several whale species have returned after centuries of hunting. Polar bears are frequently sighted, either on ice floes hunting for seals, roaming on land or swimming out to boats. Watch also for Arctic birdlife and walruses.

Explore Ny Ålesund

A 1.5km trail with interpretive panels takes you around this tiny settlement's sights. In the early 20th century several polar explorers set off from Ny Ålesund, including Roald Amundsen. There are poignant memorials to these expeditions.

What to spot...

Polar bears and walruses are possible anywhere, but gravelly Moffen Island hosts one of the largest walrus colonies on the planet; a 300m boat exclusion zone means you'll need a long lens. Other possible sightings include the Arctic fox (also known as the polar fox) and Svalbard's unusually squat brand of reindeer. The park contains numerous colonies of seabirds, and its sea cliffs and islands provide summer breeding perches for colonies of barnacle and brent geese, common eiders and black guillemots, among others.

POLAR BEAR Isbjørn (polar bears), the world's largest land carnivore, weigh up to 720kg and can measure 2.5m long, but the animals are swift and agile. A polar bear's diet consists mostly of seals, beached whales, fish and birds.

WALRUS The *hvalross* (walrus) measures up to nearly 4m and can weigh up to 1450kg; their elongated canine teeth can be 1m long in males. Although once heavily hunted for their ivory and blubber, the Svalbard population has rebounded to around 1000.

BARNACLE GOOSE The handsome barnacle goose has a striking black neck and crown, white face, a grey-white underbelly and silver-like colourings on the wings. The summer population on Svalbard numbers around 24,000; they winter on the UK's Solway Firth.

See this...

O1 Blomstrandhalvøya
Blomstrandhalvøya was a peninsula until the early 1990s when it was released from the icy grip on its northern end and it is now one of the newest islands in the world.

O2 Hot Springs
The hot springs of Troll and Jotun hot springs, along the shores of the park's Bockfjorden, are believed to be the world's northernmost hot springs; water temperatures range from 24.5°C to a positively balmy 28.3°C.

O3 Krossfjorden
Krossfjorden attracts quite a few cruise ships. Opposite the mouth of the fjord rise crowded bird cliffs overlooking one of Svalbard's most verdant spots, with flowers, moss and even grasses.

Itineraries

Your time in the park is likely to be dictated by the nature of your expedition, but there's no such thing as a bad view in this place – everywhere you turn is staggeringly beautiful.

◀ The starting point of many early North Pole expeditions, Ny Ålesund is now a centre for scientific research.
▶ Svalbard is one of the world's best places to spot polar bears.

01
A day

Most forays into the park begin at Ny Ålesund, and just about every cruise ship pulls ashore here and allows you to spend an hour or two wandering around this intriguing settlement, taking in the fascinating cultural detritus that litters the site. Watch especially for the anchor pylon which was used by Umberto Nobile and Roald Amundsen to launch the airship *Norge* on their successful flight over the pole to Alaska in 1926. Perhaps the most unusual attraction is the stranded steam locomotive near the dock. In 1917, a narrow-gauge railway was constructed to connect the coalfields with the harbour and it remained in use until 1958. The town also supports a neat little Mine Museum in the old Tiedemann's Tabak (tobacco) shop, relating the coal-mining history of this area. Back out at sea, you'll pass by Blomstrandhalvøya. If you pull ashore to Blomstrand, look for the machinery remains of an ill-starred 1911 attempt to quarry marble; the stone was rendered worthless by aeons of freezing and thawing.

02
Two days

Continuing north, you'll sail the length of Kongsfjorden, the glorious backdrop to Ny Ålesund. In summer, Kongsfjorden spectacularly contrasts bleak grey-brown shores with expansive white icefields. The distinctive Tre Kroner peaks, Dana (1175m), Svea (1226m) and Nora (1226m) – named in honour of Denmark, Sweden and Norway, respectively – jut from the ice and are among Svalbard's most recognisable landmarks. Rounding a fiercely beautiful headland and tracking northeast, Krossfjorden is another Nordvest-Spitsbergen icon and it's dominated by the splendid gravitas of Lillehöökbreen (its grand tidewater glacier). Among the historical relics that line the fjord's shoreline, at Ebeltoftbukta, you can see several whalers' graves as well as remnants of a 1912 German telegraph office. As you venture deeper into the fjord, which cuts ever deeper into the Spitsbergen interior, there is a sense of entering some forbidden kingdom somewhere close to the end of the earth.

03
Three days

By now you're well used to one jaw-dropping landscape of singular beauty after another, and if you tire of such experiences you're in the wrong place. Magdalenefjord is, quite simply, perfect and one of the most beautiful places on earth, Arctic or otherwise. Not far away, there's Danskøya, where the remains of so many broken dreams now lie scattered across the lonely beach, from the ruins of blubber stoves from a 17th-century whaling station to the ruined cottage built by English adventurer Arnold Pike, who sailed north in his yacht *Siggen* and spent a winter subsisting on polar bears and reindeer. Traversing ever more remote seas, you'll pass the island of Amsterdamøya, the site of the large Smeerenburg (meaning 'blubber town' in Dutch) whaling station and still littered with graves, on your way to the waters around Moffen Island. A look at the world map to see just how far north you've come will carry a very special kind of magic for most travellers.

36

Ordesa y Monte Perdido National Park

Here's where the Spanish Pyrenees stakes its claim to be Europe's most spectacular mountain range, with fabulous high-country hiking amid a glorious dragon's-back profile of limestone peaks.

Alamy Stock Photo | Sebastian Wasek

Your first sight of Ordesa y Monte Perdido National Park never quite leaves you, evoking as it does the jagged ramparts of some hidden mountain kingdom. Perhaps it's the name – 'Monte Perdido' translates as 'Lost Mountain' – that lends these mountains their cachet. Or perhaps it's because the park's impossibly steep summits and forbidding mountain passes have always served as a barrier to France and the rest of Europe, preserving until well into the 20th century the sense of Spain as a place apart. Then again, perhaps it's altogether simpler than that: this is one of Europe's most beautiful corners.

So impassable is the park's wall of rock that for centuries its only human inhabitants were those with something to hide. Trade routes followed easier contours east and west of here, leaving the park's difficult pathways to smugglers and bandits, who passed through safe in the knowledge that law-enforcement officials from both Spain and France would never follow. Such inaccessibility also enabled Pyrenean wildlife to flourish far from the hunters and habitat loss that stalked wild creatures at lower altitudes. Those that survive up here, the keepers of Pyrenean secrets, are real mountain specialists, but even here there are tales of woe: the Pyrenean ibex breathed its last in January 2000.

The sense of a secretive world accessible only to a select few continues, with just 1800 people allowed in the main section of the park, the Pradera de Ordesa, at any one time – a far cry from the relentless hiking traffic so common in other popular European national parks. Thus it is that there will be moments when time will seem to stand still, when this stunning mountain

realm is yours and yours alone, save for the whisper of Pyrenean winds, and birds of prey circling high above.

⬆ Aside from superb hiking, you will find stunning mountain views in the small village of Tella, also pictured on the previous page.

Getty Images |Westend61

Toolbox

◎ **When to go**
July and August are the best months for hiking, but they're also the most popular. Either side of these months (especially May, June and September) is generally OK, but the weather remains very unpredictable, particularly at high altitudes.

◈ **Getting there**
Ordesa y Monte Perdido is in northeastern Spain, in the Aragón region, which lies between Catalonia and Navarra. Torla is the main gateway village, and the nearest major airport is Zaragoza.

Park in numbers

156
Area covered (sq km)

3348
Highest point: Monte Perdido (m)

130
Bird species recorded in the park

Stay here...

 Casa de San Martín
For something a little special, look no further than Casa de San Martín, nestled in a hidden valley and along a dirt track 5km off the main Torla–Aínsa road. The handsome stone house has been beautifully renovated and the rooms are temples to good taste without being overdone. It's convenient for the park and you spend days here in perfect relaxation. Meals are as exceptional as the setting, and the welcome is as warm as the sitting room with its fireplace and roaring winter blaze. This is a stunning rural retreat.

 Hotel Villa de Torla
In the mountain hamlet of Torla, this place has tidy rooms – some are spacious and stylish, others have floral bedspreads and look a little tired. But the undoubted highlight is the swimming pool and bar terrace, which have lovely views.

 Hotel Villa Russell
Also in Torla, the last town before the national park and its mountains take hold, Villa Russell has enormous rooms that won't win any style awards but come with sofa, microwave and hydromassage shower. There's an on-site Jacuzzi and sauna.

Do this!

 Hiking
The only problem with hiking in Ordesa y Monte Perdido is deciding which trails to take, so wonderful are they all. Most are challenging treks rather than leisurely strolls, although most are accessible to hikers of reasonable fitness, and a shuttle bus runs between the car park in the village of Torla and some of the trailheads inside the park. The really adventurous could combine some of the day walks into multiday hikes, but you'll need to be self-sufficient to do this. Some trails even cross the border into France, an epic Pyrenean traverse.

 Climbing
The Circo de Cotatuero has been set up with 32 iron pegs hammered into the rock; they're more a rising traverse than a vertical ladder, but you'll need a cool head. Otherwise, Monte Perdido requires mountaineering gear and skills.

 **Exploring Torla**
This alpine village above the Río Ara is a wonderful prelude to the national park. Sample hearty mountain cooking, then wander out to the 13th-century Iglesia de San Salvador; there are fine mountain views from the small park on the church's northern side.

What to spot...

With 45 mammal species and 130 kinds of bird in residence, there's plenty to keep an eye out for. Brown bears occasionally pass through, but you'd have to be exceptionally lucky to see one. Pyrenean chamois are shy, but the chances of seeing them are reasonable. Watch also for wild boars, marmots and Pyrenean desmans. Birdlife is likely to be a feature – scan the skies for the golden eagle, bearded vulture, griffon vulture, all manner of hawks, and the rather lovely royal owl.

PYRENEAN CHAMOIS A member of the goat family, this agile creature can graze as high as 3000m and has made a spectacular recovery from near-extinction in the middle of the 20th century.

PYRENEAN DESMAN This semi-aquatic, mostly nocturnal water mole may be difficult to see, but boy will you be happy if you spot it. Just 11cm to 16cm long, it has a scaly tail and is excellent at climbing and swimming.

GRIFFON VULTURE With a wingspan of almost 3m, this unmistakable scavenging bird of prey is commonly seen surveying the high mountain valleys from rocky perches or circling high above.

Hike this...

01 Circo de Soaso
A challenging 15km walk (seven hours return) follows the Valle de Ordesa to Circo de Soaso, a rocky balcony whose centrepiece is the Cola del Caballo (Horsetail) waterfall.

02 Puerto de Bujaruelo
This long day section of the GR11 climbs to San Nicolás de Bujaruelo, then to Puerto de Bujaruelo on the French border, before descending to Gavarnie (France).

03 Balcón de Pineta
This challenging hike (eight hours return) begins near Bielsa and climbs via a series of steep switchbacks to the 'Pineta Balcony' for stunning glacier and mountain views.

Itineraries

This is serious hiking country with ample opportunity to link classic Pyrenean treks, while those in vehicles can cherry-pick some of the better vantage points to enjoy.

◀ Day hikers can visit the magnificent Cascada del Estrecho.
▶ The small town of Torla is the gateway to Ordesa.

01
A day

Numerous roads circle and dip into the park. Begin at ridge-top Aïnsa, one of northern Spain's most beautiful stone villages, and drive north to Escalona, where the road branches. First take the northern branch (turn right at the fork) for the drive up to Bielsa, from where a 12km paved road runs up the Valle de Pineta in the park's northeastern corner with stunning views all the way. Return to Escalona, then follow the HU631 that bucks and weaves west over the mountains to Sarvisé, crossing the park's southern tip in the process and passing through the dramatic, sinuous Bellos valley. If you're here from July to mid-September, or during Easter week, a one-way system operates on part of the Escalona–Sarvisé road. Continue on to Torla, then north to the Pradera de Ordesa, the starting point of so many trails and a pretty spot in its own right, lying in the shadow of high mountains; in summer and at Easter, private vehicles cannot drive this road, so take the shuttle bus.

02
Two days

After circling the park with intent on day one, stay overnight in Torla, then set off early to undertake the Circo de Soaso high-altitude trail. This marvellous Pyrenean hike begins at the eastern end of the Pradera de Ordesa, where you cross the Río Arazas, and then climbs steeply through woods on the valley's south side. This hardest part, called the Senda de los Cazadores (Hunters' Path), in which you ascend 600m, takes an hour. Then it's level or downhill all the way along the high Faja de Pelay path to the *circo* (cirque; a half-open, steep hollow at the head of a valley). The splendid views are evocatively supplemented by a beguiling sense of a mountain realm apart. Return by the path along the bottom of the valley, passing several waterfalls. The circuit takes about seven hours and you'll need to carry all your food and water. If you've time and wheels, take the detour into the gorgeous Valle de Bujaruelo that shadows the eastern boundary of the park.

03
Three days

With an extra day to spare, you could spend the first night in Bielsa, using it as a base to rest after attempting the spectacular Balcón de Pineta hike. If you take this option, drive via Escalona and Sarvisé to sleep the second night in Torla (or the Casa de San Martín), then hike the Circo de Soaso on day three. Another alternative to Balcón de Pineta is the Cañón de Añisclo, a gaping wound in the Earth's fabric. Although multiday walkers can reach it from the north, the southern approach begins 12km from Escalona on the road to Sarvisé – from the trailhead, a broad path leads down to the dramatic Puente de San Úrbez, then up the canyon. You can walk as far north as La Ripareta and back in about five hours, or to Fuen Blanca and back in about eight hours. These southern canyons of the park present a very different vision of the Pyrenees, drawing your gaze down into the abyss rather than up to the summits of these majestic mountains.

Getty Images | veger

37

FINLAND

Oulanka National Park

White water blasts forest-flanked gorges, and a unique triple act of Arctic, Siberian and European nature flourishes. Best way to see the show? Karhunkierros, Finland's most famous hike.

Oulanka National Park

The ferocity of rapids and waterfalls, the untamed nature of Finland's greatest hiking trail, the eclectic convergence of European, Siberian and Arctic flora and fauna amid the rocky valleys... it's easy to see why visitors flock to Oulanka.

In Finland's far east near the Russian border, the park owes its improbable biodiversity to the calcium-packed bedrock and the widely fluctuating air temperatures between valleys and fell tops. Species endangered or extinct elsewhere in Finland thrive here, from calypso orchids to golden and white-tailed eagles to brown bears.

The thrust of this nature-lovers' thrill ride, though, is the rivers – and even by Finland's phenomenal standards these stand out. They channel into cacophonous rapids, they plunge over and gouge through gorges, they entice the wildlife to perform and they intensify Oulanka's lushness. The 135km-long Oulankajoki River is the park's prime artery, where superb canoeing awaits for the adventurous.

Abutting these waterways is northern boreal forest: a thick fuzz of Scots pine and spruce resounding to the screech of eagles and the gurgle of warblers in summer, and drumming woodpeckers come wintertime.

It's in the forests that you'll witness the tale of how this landscape was created, unfolding as you hike through on what few deny is Finland's best batch of trails. Glaciers chiselled everything out during the last ice age, eroding the cliffs, carving dramatic valleys and depositing fine sand on the bed of the Oulankajoki River. In the past few centuries, slash-and-burn farmers created intermittent patches of pretty pastureland while felling wood to graze reindeer. Since the early 20th

century, though, no axes or chainsaws have touched these trees and the result is a richly preserved ecosystem. No better crash course in Oulanka's contrasts can be had than on the long-distance path bisecting the park, Finland's fabled Karhunkierros (Bear's Ring), which is aptly named indeed.

⬆ Oulanka National Park is famed for its wild rivers and thick, verdant northern boreal forest. Previous page: the Oulankajoki River flows for 135km.

Toolbox

When to go
Oulanka and surrounds have a reputation for one of the world's longest ski seasons (October to June) due to lingering snow coverage. June could see you skiing in the higher reaches and still striking out on some trails.

Getting there
The nearest airport is at Kuusamo, 50km south, with daily connections to Helsinki. The main park villages are Juuma (south) and Hautajärvi (northwest corner). The Kuusamo–Salla airport bus, connecting with all flights, passes through both.

Park in numbers

290
Area covered (sq km)

82
Length of longest trail (km)

7
Number of wilderness shelters

Stay here...

Basecamp Oulanka
Eighteen tasteful pine-furnished en-suite rooms (nine of decent midrange standard, with mezzanine levels, and nine with fewer mod-cons) compose the cosy accommodation here. Activities include memorable canoeing from the sandy beach outside, hiking on the Karhunkierros Trail and, during winter months, snow building and ice climbing. The complex lies on the lakeshore across from Juuma village.

Oulanka National Park Camping Ground
If you come to the wilderness, luxury isn't always an option. This campsite is nevertheless the area's best, equipped with a sauna and photogenically situated in the midriff of the park on the banks of the Oulankajoki River just 1.5km from Oulanka Visitor Centre.

Ruka Golden Cottage
Ruka, Finland's best ski resort, just over 20km southwest of Oulanka, has numerous accommodation possibilities, including this inviting wooden self-catering chalet 1.2km from the Ruka chair lift.

Do this!

Canoeing
Feeling the formidable current of the Oulankajoki River helps you understand the dominance of water in lake-littered, river-riven Finland. In Oulanka, as in much of the nation's north, waterways take precedence over roads. The park has two acclaimed canoe routes, one of which takes on a 13km section of the faster upper rapids and one that follows a 25km stretch of the lower river. There are campfire sites and a hut to overnight in en route.

Hiking
The big daddy of Oulanka's hikes is the 82km-long Karhunkierros Trail, but many shorter routes exist. Some, like the stroll to Kiutaköngäs waterfall, are a kilometre or two in length; others, like the strenuous tramp between the Karhunkierros and Oulanka Visitor Centres, necessitate a night's stay in a wilderness hut.

Snowshoeing
The national park has developed some scintillating snowshoeing routes, ranging from 2km to 26km in length. When Oulanka is beset by winter they offer a unique means of exploring the forests and reach areas even the trails cannot.

What to spot...

The rivers waylay water-sports aficionados while the forests, interrupted only by valleys or flower-filled meadows, fulfil the most intrepid hiker's expectations, but the bottom line with Oulanka is its diversity, terrain wise and temperature wise. This ensures one of Europe's most species-rich forest floors, replete with rare mosses, lichens and flowers, which in turn have boosted diversity all the way up the food chain.

BROWN BEAR An estimated 1500 brown bears can be found across Finland, and in Oulanka they rule the roost among the bigger predators. Weighing up to 300kg, the mighty beasts are mainly in evidence between April and September, and they usually mate in June.

CALYPSO Foraging is permitted in Oulanka, but the forests – and the meadows in their midst – sport their fair share of protected plants, of which the calypso, a pale-pink member of the orchid family and the park mascot, is among the most beautiful.

RED-BREASTED FLYCATCHER One of Oulanka's more elusive avian species, the red-breasted flycatcher visits annually, and can be glimpsed at Savilampi in the northwest of the park.

Hike this...

01 Karhunkierros Trail

The park's signature trail is among the toughest. The 27km route requires two to three days but runs the gamut of Oulanka's most exquisite elements, thrillingly featuring five swinging river bridges that groan under your weight as currents churn beneath.

02 Pieni Karhunkierros Trail

This demanding, 12km circular route offers rapids rampaging through rocky gorges, complemented by jaw-dropping forests and three swinging river bridges. It winds alongside the Kitkajoki River.

03 Kanjonin Kurkkaus

A 6km intro to Oulanka leads walkers through varied forest scenery and encompasses a lake and river-gorge cliffs.

Itineraries

Witness these unique, undisturbed ancient forests open up like an excerpt from Finnish folklore classic The Kalevala: *first by water, then by trail.*

◄ Hikers on the Karhunkierros Trail cross the Kitkajoki River.
➡ The Oulankajoki River is famous for its two superb paddling routes.

01
Two days

To truly experience Oulanka you can't come for less than a weekend's worth of outdoor action. Why? Because you need to feel the white water spray as you paddle the lakes and rivers *and* the soaring sensation as you hike the trails, creeping breathlessly along swinging bridges over rapids or paused open-mouthed at the lavish forest beauty.

The ideal choice (in truth, the only logical one) for accommodation is Basecamp Oulanka, on the cusp between forest and lake. On a late-June day with the flora blossoming swiftly to make the most of the short summer and trails newly snow free, this makes a heavenly HQ for activities. On your first day, you're going to get wet. Hire a canoe to follow one of Basecamp Oulanka's self-guided routes, or go for a guided paddling trip: either way the fun launches on the sandy beach right outside your room. Guided excursions will occupy either the morning or the afternoon, but the only other thing you'll want to do today is relax in the restaurant with some succulent grilled salmon or attempt a short walk. For the latter, driving north to Oulanka Visitor Centre is best: try the gentle walk to the Kiutaköngäs waterfall. You can get initiated in the park's history and geography, and the cafe here serves tasty snacks.

Next day, gather picnic supplies for an all-day tramp on the delightful but taxing Pieni Karhunkierros trail. It's a distillation of the park's charms and challenges: rapids and forested ravines hung by bridges.

02
Five days

Begin by basing yourself in the belly of the outdoor action at Oulanka Camping Ground. There is no better way to get into the spirit of the park than by embarking on a paddling adventure, and Oulanka has won praise for its two stunning routes along the Oulankajoki River. Make a choice: 13km of proper rapids on the upper section or a gentler 25km splash along the river's lower stretches. Either way, allow two days, as stopping off en route at the campfire sites and wilderness hut is integral to the experience.

Before the close of the second day, squeeze in a pootle about Oulanka Visitor Centre and a stroll to Kiutaköngäs waterfall. Stay at Oulanka Camping Ground again tonight and be sure to rest up, ready to tackle the park's classic hike tomorrow.

The park recommends that you spend two to three days hiking the trail from Oulanka Visitor Centre to Karhunkierros Visitor Centre in Hautajärvi (fit hikers can accomplish it in two). This glorious hike, one of the loveliest segments of the still-longer Karhunkierros Trail, will leave you feeling as though you have come to, seen and conquered Oulanka. Start early on your second day's tramp to hit Café Lapis at Karhunkierros Visitor Centre before closing time, and camp at the Hautajärvi Camping Ground.

The next day, it's treat-yourself time: spend your final night in relative luxury at Basecamp Oulanka. This wilderness hotel has a lakeshore location, hiking trails, canoeing and a nice restaurant.

38

— CROATIA —

Paklenica National Park

Planet Earth doesn't get better than Croatia's Paklenica National Park, with its dramatic display of peaks and canyons, caves and pits, rushing rivers and dizzying peaks.

The first sight of Paklenica is breathtaking. Viewing the two canyons – Velika (Large) and Mala (Small) Paklenica – swooping and falling before you vertiginously is unforgettable. Velika Paklenica Canyon is an impressive 14km long and almost 1km wide, walled with cliffs over 700m high at some points. You can follow the rushing river downstream to Anića luka, the canyon's narrowest point, and view the crashing water from the steep clifftop. Mala Paklenica Canyon is no less stunning, though the river is calmer here. At 12km in length, it's only 2km shorter than its bigger sister, and it's around 500m wide, but the framing cliffs are just as impressive.

The mountain ranges of Borovnik and Crni Vrh are in the central part of Paklenica. Covered in lush pine forest and karst rock, they're magical seen in relief against the sky. Two valleys, Mala Močila and Velika Močila, are cradled in the mountains' lap, green vessels for the rich flora and fauna of the park. The crowning glory of Paklenica is its highest mountain, Velebit, an imposing and steely observer pockmarked with wondrous cliffs and indentations. There are around 40 caves hidden in the mountain – Vodarica is 300m long, while Bunovac crevasse reaches 534m below, making it Velebit's deepest pit. Vaganski vrh (1757m) and Sveto brdo (1753m) are Velebit's highest peaks, and hiking to the top is a must for mountain-lovers.

South Velebit has been inhabited since Palaeolithic times, but it was the Romans who founded Argyruntum, now known as Starigrad, fortifying it with towers and making it a significant trading centre. In the Middle Ages, the Croats arrived and settled in the area. Paklenica was declared a national park in 1949.

Toolbox

☼ When to go
The park is never crowded, save for the rush of climbing enthusiasts during the warmer months. Hiking is recommended in spring, summer and autumn, while winter means harsher conditions. Spring and autumn, when the flowers are out, are particularly heavenly.

◎ Getting there
Paklenica is in northern Dalmatia, near Zadar (location of the nearest airport, a 45-minute drive away), on the southern side of Velebit mountain. Starigrad, the park's entry point, is on the coast at the park's foot.

Park in numbers

95
Area covered (sq km)

30,000
Age of an excavated cave bear's skull (years)

5
Permanent springs of fresh drinking water

⬊ A tiny chapel is dwarfed by the spectacular rock walls of Paklenica National Park.

Stay here...

 Camp National Park
Sitting right at the park entrance, on a pebble beach, this quaint camp site is shaded by bending pine trees. It's the ideal place to return to after a day of hiking or climbing: the sea is at your toes, the mountains are at your back, and there's no better place to soak tired muscles than the waters of the Adriatic. A barbecue supper under the night sky is a real treat. There's a range of great facilities, so you get the best of all worlds.

 Stone Houses Pojata and Varoš
These two traditional houses, with wooden beams and stone walls, have perfectly combined heritage with modern, comfortable and cosy lodgings. They're near the park entrance and the beach.

 Holiday Home Paklenica
This small house with wood-beamed ceiling and traditional knick-knacks is 300m from the park entrance, making it super convenient for exploring the hiking trails and enjoying the park's beauties.

Do this!

 Mountain summiting
Paklenica has around 200km of trails and paths, but most rewarding are the hikes to the high points of Velebit, both for the variety of landscapes, flora and fauna that you encounter along the way, and for the spectacular views on offer. Vaganski vrh is Velebit's highest peak and offers endless views all round on a clear day. Liburnija gives you the most stunning perspective: you can take in the entire mid-Adriatic archipelago.

 Cave exploring
Manita peć is the only cave in the national park that can be visited, and it's been admired since 1937 for its abundance of speleothems (cave formations) – stalagmites, stalactites, columns and flowstones.

Climbing and hiking the canyons
Rock climb and admire Velika Paklenica Canyon, with its jumbles of collapsed rock and boulders creating rapids and small waterfalls in the river below, and hike Mala Paklenica Canyon, observing the rock formations and rich flora.

Hike this...

01 Circular Paklenica trail
The essential Paklenica route, this six-hour hike passes along Velika Paklenica Canyon, through pine and beech forests via Kapljarka cave, and back alongside Mala Paklenica Canyon.

02 Manita Peć trail
This trail is a great way to incorporate a visit to Manita Peć cave into a light, 1½-hour walk, with some great views of the karst cliffs at Anića kuk.

03 Pjeskarica educational trail
Great for families, this undemanding 1.5km trail to Velika Paklenica Canyon takes you through dramatic landscapes occupied by diverse fauna.

What to spot...

Paklenica's diversity of habitats offers a wealth of flora and fauna. There is a variety of butterflies, as well as amphibians and snakes, including Orsini's viper and the spotted salamander. There are 254 species of bird, including the elusive white-backed woodpecker. Rarely spotted mammals are the brown bear, wolf and lynx. Out of 1000 plant species and subspecies recorded to date, 79 are endemic, the most exemplary being the columbine.

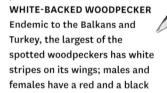

ORSINI'S VIPER This poisonous snake is also Europe's most endangered. It has a thick body, a narrow head and a scaly appearance, its grey, beige or yellow body striped with a black, zigzagging line.

WHITE-BACKED WOODPECKER Endemic to the Balkans and Turkey, the largest of the spotted woodpeckers has white stripes on its wings; males and females have a red and a black crown, respectively.

COLUMBINE Said to resemble the eagle – 'aquila' in Latin – with its five-point shape, this delicate but hardy flower blooms from cracks in the karst that enable its growth with their specific microclimatic conditions.

Itineraries

Hike and visit a splendid cave in a day, or spend four days hiking up to a Velebit mountain peak, spending the nights camping and in a mountain hut.

◧ Velika Paklenica Canyon is perfect for hikers who love to explore.

◩ The limestone walls of Paklenica are very popular with rock climbers.

◨ A WWII shipwreck lies submerged in the emerald-green waters of Zavratnica inlet.

01

A day

Get into the park early to hear the birdsong, starting your hike inside Velika Paklenica Canyon and taking in the flora that sprouts from the cliffs around you. As you go along the stream path you will have the chance to see the dramatic rock face of Anića kuk from Anića luka; the cliff dominates the park from afar and attracts many climbers. Go inside Manita Peć cave for a 30-minute tour of the marvellous underground formations and fauna, and spot the various stalagmites, stalactites, columns and flowstones. Take some warm clothes for the tour since the temperature inside the cave is a constant 9°C throughout the year. Back outside, have your lunch under the trees and let your eyes adjust to daylight again, and then start making your way back down towards Starigrad. Dip into the Adriatic at one of the pebble beaches to perfectly cap off your day.

02

Four days

This four-day hike up to Velebit's highest summit of Vaganski vrh (1757m) is the best way to really take in Paklenica's beauty. The hike includes staying in a mountain hut and camping on the mountainside. Start off early, amid the dawn chorus, and walk from Velika Paklenica Canyon, admiring the stream's waterfalls; you'll reach the Paklenica Mountain Hut in time for lunch. Another three hours' hike to Struge takes you through beech forests and glacial deposits, as well as through some incredible plant and animal life. Spend the night in the Struge shelter, a cottage-type hut where you can have your supper out under the stars. The next morning should be an early start since the seven-hour hike to the top is a demanding one, taking your breath away with the incredible views that stretch all around. Once you're atop Vaganski vrh you'll be able to spot the highest peaks of the Dinara mountain range. On the way back down, spend the night camping on the mountainside.

39

Peak District National Park

England's Peak District is more than just a landscape – these rolling dales and rugged crags were the very crucible of the Industrial Revolution.

Peak District National Park

500px | Mat Robinson

A handsome ruck of green hills tucked between the industrial centres of northern England, the Peak District has a wonderfully split personality – this is a land of Dark and White, hill and dale, limestone and grit, nature and human ingenuity. To the north, the Dark Peak is an atmospheric carpet of purple moorland and gritstone outcrops, a rival to the Lake District for English natural beauty. To the south, the White Peak rises over limestone bedrock, pockmarked with caves, sliced by rocky gorges and dotted with relics from the Industrial Revolution.

The Peak District – that's 'Peak' singular, never 'The Peaks' – was the first national park in Britain, founded in 1951, and the birthplace of hill-walking, thanks to the Kinder Trespass of 1932, which liberated the British countryside from the landed gentry and handed it to the people. This national park doesn't just preserve animals and plants, though many of England's most enigmatic creatures are found here. It also preserves the very history of industry – the mills that produced the first ever bolts of machine-made cloth, and the mines and quarries that turned metal-working from a cottage industry into a national endeavour.

How you experience the Peak is up to you. You might want to stand in serene silence, surrounded by its natural beauty and buffeted by the wind that scours the desolate moors of the Dark Peak. You might want to pit mind and muscle against some of England's most gruelling climbing and mountain-biking routes. You might decide to wriggle through the twisting caves that wormhole through the White Peak. You may prefer to hopscotch around the mills, quarries and philanthropic institutions of

Richard Arkwright's Industrial Revolution. Or there's always the genteel option: exploring historic market towns, sipping real ale in country pubs, and wandering around fabulous stately homes.

⬆ Rock climbers tackle the historic gritstone cliffs of Stanage Edge in 1964.
➡ Wind-worn gritstone edges on Kinder Scout overlook Kinder Reservoir.
Previous page: Winnats Pass.

When to go
It's a hardy soul who takes on the windswept moors of the Peak District in winter. Summer is peak season (as it were) for outdoor activities and natural beauty, but the crowds diminish in spring and autumn, when flowering heather paints the Dark Peak a rich purple.

Getting there
The park spills from Derbyshire into most neighbouring counties. Manchester and Sheffield are the main gateways, and four railway lines provide access to the heart of the Peak.

Park in numbers

1437
Area covered (sq km)

636
Highest point:
Kinder Scout (m)

1733–70
Years that gave birth to the Industrial Revolution

Stay here...

◀ The natural limestone cave of Poole's Cavern near Buxton is estimated to be 2 million years old.

🏠 Old Hall Hotel

Mary, Queen of Scots, was a resident at the Old Hall, which claims to be England's oldest hotel. Dripping with ivy and serving award-winning breakfasts, it's the pride of Buxton, the unofficial capital of the Peak. Rooms have been modernised since this place was used as an Elizabethan gaol, but there's still plenty of frilly brocade in Mary's Bower, the room where the unfortunate royal is said to have been interned.

🏠 Hartington Hall YHA

Budget travellers can live like the lord of the manor in this wood-panelled 17th-century manor-house hostel that hosts its own beer and music festivals. There are gorgeous gardens for picnics, and welcoming wood fires to warm your toes after damp hikes.

🏠 Hassop Hall Hotel

This grand 17th-century pile is within walking distance of Bakewell (of tart fame) and it offers the full country-house package: wood panelling and heirloom antiques, silver-service dinners, sprawling parterre gardens, and its own neoclassical church in the grounds.

Do this!

🥾 Walking over hill and dale

You'll have plenty of company on a Peak District walk, but isolation was never the main appeal here. Trails pick their way between country villages, so there's a roaring fire and a refreshing pint waiting at the end of every hike. En route, you can climb to rocky viewpoints, scramble down swampy dales, duck into historic mills and quarries, and even pause to cast a line in the reservoirs where the Royal Air Force practised for the Dam Busters raids in WWII.

⛰ Climbing

Climbing in the Peak District doesn't actually involve climbing many peaks. Climbers are more interested in the park's exposed gritstone escarpments and narrow limestone gorges. The White Peak is studded with bolted sport routes, but the gritstone Dark Peak is trad all the way, with classic 'edges' like Stanage, Froggatt and Curbar.

🚲 Cycling a former railway line

The 13.7km Monsal Trail follows the route of the vanished Manchester, Buxton, Matlock and Midland Junction Railway line, passing abandoned stations, ruined mills, and dark and spooky tunnels and viaducts. Bike hire is available at Hassop station and Blackwell Mill.

What to spot...

While sheep are the most common residents of the Peak District, proper wildlife abounds on the higher ground. Hares box on the hillsides, otters gambol in the brooks, foxes and hedgehogs pick their way along the hedgerows, bats swoop out of hidden caves, and owls, kestrels and buzzards mop up any smaller animals foolish enough to venture within swooping distance. Some 161 species here have been identified as endangered, including Derbyshire feather moss, found only in a single stream.

HEDGEHOG Once so common as to be almost a cliché, hedgehogs have been poisoned, de-homed and flattened out of many of their former habitats, but they still thrive in the dales of the Peak District.

ERICACEAE (HEATHER) Without heather, there would be no Dark Peak: the area takes its name from the heather-clad moorlands that burst into flower every autumn, adding a distinctive maroon wash to the landscape.

DERBYSHIRE FEATHER MOSS The entire world stock of Derbyshire feather moss can be found in a single square yard of stream bed in Cressbrook Dale. The exact location is kept secret to deter collectors.

Hike this...

01 Limestone Way
This 73km trail rambles over the rolling hills and dales of the White Peak, starting from picturesque Castleton and ending up in Ashbourne.

02 Tissington Trail
A rewarding 21km tramp or cycle from Ashbourne to Parsley Hay follows the path of the vanished Ashbourne Line, once used by Victorian holidaymakers fleeing the smog-filled cities.

03 High Peak Trail
Following another vanished railway line, this time for the Cromford and High Peak Railway, this walk climbs to stunning views along the 27km between Dowlow and Cromford.

Itineraries

Ramble from country house to country house, rent a bike and roll through the heartland of the Industrial Revolution, or get far from the crowds on the solemn moorlands of the Dark Peak.

◄ The Peak District has superb mountain biking; a rider climbs Mam Tor with Edale Valley below.
► The rather grand Buxton Opera House hosts an eclectic range of performances in its 902-seat theatre.

01

Two days

If you only have a few days in the Peak, get right to the heart of things in Buxton. This historic town is a photogenic jumble of Georgian and Victorian buildings, like a Peak District version of Bath transplanted to the Derbyshire dales. It's a gorgeous place to wander, with a famous opera festival every July. Predictably for a Victorian resort, you can also sample the local spring water. Just 1.6km from the centre is Poole's Cavern, where 28 steps drop into a limestone garden of stalactites and stalagmites, and a 20-minute climb above the cavern car park will take you to Solomon's Temple, a Victorian folly that offers sweeping views over Buxton and the dales. That should give you the appetite for a boozy evening of local cask ales at the Buxton Tap House, or a more refined meal with the opera set at Columbine Restaurant.

Start early on the second day and follow the back roads to Eyam, whose medieval villagers voluntarily quarantined themselves and succumbed to the Black Death in order to protect their neighbours. Fill up on carbs in nearby Castleton – if you come on 29 May, for the agreeably Wicker Man–esque crowning of the Garland King, all the better – then point your compass north over the ridge to Edale, following the 4.5km trail via Mam Tor. On your way back to Castleton, there should just be time enough to duck into Speedwell Cavern, for a *Lord of the Rings*-style ride through flooded tunnels to a secret subterranean lake.

02

A week

A week gives you time to daisy-chain some of the splendid walking, cycling and horse-riding trails that criss-cross the national park. Kick off by cycling the Tissington Trail, starting at Ashbourne, and feel like a Victorian holidaymaker as you pedal north under a canopy of trees. At Thorpe you can duck off the trail to visit Dovedale, where an oft-photographed line of stepping stones crosses the Dove River. At Parsley Hay, jump tracks to the High Peak Trail, continuing on to Buxton, the heart of the Peak District. Take the waters and see an opera, then roll on to Bakewell to sample the Peak District's most famous pud. After a night in Bakewell, take tea at Chatsworth House, the lavish 16th-century residence of the phenomenally wealthy Bess of Hardwick, then pick up the Monsal Trail, which meanders east through a string of eerie old railway tunnels. Along the way, you can duck into such 18th-century landmarks as the model cotton-millers' village at Cressbrook, and Litton Mill, where orphans were worked to an early grave by the villainous Ellis Needham. From the end point at Blackwell Mill, it's a short hop to pretty little Chapel-en-le-Frith and on to Castleton, with its ruined castle and caverns. Squeeze through Winnats Pass to reach Edale, starting point for walks onto the Dark Peak, tracing the routes followed by the Kinder trespassers. Finish up with a day's rock climbing at Stanage Edge or a peaceful stroll around the lovely Derwent reservoirs.

40

Pembrokeshire Coast National Park

Clifftops, castle ruins and moody, windswept heath: Britain's only coastal national park casts its indelible, edge-of-the-Earth spell on all who visit.

Getty Images | joe daniel price

Travelling through Pembrokeshire Coast National Park is like observing the work of a wizard who has cherry-picked his favourite places from around the world and plunked them down in Wales: turquoise Grecian waters, glacial ridges from Scandinavia and winsome villages from the south of France, hemmed in by the volcanic mounds of Hawaii. And unlike most national parks, the preserve, too, seems to play hopscotch through the peninsula, protecting only the most coveted tracts of land and sea.

Like the region's natural assets, Pembrokeshire's elaborate human history plays out in striking fashion. Neolithic tombs, Iron Age Celtic weapons, Roman copper hoards, cornerstones and the more obvious stone castles, vestiges of the Norman invasion and the growth of medieval England, tell the tale of almost 30,000 years of human occupation.

Pembrokeshire's elemental symphony of sea, wind and stone has a stirring effect on the soul and the region has been Wales' veritable holy land for over 2000 years. The country's patron saint was born within the confines of today's national park, and it is commonly believed that a journey twice undertaken to the cathedral in St Davids bears as much religious gravity as a pilgrimage to Rome. It's easy to fathom why the western recesses of the country have become so hallowed – even beyond the area's birthright.

The modern-day Pembrokeshire coast now lures different devotees: holidaymakers from around the United Kingdom, and sometimes beyond. They perform their pilgrimages in droves, especially during the warmer months, worshipping the dozens of broad Blue Flag beaches with cool tropical-

blue waters, visiting the tiny towns cheered by a disorganised canvas of primary and pastel colours, tasting stellar fresh food that firmly refutes any stigmas about British cuisine, and experiencing the trademark Welsh hospitality – the cosiness of the reserve personified.

⬆ The remote Marloes Sands is popular with bodyboarders.
➡ The uniquely Welsh sport of coasteering – traversing the coast via swimming and climbing.
Previous page: this limestone arch is called the Green Bridge of Wales.

Toolbox

When to go
Summer is the undisputed best time to visit the park, when, if you squint just a little, the beaches could be the subject of a Caribbean postcard. The shoulder months promise fewer travellers and discounted accommodation, while early spring and late autumn are hatching season for the park's various critters.

Getting there
The national park blankets the entirety of Wales' southwestern coastline, including the notable townships of Tenby and St Davids.

Park in numbers

612

Area covered (sq km)

1841

Population of St Davids – Britain's smallest city

58

Number of letters in the longest word in Welsh – a town in the northwest

Walking one of Pembrokeshire's many beautiful coastal paths, this time in Abercastle.

Stay here...

🏠 Roch Castle Hotel
Erected in the 12th century by Norman knight Adam de la Roche, this stone fortress has changed hands countless times since the Roche dynasty ended in 1420. Today it is a luxury hotel with six bedrooms. The interior is strikingly modern, with a monochromatic theme that lets the historical accents shine through. Breakfast is served overlooking the countryside and the coastline just beyond the little township below.

🏠 St Brides Spa Hotel
Overlooking Saundersfoot's quiet harbour, the modern yet cosy accommodation here uses blonde wood and blue-and-white accents to create a tasteful nautical theme highlighting the property's centrepiece: a soothing spa featuring an outdoor heated infinity hydro pool – the perfect end to a day spent hiking the nearby crags.

⛺ Fforest
Near Cardigan, Fforest's 80 hectares promise a fantastical collection of accommodation – geodesic domes, shacks, lofts and giant tents – that champion outdoor living. Waterfall walks, canoeing and marsh treks are but minutes away.

Do this!

🗺 Coasteering
Like some sort of amphibious parkour through the rugged coastline, coasteering was invented in Wales in the 1980s by surfers who turned negotiating shifting tides into a sport unto itself. Armed with wetsuit, helmet and flotation device, participants swim, bodysurf, explore caves, skip through rock pools and jump off cliffs along a designated trail that weaves in and out of the sea. Every trip (guided by an accredited local operator) is a different experience as neophytes negotiate naturally occurring eddies nicknamed 'the toilet' or 'the washing machine' in the name of blood-pumping fun.

🪧 Visiting St Davids
The smallest city in Britain, St Davids is named for the eponymous patron saint of Wales, born just steps away at St Nons, and it's regarded as exceptionally holy.

🏄 Surfing
More than 50 pristine beaches throughout the park add up to plenty of prime surfing spots for every level of ability. Pembrokeshire's coastline is generally considered the best for the sport in the entirety of Great Britain because the island's prevailing winds – from the southwest – foster consistent, broad waves.

What to spot...

With habitats ranging from ocean to upland pasture, the Pembrokeshire coast fosters a diverse array of organisms that includes large marine mammals and delicate highland flowers. The park's southern limestone cliffs and golden beaches slowly give way to terrain marked by more severe geological activity, such as glacial floodplains and curved volcanic hills. The landscape and its inhabitants weather drastically changing seasons that can yield daunting blizzards and steamy summer afternoons in equal measure.

RISSO'S DOLPHIN The rare Risso's dolphin, best distinguished by white scars from battling its prey, is the world's biggest dolphin, reaching up to 4m long; it's closely related to the pilot whale. A large pod dwells near Bardsey Island in Wales' north.

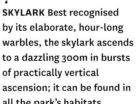

SKYLARK Best recognised by its elaborate, hour-long warbles, the skylark ascends to a dazzling 300m in bursts of practically vertical ascension; it can be found in all the park's habitats.

ATLANTIC SEAL Larger than the common seal, the Atlantic (grey) seal is distinguished by its more pronounced sloping nose. The seals spend most of their time at sea, except during the autumn calving season.

Hike this...

O1 Stackpole Head
Follow an 8km, 2½-hour coastal route down to Barafundle Bay, out to Stackpole Head, over wild dunes at Broad Haven South and then back through lily ponds.

O2 Solva to Whitesands Bay
Coves and cliffs punctuate the 18km of coastline around St Davids, each inlet a little secret between scenic, glacially carved Solva harbour and broad, peach-coloured Whitesands beach.

O3 Cemaes Head
An 8km circle takes in some of the park's most tortured landscapes – evidence of geological activity aeons ago. Grazing livestock and populous bird cliffs lend the escarpments a safari feel.

Volunteers from St Davids Lifeboat Station have been saving the lives of seafarers since 1869.

Itineraries

Although the Pembrokeshire Coast may not be one of Europe's largest parks, its series of saw-toothed peninsulas means that the possibilities for exploration are endless throughout each cliff-ridden enclave.

▶ A parliament of puffins on Skomer Island.

01

A day

In some respects, Pembrokeshire Coast National Park lends itself well to exploration by private vehicle, but the roads are often impossibly narrow and windy, making travel times rather lengthy. To ensure minimal time spent stuck behind the wheel, it's best to centre your trip on one of the park's major villages, from Cardigan in the north down to Fishguard, over to St Davids, or further down to Milford Haven, Pembroke or Tenby. St Davids' strong pilgrimage pull makes it a worthy choice for natural and cultural reasons. Britain's smallest city is the gateway to the region's most stunning headland – part of the 18km of coastline that undulates between Solva and Whitesands Bay. From the city centre you can perform an abridged walk – perfect for day trippers – that loops through the heath in about an hour and 20 minutes, moving from St Patrick's Chapel across two broad, sandy beaches, up to a lookout point with views all the way to Cardigan, and then down to the cliff's edge, where the remains of an Iron Age stronghold can be glimpsed. Return to town, the birthplace of Wales' patron saint, to appreciate the large cathedral, then follow the road by car for an oversized fish-and-chip burger at the Cambrian Inn and seriously cool digs at Roch Castle – a converted stone fortress that now features six suites – where you can watch the sun set while you sip a well-deserved glass of wine.

02

Three days

With the luxury of a long weekend up your sleeve, it's far easier to delve deeper into the different pockets that make up the park's arcing landscape, which stretches across dozens of cliffs and the beaches they keep hidden in their grasp. Start in the Tenby area, enjoying the broad public beach below and the colourful holiday houses carved right into the rock face. There are sweet shops and cosy pubs in the civic centre, lending the village a utopian feel when the sky is free of clouds. Saundersfoot, just 10 minutes down the road, is decidedly less cheery, but its St Brides Spa Hotel – perched atop a bluff – promises all the country charm you could want in an inn, and it boasts a fully kitted-out spa to boot. Stretch your legs by making the trek out to Stackpole Head, which takes in a handful of the park's top beaches, including Barafundle Bay, and winds past several of Pembrokeshire's best lookout points. Spend your remaining time near St Davids, staying at Roch Castle and following the coastal hiking path as it veers north, offering great photo opportunities all the way up to Fishguard (and beyond, if you have the stamina). For those making their way back to Cardiff, Swansea or western England, the following two stops are a must: the Carreg Cennen Castle ruins (don't miss the dungeon down below!) and Wright's Food Emporium, serving nouveau Welsh rarebit – both are located just a stone's throw beyond Llandeilo.

41

Peneda-Gerês National Park

The granite massifs, oak forests and medieval stone villages of Portugal's only national park protect both endangered species and a unique, rural way of life.

Steep mountains tower above deep valleys, the slopes dense with pine trees, the rocky peaks bare, the valleys lush with oak forests. Thermal springs bubble out of the ground, a hint of geothermal activity below. You're making your way along a narrow trail, high up in the mountains. A movement catches your eye. Several wild Garrano horses are grazing a short distance away. They see you, and unhurriedly make their escape. At night, when you're camping, you hear an eerie, distant howling. Wolves are out hunting.

About 300 million years ago, a continental collision pushed together the Iberian Peninsula and Europe, resulting in the amphitheatre of the Serra da Peneda, Serra do Soajo, Serra Amarela and Serra do Gerês mountain ranges, dominated by immense granite cliffs and slabs. The glacial fields that covered these mountains during the ice age of the Pleistocene era are nowhere to be seen. Still, the moraines, glacial deposits and deep, U-shaped valleys hint at the violent climatic events that shaped this land.

The first signs of human presence here date to around 6000 BC. Later inhabitants left behind dolmens, megalithic stone tombs and hints of ancient agriculture and animal husbandry. Two thousand years ago, Romans made their mark, with the remains of their stone roads and millenarian markers still dotting the landscape. The Buri, a Germanic tribe, settled in these mountains in the 5th century AD after invading the Iberian Peninsula, before the region was incorporated into the kingdom of Galicia and León and finally became part of Portugal.

Portugal's first – and only – national park came into being in 1971, in a bid to conserve the unique environment and the traditional way of rural life at the same time.

⬆ Summer visitors to Peneda-Gerês will find plenty of stunning rivers to swim in.
Previous page: the Cávado River winds its way through the peaks.

Toolbox

When to go
April to May, when flowers are in bloom, is great for walking. July to August is the busiest and least rainy time but can be hot in the countryside and cold in the highlands. From September through October you can observe grape harvesting.

Getting there
Peneda-Gerês forms a horseshoe shape in the north of Portugal along the Spanish border. The town of Braga, 36km away, is the departure point for buses to the park. With your own wheels, you can drive the winding mountain roads.

Park in numbers

703

Area covered (sq km)

1559

Highest point: Pico da Nevosa (m)

6000

Years that humans have been active in the park area

Stay here...

🏠 Casas de Soajo
Scattered around the village of Soajo, famous for its ancient *espigueiros* (stone granaries), and with views over Rio Lima, these restored village houses are perhaps the most atmospheric option for those interested in immersing themselves in the vanishing way of Minho life. Their sturdy stone interiors accommodate up to eight people; the fireplaces, low ceilings and antique furniture add character; and fresh bread is delivered to your doorstep every morning. Don't wish to cook? Village restaurants serve such local specialities as Portuguese stew and Soajo-style grilled goat.

🏠 Peneda Hotel
This mountain lodge overlooks the Peneda village across the picturesque ravine and a roaring creek below. Formerly a refuge for pilgrims visiting the historic Senhora da Peneda church, the hotel is bright and cosy and has a good restaurant.

🏠 Hotel Baltazar
In the centre of Gerês village, this family-run, 19th-century granite hotel accommodates guests in large, modern rooms overlooking a woodland. The in-house restaurant serves exemplary regional cuisine and the hotel is a stone's throw from the hot springs.

Do this!

🪧 Exploring villages
Visiting mountain villages in the Serra da Peneda is a step back in time, with packhorses carrying supplies along the trails, oxen working the fields and black-clad widows walking the cobbled streets. In Castro Laboreiro and Montalegre, explore the striking castle ruins. In Soajo, look for the mausoleum-like 18th-century *espigueiros*. Pitões das Júnias is an excellent place to observe traditional farming techniques. In early September, catch the Nossa Senhora da Peneda festival in Peneda, with candlelit processions and music put on by thousands of pilgrims.

🐴 Horse riding
Wild Garrano horses are native denizens of the park; a number of them have been tamed and can be ridden along the shepherds' trails or into the mountains. Equestrian schools in Gerês offer lessons and day rides.

🚲 Mountain biking
The area's winding mountain roads, precipitous dirt tracks and the ancient stone slabs of the Geira Romana are popular with cycling tours and independent cyclists. Combine steep climbs to viewpoints with rides through forests and dips in waterfalls and thermal springs.

What to spot...

Peneda-Gerês National Park encompasses high mountain plateaus and deep valleys; rainfall is high. The climate is cool in the highlands and mild in the valleys, with hot summers. Habitats include regenerating oak forests, riparian areas and peat bogs, with lots of granite formations in between. Large diurnal mammals include Spanish ibex, Garrano horses and roe deer, while nocturnal hunters include wolves. In the sky, look out for hen harriers, yellowhammers and European honey buzzards.

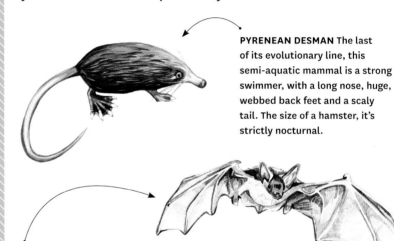

PYRENEAN DESMAN The last of its evolutionary line, this semi-aquatic mammal is a strong swimmer, with a long nose, huge, webbed back feet and a scaly tail. The size of a hamster, it's strictly nocturnal.

MEDITERRANEAN HORSESHOE BAT
Named after its horseshoe-shaped noseleaf, this medium-sized, gregarious bat roosts in colonies of up to 2000 individuals in woodlands, olive groves and caves. These nocturnal hunters prey on moths and other insects.

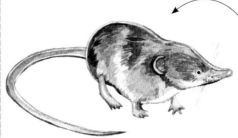

IBERIAN SHREW These small, mole-like mammals are nocturnal and feed mainly on insects. Endemic to the Iberian Peninsula, they are among the few mammal species besides whales that communicate through a series of ultrasonic squeaks.

Hike this...

O1 Geira Romana
The longest hike in the park, this 29.7km trail follows the 2000-year-old Roman road through oak woods from Portela do Homem through to Lobios, near to the Spanish border.

O2 Cidade de Calcedónia trail
Climb up to the Cabeço Calcedónia viewpoint for all-encompassing mountain views from the road that snakes over the ridge from Gerês village. It's a 7km loop in total.

O3 Trilho Castrejo
This strenuous 17km hike climbs up from the castle ruins of Castro Laboreiro and follows centuries-old shepherds' trails through the mountains.

Itineraries

Hike the old shepherd trails and the Roman road through Portugal's only national park, explore ancient villages and swim in hot springs. Grilled goat? That's on offer too.

← Pedra Bela Trail is a popular walk near the spa town of Vila do Gerês.
→ Traditional ways still continue in Peneda-Gerês; a goat herder with his flock.

01
A day

If you're short on time, drive from Braga to Serra da Peneda's most beautiful village, Peneda, halfway between Lamas de Mouro and Soajo – the trip takes less than two hours. Peneda's granite houses cluster on both sides of a precipitous ravine, against a mountain-and-waterfall backdrop. In the village, you can explore the Igreja Senhora de Peneda, a historic church that attracts thousands of pilgrims each year. A short, steep 1km trail starts behind the church and winds its way up the mountain to the human-made lake high above the village. If you're lucky, you may spot some wild Garrano horses grazing in the grasslands. If you're feeling energetic, the 8km trail past the lake makes for a pleasant and not too difficult walk that leads you through some woodlands and takes you back to the highway just above Peneda. On the way back to Braga, stop at Soajo to admire the 18th-century *espigueiros* – granite caskets on stilts that look like mausoleums but were used to protect corn harvests.

02
Three days

Get the best of the park by mountain bike by climbing up to the Pedra Bela viewpoint from Caldas do Gerês via a 35km trail. Then make your way down dirt trails to Rio Arado for a swim in the Cascata do Tahiti, returning to the starting point via rural roads and small, picturesque villages. Overnighting in Caldas do Gerês, test your mettle with a fairly strenuous 50km loop the following day. The Rota de Sombras takes you up into the high mountains, alternating between paved, narrow roads and bumpy dirt trails, and the views of the surrounding mountain range are second to none. Descend along a dirt trail to Rio Caldo and reward yourself with a soak in the river's thermal pools. On the last day, climb up to the Mata de Albergaria, one of the region's oak forests. The trail crosses into Spain and cuts across the Geira Romana. Then make your way to Campo do Gêres past Vilarinho da Furna, an eerie village flooded by a 1970s dam.

03
A week

Having your own wheels lets you make the most of the park's three mountain ranges. In Serra da Peneda, spend a day or two exploring Soajo's *espigueiros* and Peneda's church before heading north to Castro Laboreiro, hiking up to its 16th-century castle and taking on the 17km Trilho Castrejo. Then drive south through Lindoso, with its own impressive castle, and Ermita, a traditional mountain village that sees few visitors, before heading east to Campo do Gerês. In the reservoir nearby, you can spot the eerie ruins of village-made-Atlantis Vilarinho da Furna. Two excellent loop trails and horse-riding excursions are reasons to linger. More great hiking, including a tough trail to Arado waterfall and trails that link to the Geira Romana, is found around Vila do Gerês. Finish your tour with a day or two in the eastern part of the park, stopping in Cabril for grilled *cabrito* (baby goat) and heading up to Montalegre, the park's eastern gateway, to marvel at its beautiful 14th-century castle.

42

Picos de Europa

The 'Peaks of Europe' might seem a presumptuously grand name, but this northern Spanish national park lives up to its billing.

Shutterstock | Arseniy Rossikhin

You're standing by a glacial lake. Soaring, jagged peaks surround you, as do some indifferent cattle. And in your head swim two startling facts: this is the place where the Spanish Reconquista started 1300 years ago, and just a few kilometres away a brown bear could be taking a nap. If that doesn't make you take note, then some of the mouth-numbingly strong Cabrales cheese and the local firewater, *orujo*, should do the trick. The Picos de Europa straddles three Spanish regions (Asturias, Cantabria and Castilla y León), and packs history, activities, wildlife and culture into a small space.

In the early 8th century the area was the stronghold for Pelayo and his band of Visigoths who, against the odds, defeated the invading Moors and established a Christian kingdom here. Today, the park is now a refuge of a different kind – endangered species like the Cantabrian brown bear and the Iberian wolf roam here, as do Pyrenean chamois and an array of amphibians and birds, including the reintroduced lammergeier (bearded vulture).

Spain's first national park offers dozens of outdoor options. Hike the famous – and famously popular – Garganta del Cares gorge, or pick a quieter trail where wild flowers and birds are your only companions. Climb one of the limestone mountains, maybe Naranjo de Bulnes, the region's best-known peak, with a distinctive shape and a name that translates to the Orange Tree of Bulnes village. Get out on the water with a kayaking expedition down the Sella River. Go canyoning in the ravines. Or get up in the clouds the easy way with the Fuente Dé

cable car, before enjoying dinner in one of the Picos' pretty villages. There you can recount tales of bear-paw prints and blisters.

↑ Fuente Dé cable car whisks visitors up 753-vertigo-inducing-metres in four short minutes. Previous page: the Picos as viewed from Riano lake.

Toolbox

When to go
Come in April or May for the wild flowers, June or September for good weather without the peak summer-season crowds and heat.

Getting there
The Picos are in the north of Spain, just 20km from the Atlantic coast and spread across three provinces: Asturias, Cantabria and Castilla y León. The nearest airports are Asturias and Santander, both 90 minutes from the park. Madrid is a five-hour drive away.

Park in numbers

671
Area covered (sq km)

2650
Highest peak: Torre Cerredo (m)

30
Estimated number of brown bears

Shutterstock | Jose Ignacio Soto

Stay here...

Parador de Cangas de Onís
Spain's national hotel chain likes its historic buildings, and its parador in the town of Cangas de Onís, former capital of Asturias and current hub for the western Picos, doesn't disappoint. The former San Pedro monastery is now a stylish sleeping option where the spacious, comfortable rooms, some with four-poster beds, are a far cry from what the monks would have enjoyed. A beautiful garden, an old church with medieval carvings, and a great restaurant serving local specialities add to the appeal.

La Casa de las Chimeneas
The 'Chimney House' is actually a collection of apartments in a farmstead that dates back centuries. Original architectural features have been retained, and a social room, pool and garden allow mingling with other Picos-goers and wonderful mountain views.

Posada del Valle
Great design and eco-friendly credentials make this one of the best sleeping options in the area. Meals use produce from the organic garden; decor takes its cue from local culture; and the hosts are a wealth of information on the Picos.

Do this!

Walking the Garganta del Cares
The 'Throat of the Cares' walk is the most popular hike in the Picos. Best walked from north (Poncebos in Asturias) to south (Caín in Castilla y León), the route cuts a relatively short 10km trail through kilometre-high cliffs, following the Cares River. The trail is a mix of steep paths, bridges and tunnels that take you alongside and sometimes through the limestone walls, while alternately barren and green landscapes provide a stunning, picture-perfect backdrop.

Taking the Fuente Dé cable car
For a lammergeier's view of the southern Picos, take an exhilarating ride on the Fuente Dé cable car. Whizz up an ear-popping 753m in just four minutes to soak up the views at the cafe or head out on a trail.

Eating cheese and drinking cider
Traditionally wrapped in sycamore leaves and left in local caves to ripen, pungent Cabrales is a blue cheese to be reckoned with. Wash it down with some potent local cider (after gaping in awe at how it's poured) for a true Picos experience.

What to spot...

Four distinct seasons, traditional and sustainable farming practices, and large sections that are too isolated for human encroachment mean a huge variety of flora and fauna exist in the Picos. Deer, badgers and even wild boar are commonplace. Pyrenean chamois are the animals you're most likely to see; elusive Cantabrian bears and Iberian wolves, the least. Alpine plants thrive in the climate here, as do many species of bird, including several types of bird of prey, and around 150 types of butterfly.

LAMMERGEIER Once extinct in the Picos, the lammergeier (bearded vulture) is making a slow comeback thanks to a recovery programme that began in 2002.

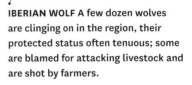

IBERIAN WOLF A few dozen wolves are clinging on in the region, their protected status often tenuous; some are blamed for attacking livestock and are shot by farmers.

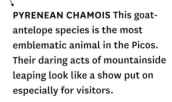

PYRENEAN CHAMOIS This goat-antelope species is the most emblematic animal in the Picos. Their daring acts of mountainside leaping look like a show put on especially for visitors.

See this...

O1 Basílica de Covadonga
This 19th-century church commemorates 8th-century events and the start of the Spanish Reconquista. Visigoth leader Pelayo prayed to the Virgin Mary here and subsequently defeated a Moorish force.

O2 Lagos de Covadonga
Glacial lakes Enol and Ercina have 360-degree mountain views, grazing cows and easy hikes. The Mirador de la Reina on the twisty road up has views fit for a queen.

O3 Bulnes
Inaccessible by road, for centuries this pretty village could be reached only via an uphill hike. These days a tunnel railway does the hard work.

Itineraries

Though small, the Picos deserve at least a few days' exploration. The park can be approached from different sides, but whichever way you explore it you're guaranteed a thrilling trip.

◀ With stunning scenery, long climbs and little traffic, Picos de Europa is a cyclist's paradise.
▶ The cliff-side shrine of Santa Cueva de Covadonga is dedicated to the Virgin Mary.

01

A day

If you really only have a day to spend here then you have two choices for getting a taste of the Picos that will have you planning your next visit before you've even finished this one. For an easy overview of the best of the park, take the scenic road up to the Basílica de Covadonga to see why this bit of Spain has such historical significance. Continue up to the Covadonga lakes and strike out on one of the easy hikes in the area, before dining in true Asturian style at El Molín

de la Pedrera in Cangas de Onís. Alternatively, be wowed by nature and get a good workout for your legs by heading straight for the park's most famous walk, the Garganta del Cares. You'll have to double back on yourself to finish in one day, but with views like this you really won't mind, especially when you can replenish those lost calories at the Restaurante Cares, near the start of the walk in Arenas de Cabrales.

02

A long weekend

Start your weekend with a Friday night of monastic splendour at the Parador de Cangas de Onís, unofficial capital of the Picos and a good jumping-off spot for exploring the park. An early start the next morning will have you hitting the famous Garganta del Cares trail before the crowds, allowing you time for a delicious dinner in Restaurante Cares before bedding down in the rustic charm of La Portiella del Llosu hotel in Pandiello. After a hearty home-cooked breakfast, it's a winding but stunning couple of

hours' drive to Fuente Dé, where after yesterday's exertions you can let the cable car take the strain. Head heavenwards to a height of over 1800m to enjoy unsurprisingly spectacular views across the southern section of the Picos mountains and, if your legs are game, head out on another hike. Finish the weekend with a night of rural comfort in La Casa de las Chimeneas, where medieval-inspired murals decorate the walls and light meals are available in the 'English Tavern' bar.

03

A week

With no roads entirely crossing the national park, you need to do a circuit around the Picos, detouring off down dead-end side roads, to fully appreciate everything the region has to offer – and a seven-day itinerary gives you time to do that. Enjoy a couple of nights in what passes for a big town in these parts: Cangas de Onís. It has plenty of sleeping and eating options, and it's a perfect base for expeditions to Covadonga's history-heavy basilica and beautiful lakes, as well as activities like kayaking down

the Sella River from nearby Arriondas. Next, walk the Cares trail – at a leisurely pace because you have time to overnight in Caín before returning the following day, stopping off for some Cabrales cheese, cider and a rest in Arenas. Loop round to the Fuente Dé cable car for jaw-dropping panoramas, before staying over in the Casa del Oso, where you can also learn about local brown bears. Finally, potter around Potes and the Santo Toribio monastery, which has been here for more than a thousand years.

43

Pirin National Park

Hear the rumble of the thunder god in Bulgaria's wild southwest, where ancient pine forests cluster between glacier-carved peaks.

As you walk through Pirin National Park, twigs fallen from millennium-old trees snap underfoot. Your ears prick at the sound of mountain goats scrambling out of view. Claps of thunder echo in the valleys and winds brew seemingly from nowhere, making tree branches sway.

To some ancient Slavic cultures, this chorus of sounds augured the presence of thunder god Perun, for whom the Pirin mountains are thought to be named. This wilderness's fierce weather changes and towering mountains – more than 100 peaks top 2000m – make this bearded, axe-wielding god an apt figurehead.

Perun was part of a pantheon worshipped across Eastern Europe until Christianity began to dominate from the 10th century. The god is associated with high winds, soaring eagles and sacred trees, which remain part of the park's timeless backdrop.

The ancient is omnipresent in Pirin National Park: one of the most popular sights is the Baykuchevata Macedonian pine, a tree well over a thousand years old. For pagan worshippers centuries ago, ancient trees were a sacred calling card of Perun, thought to have their roots in the world of the dead, their trunks representing the living, and their branches stretching heavenward.

Further back in the park's timeline, scars from the last ice age are still vivid. Dozens of glacial lakes hark back to the grind of ice that shaped the Pirin region into chasms of granite and soaring limestone peaks.

Though established as a national park in 1962 and gilded with Unesco World Heritage status 31 years later, this place

has been impossible to tame. Expect raw wilderness, simple hiking huts and a patchy phone signal. Unleash your inner explorer and get ready to march in the footsteps of gods.

⛰ Studded with peaks up to nearly 3000m, – Vihren (2914m) being the highest – Pirin National Park is popular with mountaineers. Previous page: nearby Babyak.

Toolbox

◎ **When to go**
Hiking season is June to October. Visit in early August for the Pirin Sings festival, when locals shake crimson skirts for a folklore spectacular. Wear layers in September and October for treks without the crowds.

🧭 **Getting there**
Most visitors arrive from lively Bansko on the park's northeastern border; the gate to the park is 2km southwest of town. Bansko is a 160km drive from capital Sofia (Bulgaria's main air hub), south along the A3 and then east.

Park in numbers

400
Area covered (sq km)

176
Number of lakes

1380
Estimated age of the oldest tree, the Baykuchevata Macedonian pine (years)

Stay here...

🏠 **Saint George Palace**
After the spartan pleasures of hikes, protein bars and mountain huts, this apartment-hotel will be a restorative. The building is styled in brooding granite, and its apartments are simple but chic, with pop-art flourishes and huge windows overlooking Bansko's rooftops. Spa offerings include a luxurious Jacuzzi and sauna, plus mountain views right from the pool. Best of all, you can muse on a tough day of hiking from an outdoor terrace bar, to a soundtrack of ice clinking merrily in your cocktail.

🏠 **Hotel Alpin**
Simple rooms fill this cheerful, chalet-style hotel in Bansko. Summer guests can scorch their supper on barbecue equipment, and there's ski storage for winter. Snow or sunshine, there's a sauna to work up a sweat, and a tavern awash in *rakia* (fruit brandy) if you need topping up.

🏠 **Tofana Hotel**
Just within the boundary of the national park, this homely hotel is surrounded by prickly pines and located roughly 300m from the nearest lift in the Chalin valog ski area – you can schuss right to the door.

Do this!

🥾 **Snowshoeing**
Between January and March, the Pirin Mountains slip on a downy coat of snow. Busy Bansko lies just north of the park, as notorious for its nightlife as for its skiing. But the national park's high-altitude plateaus offer serenity in the snow. Clamp on snowshoes and trudge through miles of white, pillowy countryside; some of the loveliest views are around frozen Popovo Lake. The risk of avalanche in this pristine place makes a local guide essential (reserve ahead). Some operators offer night walks, allowing you to see snowdrifts sparkling under moonlight.

🚲 **Mountain biking**
Steel your nerves for a dizzying descent: from the Bezbog chairlift in the eastern part of the park, you can access thrilling downhill biking trails. Several outfits run guided biking day trips from Bansko.

🔭 **Birdwatching**
Pirin is home to more than 170 species of bird; the most colourful are rock thrush, wallcreepers and robins. Prime your binoculars for peregrine falcons and golden eagles in the valleys, and listen for the rattle of four kinds of woodpecker in the forests.

What to spot...

Jackals, bears, wolves and boar all bare fangs in Pirin's forests and mountain passes, and chamois gather in herds. Less prone to bolting from human company are Hermann's tortoises – you'll know it's mating season if the bushes shake and you hear a comical chirrup (really). Almost 40 percent of Bulgaria's bird species fly through: forest dwellers include woodpeckers, robins and pygmy owls, while falcons and golden eagles soar over ravines. Endemic plants include bright Pirin poppies and Pirin thyme, and look out for lucky edelweiss.

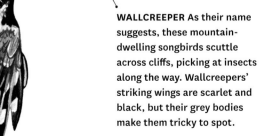

EURASIAN OTTER These sleek little mammals can be seen gnawing on fish and cavorting in streams at numerous places in the park; keep your eyes open along the waterways threading the Banderishki Lakes area.

EDELWEISS See this star-shaped flower – a Pirin emblem – bloom in park meadows during July and August. Like Pirin's hikers, edelweiss dresses for the weather: a woolly down protects its petals and leaves.

WALLCREEPER As their name suggests, these mountain-dwelling songbirds scuttle across cliffs, picking at insects along the way. Wallcreepers' striking wings are scarlet and black, but their grey bodies make them tricky to spot.

Hike this...

O1 Banderishki Lakes
An 8km route circles some of the park's glacial lakes. The smallest, Eye Lake, is so tiny you won't spot it until you're metres away.

O2 Prevalski to Popina
This two- to three-hour 10km trail from the Prevalski Lakes climbs mountain and forest paths to reach the Popina area at the park's southwestern fringe.

O3 Red Route 1
A challenging two-day 25km route slices south from Vihren Chalet to Pirin Hut via lakes and plateau; stay overnight in Tevno Ezero shelter.

Itineraries

Lace up your toughest hiking boots and forget about home comforts. Pirin National Park rewards the intrepid with views of glacial lakes and cloud-scraping mountains.

◄ An old Ottoman konak (administrative building) in Melnik is dwarfed by one of the spectacular Pyramids of Melnik towering above.
➡ Hiking is one of the park's most rewarding activities.

01
A day

Dip into the park on a packed day trip from Bansko. Start early at Bansko's park information centre to get hiking maps and advice on weather conditions. While you're in town, stuff your rucksack with picnic provisions: spinach *banitsa* (pastry), cured hams and energy-boosting *halva* (sesame nougat) should do the trick. Take ulitsa Pirin southwest out of town for around 15km, towards Banderitsa Hut in the midst of the park. From here you can set out on a five-hour hiking circuit, heading west through glades and scrambling up mountain paths to Premkata Saddle. After the challenging uphill climb, and beneath Mount Vihren (2914m), your (now squashed) *banitsa* will taste all the better. Return the same way and refresh yourself with a cold lemonade at Banderitsa Hut before taking the road out of the park. Make a short diversion at the edge of the park to 'the Secret Hotel', known for its party atmosphere, and toast the day's hike before returning to Bansko.

02
A weekend

Fill your pockets with hiking snacks in Bansko before driving towards Vihren Chalet, the centre of the park and the starting point of numerous trails. Spend the day hiking a circuit around the Banderishki Lakes, pausing at Fish and Frog Lakes, cobalt Long Lake, and blink-and-you'll-miss-it Eye Lake. Long Lake has some of the best views of Mount Vihren, so it's an ideal place to picnic before returning to Vihren Chalet.

On day two, set out from the chalet to tackle Mount Vihren herself. Reaching the summit from the southwestern slopes is an energy-sapping three-hour hike, but you'll quickly forget your blistered feet as you contemplate the resulting Pirin panorama. After climbing down, drive back into Bansko to unwind. Give the town's casinos and English-language menus a wide berth; instead, settle in at a *mehana* (traditional tavern) for hulking portions of grilled meat, *shopska* salad (cheese, tomatoes and cucumber) and generous splashes of Melnik wine.

03
Four days

Consider yourself a hardened hiker? Take a taxi from Bansko to Vihren Chalet, and enjoy your pick of trails on the slopes of the park's loftiest peak, keeping an eye out for edelweiss. Spare some time to muse on your mortality at the 1380-year-old Macedonian pine, a half-hour walk from the chalet.

After resting in Vihren Chalet overnight, take a long, meandering hike among the Banderishki Lakes, aiming to finish the day at Demianitsa Hut, 5km southeast.

On day three, set your sights on Bezbog Lake, 5km east. A tough, indirect, but very scenic route dips south to 30m-deep Popovo. The largest lake in the park, Popovo is backed by mountains that are snow streaked well into summer. From here, take the trail northeast to Bezbog; the hut is reachable by a scenic chairlift and makes a comfortable overnight stop.

On your last day, trek back in the direction of Vihren Chalet, where you can arrange transport to Bansko. Back in town, you can glug a well-earned bottle of Kamenitza beer.

44

Plitvice National Park

Lose yourself in a maze of turquoise lakes, small and large waterfalls, green woods and heart-stopping biodiversity inside Croatia's most popular national park.

Getty Images | Kelly Cheng Travel Photography

Perennially changing and adapting, Plitvice dazzles with a beautiful dance of water, air, light, rock formations and flora; the 16 lakes, waterfalls and cataracts, and the lush vegetation that surrounds them, are simply divine. But rather than being separate entities of still waters, the lakes are in fact one body of constantly flowing, confluent rivers, separated by natural dams – a collection of travertine or tufa (chalk rock) deposits, packed with moss, algae and various forms of bacteria. The colour of the lakes – divided into 12 upper lakes and four lower lakes – shifts from turquoise to pea green, steel grey or deep blue, depending on the current make-up of the organisms in the water, its mineral composition, and sunlight. The 18km of wooden pathways and bridges makes it possible for visitors to meander among the lakes at their own pace. Plitvice also has abundant forest flora and is home to such wildlife as brown bears, wolves and lynx, and a variety of deer.

The area reflects the many invading and settling populations that have crossed the greater region, among them the Illyrians, Celts, Romans, Avars, Slavs and Ottomans. The Croats arrived in the 6th century, and Plitvice formed part of the medieval kingdom of Croatia, remaining thus until 1528, when the Ottomans took over for 150 years. After its stint as an important site for the anti-Fascist movement in WWII, Plitvice Lakes was declared a national park in 1949, and it was placed on the Unesco World Heritage List in 1979. Unfortunately, Plitvice was embroiled in the 1990s conflict, when, due to the apparent risk of mines, the park found itself on Unesco's List of World Heritage in Danger. After the

conflict ended, the park bounced straight back and it's now visited by more than a million tourists a year.

⬆ Plitvice is full of paths to explore. Previous page: the park is blessed with umpteen waterfalls.

➡ Boating on the idyllic Kozjak Lake.

Budget Travel | allmann, Shutterstock | evronphoto

Toolbox

☼ When to go
The park is crushed with tourists from June to August, and sometimes even September is busy, so try to visit in spring and autumn, which is also the best time for bird and wild-flower spotting.

🧭 Getting there
Plitvice Lakes is in central Croatia, between the Adriatic and the inland region, and borders Bosnia and Hercegovina. It sits in a depression of the Dinaric Alps, and is surrounded by glorious mountains. Zagreb and Zadar are equidistant airports.

Park in numbers

296.85
Area covered (sq km)

321
Species of butterfly

6000
Estimated age of the tufa deposits (years)

The lakes and waterfalls of Plitvice are truly majestic.

Stay here...

🏠 **House Biba & Leona**
There are hotels inside the park, but this place is a 15-minute walk from the entrance and sits in the middle of a peaceful valley, giving you endless views of the countryside. It's perfect as an outpost for exploring the park, and for having a quiet space to get back to in the evening; the hosts are friendly and can recommend good places to eat nearby. There are rooms and apartments. If you're travelling with children or pets, they can run wild and free.

🏠 **Hotel Jezero**
Stay at this 1980s throwback if you want to travel to the Yugoslavian yesteryear and have a room overlooking the largest lake in the park, within earshot of the waterfalls. Don't expect much from the restaurant.

🏠 **Hotel Plitvice**
Right at the entrance to the park and built in 1958, this place has a look of functional architecture that relies heavily on the cubic form, but the effect is relieved by the lush surroundings. The hotel was recently refurbished and aims for modest modernity.

Do this!

🥾 **Exploring the lakes**
The 18km of pathways and wooden footbridges around the 16 Plitvice lakes is best explored out of the high season, away from the summer crowds; the paths can be walked in around six or seven hours. The lakes of Prošćansko and Kozjak are the largest, and among the 12 upper lakes. See the gorgeous Labudovac waterfall, which is over 20m high, at Okrugljak Lake, and the Cave Garden below. Get a boat from Kozjak to the lower lakes, where you can stand in awe of the Veliki Slap, Croatia's tallest waterfall.

📷 **Veliki Slap**
Cascading down several levels of karst rock and stretching up 78m, the Veliki Slap is bound to leave you gawping in awe; the jade-green water and emerald vegetation will make you feel as if you're in the middle of the Amazon.

⛑ **Šupljara cave**
Going underground into Šupljara you might spot (or miss) the tiny, 1mm snail *Zospeum isselianum*, or the minuscule *Meusel pseudoscorpion*, both endemic to Croatia. The cave was used in Italian and German spaghetti Westerns, filmed in the 1960s in Plitvice Lakes.

What to spot...

The park has a mild Continental climate, with the mountains at the back cooling the coastal temperatures, and blessing the region with a wonderful mixture of alpine and Mediterranean vegetation. Plitvice is dense with beech and fir forests, and the unique combination of microclimates and differing soils and altitude levels makes for abundant flora – there are 55 species of orchid, for instance. The park is one of Europe's last resorts for the brown bear and wolf.

EURASIAN EAGLE-OWL
The eagle-owl is one of the largest of the owl species, and has a tawny body and protruding ear tufts. You might spot it by its glowing orange eyes.

LADY'S-SLIPPER ORCHID This limestone-keen beauty is a protected species; its crimson and yellow flower traps insects in its pouch so they fertilise it by having to climb inside.

EUROPEAN POND TURTLE
A lover of wetlands and wooded landscapes, the pond turtle is semi-aquatic and dark in colour. It nests near water and can live up to 60 years.

Hike this...

O1 Medveđak trails
Choose between the two 800m-plus peaks: Oštri Medveđak (889m) or Tupi Medveđak (868m), connected by untouched 700-year-old beech forests.

O2 Turčić trail
The Turčić peak (801m) is reached via a mild 8km karst track that is occasionally shaded by spruce woods. You'll have views of the Veliki Slap and Kozjak Lake from the top.

O3 Čorkova Bay
A fantastic way to get a good look at the park's flora and fauna is this 21km hike through large forests teeming with wildlife and vegetation. Listen out for the woodpeckers.

Itineraries

Spend two days exploring the park and walking its diverse trails, where bird- and plant-spotting opportunities abound; you can hike to mountain peaks on day three.

◄ Hikers exploring around Galovac Lake.
► The dense beech and fir forests of Plitvice are home to abundant plant and animal life.

01
Two days

The first day should be spent making your way around the Plitvice Lakes. Wake up early and have breakfast on a terrace as you listen to the majestic birdsong that brings the morning woods to life. Take a packed lunch and head out to the main area of the park to walk around the 18km-long wooden footbridges, making sure you take in the Veliki Slap and all of the upper and lower lakes. Don't miss a visit inside the Šupljara cave for a glimpse of the underground life. Since a thorough going-through of the park can take most of the day, you can eat your picnic lunch in a shaded, wooded spot, by one of the smaller lakes, while the jade-green waters shimmer below. Head back and get an early night so that on day two you can start early, choosing one of two walking trails – either the Čorkova Bay trail (21km) or the shorter Plitvica trail (9km) – both of which start and end at Labudovac Lake. Panoramic views abound on both walks, the paths leading you through centennial forests and valleys that abound with wildlife and various plant species, and you can look out for a variety of butterflies and birds, and even spot a wild beast if you're lucky. You can do the walks alone or go with a park ranger. Head back to the park's centre to enjoy dinner under the stars, set to a soundtrack of frogs, insects and hooting owls.

02
Three days

Day three should be spent hiking up to one of the three peaks of the national park: Oštri Medveđak, Tupi Medveđak or the Turčić peak. The latter is the shortest option, at 1½ hours, whereas the Medveđak hikes take around 2½ hours each. These are light hikes for the most part and they can easily be enjoyed in a day. You'll need to take all food and water with you. The hikes take you through beech and maple forests, and it's a good idea to bring along binoculars to give yourself the best chance of spotting woodpeckers, butterflies and other fauna. The views from Oštri Medveđak are incredible, giving you the sight of valleys of the Korana River and of neighbouring Bosnia-Hercegovina's Una River, a beautiful, glimmering stream that snakes through lush forests. Getting to the Tupi Medveđak peak is even more rewarding: from here, six of the Plitvice Lakes can be seen from above. The Turčić peak, although the lowest, offers you the sight of Kozjak Lake and the Veliki Slap from the top, as well as vistas of the surrounding mountain ranges. The best time to hike is early spring and especially autumn, when the leaves change colour and the beech and maple forests paint the landscape in glorious reds and golds. Head back down into the park and, if you have the energy, rent out a rowing boat to cap off the day by taking in the view of the lakes at dusk.

45

Port-Cros National Park

Two islands and a swathe of deep-blue sea, Port-Cros National Park in southern France is postcard Mediterranean paradise.

From the mainland, Port-Cros, Porquerolles and Le Levant seem to shimmer in the distance. It's the mica-rich rock of these three small islands off the French Côte d'Azur that has given them their name of Îles d'Or (Golden Islands). Port-Cros and most of Porquerolles now make up Port-Cros National Park, a marine and terrestrial park. The park is a concentrate of Mediterranean beauty: crystal-clear waters, beaches of fine sand, magnificent pines and fragrant scrubs, the air filled with the song of cicadas in summer. The northern shores of both islands are characterised by sandy beaches and sheltered coves, whereas the southern coasts feature cliffs and rugged terrain and are much more exposed to the swell and wind.

There are no cars on either island, although Porquerolles is criss-crossed by a series of wide tracks perfect for cycling. Port-Cros, on the other hand, has just a few buildings and then nothing but 30km of trails and glorious landscapes. The sea is equally serene, with boats required to limit their speed and nary a jet ski in sight. Most visitors are day trippers from the mainland, so staying in the park overnight offers a unique experience. (However, it's expensive and requires advance booking.)

Both islands have been settled since at least Roman times (even earlier for Porquerolles), although most of the historical sights (forts mostly) date from the 17th century onwards. The islands were bastions of piracy before Louis XIV, and later Napoleon Bonaparte, used their military might to weed out undesirable residents. Over the course of the 20th century, agriculture and tourism emerged as the islands' new raison d'être.

Nowadays the national park is beloved by the French, but foreign visitors remain a minority – now's your chance to get in on this Mediterranean secret.

⬆ Cycling is one of the best ways to get around flat Porquerolles. Previous page: the turquoise waters of a Port-Cros bay.

Getty Images | David C Tomlinson

Toolbox

 When to go
Due to school holidays, July and August are peak season. June and September are probably the best months to visit, with warm weather and fewer visitors. Winter is very quiet, with limited boat services.

Getting there
The park is located on France's southern coast; it comprises a swathe of the Mediterranean and two islands, Port-Cros and Porquerolles, accessible by boat from Hyères (one hour and 20 minutes, respectively). The nearest international airport is Toulon-Hyères, next to Hyères port.

Park in numbers

17/29

Land/marine area covered (sq km)

350

Permanent inhabitants

6

Shipwrecks in the park

Stay here...

🏠 **Le Mas du Langoustier**
Located on Porquerolles, this glamorous boutique hotel goes back to the days when the island was run as an agricultural estate, as the nearby vineyards attest. Set amid 40 hectares of scented Mediterranean greenery, with access to an idyllic cove, the Langoustier prides itself on its creature comforts – a beautiful pool, a Michelin-starred chef, a helipad (yes), spa treatments and glorious views: if you want to do the national park in style, this is the place to come. Open May to September.

🏠 **Le Manoir**
In a charming 19th-century building, this lovely establishment (one of just three on the island of Port-Cros) feels like a cross between a family pension and a boutique hotel. The rambling gardens are divine and the restaurant is sumptuous too. Open May to September.

🏠 **L'Oustaou**
If you want to get a sense of what island life is like, you can't beat this lovely guesthouse. Located in the village on the island of Porquerolles, it is the only establishment open year-round. It also runs a restaurant.

Do this!

🥽 **Snorkelling on Port-Cros**
Port-Cros is first and foremost a marine national park, so what better way to explore it than by going snorkelling? The park has an underwater trail for visitors to discover the island's wonderful marine life. It is marked by buoys and takes about 40 minutes to complete. There are six stops with explanatory panels; you can also pick up a leaflet about fauna and flora at the Maison du Parc in the village (where there's also snorkelling gear for hire).

🚲 **Cycling on Porquerolles**
With its relatively flat terrain and well-maintained tracks, Porquerolles was made for cycling. Tracks wind through fragrant pine forests, scrubland and vineyards and along dreamy coves and beaches. The tourist office has signposted four circuits ranging from 6km to 15km.

🍇 **Wine tasting on Porquerolles**
Not your typical national-park activity, but so typical of the region! The island has three vineyards, which produce mostly rosé wines. They all offer tastings, although advance booking is usually required. You can, of course, buy the local vintages too.

What to spot...

Port-Cros National Park is a pocket jewel of Mediterranean climate, fauna and flora. It's sunny year-round, with mild winters and hot summers. Port-Cros is mountainous, while Porquerolles is more level. The dominant vegetation is maquis, a mixture of hardy scrub, Aleppo pines and evergreen oaks. Underwater, the park is best known for its posidonia oceanica (seagrass) meadows, which play a crucial role in Mediterranean biodiversity. Fish and molluscs are abundant, and it's not unusual to see dolphins and whales.

BLACK SCORPIONFISH This fearsome-looking fish usually hangs out near the sea floor to make the most of its camouflage. The spikes on its dorsal fin are poisonous, so don't get too close.

FAN MUSSEL One of the largest seashells in the world, this mollusc likes to nestle among the seagrass. Its byssus (the tuft of filaments at its base) is said to have been used to make the golden fleece.

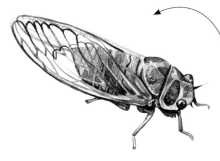

CICADA From June to August, the song of this dark, long-winged insect fills the air. For many, this is the sound of summer. Find cicadas on tree trunks and branches.

Hike this...

O1 Circuit de Port-Man, Port-Cros

A four-hour hike, this route takes in the secluded Baie de Port-Man in the east of the island and a number of historic buildings.

O2 Sentier des Crêtes, Port-Cros

This demanding three-hour walk in the steep western half of the island culminates on Mount Vinegar (196m) and features great views of the rugged southern coastline.

O3 Sentier des Plantes, Port-Cros

An aromatic (and steep) 4.5km option, this trail winds its way past the park's signature plants – wild lavender, euphorbia, mimosa, rosemary and the like – and offers stupendous views.

Itineraries

Learn your seagrass from your algae, wine and dine in superb settings, give your legs a workout on foot and by bike – it's all on just two French Mediterranean islands.

 Hikers will find interesting terrain matched with serene ocean views on the north coast of Port-Cros.

 A shoal of salema porgy; the park has superb snorkelling, including a specially marked underwater trail.

01
A day, Port-Cros

As you get off the boat, pop into the Maison du Parc (national-park office) to buy a map of the island and hire some snorkelling equipment in one of the shops. Head inland on the Circuit de Port-Man (orange trail) towards Fort de l'Estissac and Fort de l'Eminence. This four-hour hike across the island will give you a wonderful overview of its natural as well as historical heritage (because of the island's location, the French have used it as a military base for centuries). Bring a picnic (and plenty of water) and break off at the secluded Baie de Port-Man (popular with private boats). The path then follows the northern coast back towards the village, via the exquisite Plage de la Palud, where you can put on your snorkel and explore the park's underwater trail. It's a 30-minute walk back to the port, where you should sit down for a well-earned drink at a terrace before hopping back on the boat.

02
A day, Porquerolles

The first thing you should do is hire a bike – Porquerolles wouldn't be Porquerolles without cycling! Get a map of the island at the tourist office and pedal off on the three-hour blue circuit towards the western half of the island. The route takes in the vineyards and two fabulous beaches: the Plage d'Argent and the Plage du Langoustier. Plan a rest (including a swim!) at the latter, which is roughly halfway on the circuit. On your way back to the village, stop at Domaine Perzinsky for wine tasting (and purchasing!). You could have lunch in the village if you wish, or if you've planned a picnic, cycle on to your afternoon destination, the exquisite Plage de Notre-Dame (20 minutes' cycling). The beach is a fine arc of white sand fringed by pines and is the perfect setting for a couple of hours of sunbathing, swimming and contemplation. Make sure you leave enough time to cycle back to the village and return your bicycle before getting back on the boat.

03
Four to five days, both islands

Spending four to five days in the park means that you'll get to experience both islands after the day trippers have gone, a treat few visitors enjoy. On day one, catch an afternoon boat to Porquerolles and book yourself in for a couple of nights at Le Mas du Langoustier. Spend the rest of the afternoon and early evening enjoying the glorious setting. On day two, hire a bike and explore the eastern half of the island (yellow trail). On day three, head to Port-Cros. In July and August, there are direct boats; the rest of the year, you'll need to head back to the mainland first. Check in at Le Manoir and head out to the Plage de la Palud for the afternoon and follow the underwater trail. On day four, explore the Sentier des Crêtes before spending the rest of the afternoon by the pool or at the beautiful Plage du Sud. Head back to the mainland on day five.

46

Pyrenees National Park

France's Pyrenees National Park is a mountain kingdom of craggy peaks and lush valleys where birds of prey soar overhead and sure-footed chamois roam the rocky slopes.

Getty Images | Sasha64f

Older than the Alps, the French Pyrenees offer a portal into one of the great unblemished wilderness regions of Western Europe. Come for a weekend foray here and you'll be awed by the dramatic scenery: alpine lakes, glacier-carved valleys and windswept heights that offer startling views over this mountainous landscape of southern France. For the French (and neighbouring Spanish and Andorrans), the Pyrenees have long been an adventure-loving playground: with white-water rafting in spring; trekking, horse riding and mountain biking in summer; and skiing in winter – perhaps followed by a rejuvenating soak in a hot spring.

The hiking here is famous, and you'll agree that that's rightly so when you contemplate a day's outing on one of the park's myriad trails. The modern world slowly disappears into the rear-view mirror on the drive to the trailhead. Then you disembark, the crunch of well-packed dirt underfoot as you wind your way along a curving path through wild flowers lit by the sun and flittering swallowtail butterflies, a great-winged griffon vulture spinning slowly overhead. The rewards of a day's exertion: picnicking beside crystal-clear lakes glittering like jewels amid a cradle of soaring peaks, or reaching the summit of a rocky peak where all the world seems to stretch out beneath you.

Yet there's much more to the Pyrenees than its varied terrain for outdoor activities. Dozens of small villages lie scattered around the park's valleys, and old-fashioned industries like cheesemaking are still part of the Pyrenean way of life. Indeed, you may find your passage temporarily blocked as enormous flocks of sheep trundle across

the road from one field to another. Come in June and you may even stumble upon the transhumance, an age-old practice by which shepherds drive their flocks to high pastures for prime summer grazing.

⬆ Cheese made from unpasteurised ewe's milk in a cellar in the village of Laruns. Previous page: Pyrenean splendour at Lac de Fabrèges in Vallée d'Ossau.
➡ A hiker strides towards Vignemale (3298m), the highest of the French Pyrenean peaks.

Toolbox

When to go
Skiing aside, the best time is June to September, when the weather's warm, all the trails are open, and available activities include rafting, biking and horse riding. Skiing is best from late January to March.

Getting there
Stretching along the border with Spain, the park has several key access points, including Pau and Lourdes. Both have train and flight connections. The main access roads from Spain are the N134 south of Accous and the D934 south of Laruns.

Park in numbers

457
Area covered (sq km)

3298
Highest point: Vignemale (m)

86
Number of villages in and near the park

Stay here...

🏠 Le Lion d'Or

This *Heidi*-esque hotel is deliciously eccentric, with charming old rooms in polka-dot pinks, sunny yellows and duck-egg blues, and mountain-themed knick-knacks dotted throughout. Breakfast includes homemade honey and jams, and the restaurant serves hearty Pyrenean cuisine. Located in Cauterets, it's a fine base for exploring the park's western section.

🏠 Auberge Cavalière

You'll really feel part of valley life at this rambling old horse farm 3km south of Accous, which offers five floral rooms and a cosy family *gîte*. The stone house is a picture of rustic character. The friendly hosts cook up delicious dinners on request (and can also arrange horse rides).

⛺ Camping Le Gave d'Aspe

Beautifully situated alongside the gurgling Aspe River, in a forested site near the mountain village of Urdos, this is a superb family-friendly campsite. There's a choice of timber bungalows or canvas-roofed chalets, or you can pitch your own tent.

Do this!

🎿 Skiing

Picturesque resorts are sprinkled throughout the Pyrenees, and you'll find much more laid-back, family-friendly (and wallet-friendly) skiing than at better-known destinations. Fine bases for downhill skiing and other winter activities (including snowshoeing and cross-country skiing) include Cauterets and Bagnères-de-Luchon. As an added bonus, these two Pyrenean resorts also have appealing hot springs. There's nothing quite like the refreshing warmth of a steaming thermal pool after a day's skiing.

〰 Rafting

The Gave d'Ossau, Gave d'Aspe and Gave d'Oloron are three of the best Pyrenean waterways for an outing and offer everything from leisurely paddles with the family (suitable for ages six and up) to churning class-IV rapids for more experienced paddlers.

🚲 Mountain biking

Once the snow melts, those crisp mountain peaks form the backdrop to rugged off-road biking. This is an adventurer's playground, offering adrenaline-fuelled rides with jaw-dropping views of the valleys laid out before you. Many resorts open their trails to mountain bikers, and well-signed *sentiers balisés* (marked trails) provide endless action for the VTT (*vélo tout terrain*) crowd.

Getty Images | BSIP/UIG

What to spot...

◀ Transhumance in action; sheep are moved to higher summer grazing pastures.

Lower elevations are covered in fir, beech and pine forest, while the subalpine slopes feature birch and mountain ash, and flowering species like the lily, rhododendron and purple Pyrenean iris. Above 2400m, the alpine landscape is largely bare save for poppies, hardy lichens and the odd dwarf willow. Some 70 animal species (plus 300 butterfly species) inhabit this varied terrain, from the tiny, mole-like Pyrenean desman to the brown bear, with golden eagles and vultures (including the rare Egyptian vulture) soaring overhead.

PYRENEAN CHAMOIS The *isard* (as it's called in French) is a horned goat-antelope with a russet-brown coat and dark eye patches. It was nearly hunted to extinction in the 1940s but flourishes today in the Pyrenees between elevations of 1000m and 2800m.

GRIFFON VULTURE Soaring over the valleys, the massive *vautour fauve* with its wingspan of up to 2.8m is an awe-inspiring sight (its scavenger's diet of animal carcasses is somewhat less so).

ALPENROSE Growing just above the tree line, this vibrant flowering shrub (a rhododendron species) reaches heights of up to 1m and produces bright-pink flowers throughout the summer.

Hike this...

O1 Cirque de Gavarnie

It's an easy hike (about an hour) to this breathtaking mountain vista: a natural amphitheatre carved by glaciers and framed by saw-toothed, snow-covered peaks.

O2 GR10

One of France's most fabled routes, this *grande randonnée* stretches 900km across the length of the Pyrénées from the Atlantic to the Mediterranean. For pure bragging rights, the GR10 can't be topped.

O3 Tour des Lacs d'Ayous

Setting off near Laruns, this gorgeous six-hour-return hike takes in sparkling blue alpine lakes, with the chance to spot chamois, marmots and birds of prey.

Itineraries

Immerse yourself in the grandeur of soaring peaks and flower-filled valleys, with magnificent hikes, memorable wildlife watching and picture-book villages all part of the great Pyrenean adventure.

◄ Pont d'Espagne spans the Gave de Marcadau at its confluence with the Gave de Gaube.
→ One of the highest railways in Europe, Petit Train d'Artouste carries passengers to beautiful Lac d'Artouste.

01

A weekend

Start the journey in Lourdes, which makes a fine Pyrenean gateway with its rail and flight connections to other parts of France. Treat yourself to a quick peek at the soaring spires of the Sanctuaires Notre-Dame de Lourdes, and assemble a picnic hamper at the town's sprawling cast-iron market before hopping in the car for the scenic drive south. The first stop is the Parc Animalier des Pyrénées, where you can spy giant otters, ibex, wolves and other native creatures in a protected mountain setting.

Afterwards, continue to Pont d'Espagne for some spectacular mountain hikes. Take the trail to Lac de Gaube for jaw-dropping views of a sparkling lake surrounded by chiselled peaks. Have your picnic there amid the grand alpine landscape. It's a short trip from there down to Cauterets, a pleasant village and a fine base for the night. In the morning, have a refreshing soak in thermal waters at Cauterets' Thermes de César before heading on winding roads through mountain passes

to the wondrous Pic du Midi, an observatory reached by cable car that affords some of the most breathtaking views in the Pyrenees from its 2877m-high perch. Have lunch at the restaurant there, then continue to Le Donjon des Aigles, with an 11th-century chateau and a refuge containing one of the world's largest collections of birds of prey. Afterwards, treat yourself to a feast at the gastronomic hideaway (with guesthouse) of Le Viscos in St-Savin, before ending the trip back in Lourdes on the following morning.

02

A week

Start this scenic ramble across the mountains in the pleasant city of Pau, well situated near the western edge of the park. After taking in Pau's fine Renaissance castle (the birthplace of Henri IV), make the drive to the Vallée d'Aspe, the westernmost of the park's six mountain valleys. Hike one of the many trails near Bedous, then visit one of the folk museums in the valley – among our favourites is Les Fermiers Basco-Béarnais, where you can sample cheese

made from the milk of local ewes, goats and cows. On day two, cross over to the Vallée d'Ossau, and learn about Pyrenean high flyers in La Falaise aux Vautours – an 82-hectare reserve that's home to some 120 nesting pairs of majestic griffon vultures. Afterwards, hop aboard the Petit Train d'Artouste for one of France's most scenic train journeys. The view over the sparkling waters of Lac d'Artouste at the end is downright cinematic. On days three and four, tack on the weekend itinerary

for majestic scenery amid soaring peaks. End the great Pyrenean odyssey with a multi-day adventure out on the mountain trails. You can sign up for a horse-riding expedition through pristine swathes of the national park with Auberge Cavalière or head off on a donkey-trekking adventure (with outfitters like Parc aux Anes), camping or sleeping in *gîtes* (self-catering cottages) along the way. Thanks to your hardy donkey pal, you won't even have to carry your bags.

47

Retezat National Park

Rugged and mythical even by Romania's high standards, the nation's first national park is its foremost: fabled for glacial lakes and sublime surrounding alpine peaks.

The Romanian word *retezat*, translating as 'cut off', does not refer to the region's isolation but rather to the blunted appearance of the summit, which gives its name to both this tract of the Carpathian mountains and the national park encompassing them.

Yet remote this wilderness is. More significantly for nature-lovers, it's also pristine. Europe's most intact mixed forest cloaks the lower slopes. Higher up, the trees give way to a stunning series of cerulean tarns, clustered below peaks and ridges regularly cresting the 2300m contour.

The Retezat Mountains are generally seen as the diamonds in the Carpathian jewel box. The striking landscape has given rise to a rich vein of legend – giants that smite mountaintops in rage and dragons that lay waste to vegetation, leaving only rock in their wake – but the drier geological explanation is that this landscape took

shape after huge quantities of snow and ice were deposited during the Pleistocene era. Glaciers chiselled out the gorges, caves, craters and lakes that distinguish Retezat today. It became a national park in 1935; Unesco biosphere reserve status arrived in 1979. One part of Retezat – Gemenele Scientific Reserve – is so protected that there is no public access whatsoever.

There's a lot to protect, and Romania's rigour in so doing means a star cast of animals, including the grey wolf, brown bear, lynx, chamois and otter, is present in the park. But the lakes festooning this massif provide the most obvious eye candy, filled with summit snow-melt and reflecting the park in stark, moody symmetry. Romania's biggest glacial lake, Bucura, is the most visited, but across the year there are some 80 glacial bodies of water hereabouts. As you camp lakeside, with the wind singing through the boulder fields, the call of the wild is as near and clear as this continent gets.

Toolbox

When to go
Snow lingers on Retezat's mountains until mid-June, when trails become accessible and rhododendrons set the slopes ablaze. Almost immediately the crowds (not large) arrive, but by September they're declining and the weather remains clement.

Getting there
Sequestered away in Romania's rural southwest, Retezat is closest to airports Timişoara (west) and Cluj-Napoca (north); the latter is the country's second-largest. Petroşani, with rail and bus links, is the park's gateway town.

Park in numbers

362
Area covered, including buffer zone (sq km)

2509
Highest peak: Peleaga (m)

900–1300
Annual precipitation (mm)

Hike this...

01 Cabana Pietrele to Pelegea loop
A 22km initiation into the park's best-of, this trail includes a visit to Lake Bucura (where you can camp) and the summiting of Peleaga, from where you'll appreciate why Retezat's smorgasbord of lakes, sparkling below, get called 'God's eyes'.

02 Lake Bucura to Retezat peak
This 10km out-and-back goes from Bucura Lake campsite to the iconic 'cut-off' peak that lends the park its name.

03 Poiana Pelegii to Bucura Lake
A 6km out-and-back trail, this is probably the easiest means of experiencing a hike that includes the park's loveliest lake.

Stay here...

Toomarahva Turismitalu
This is about as high end as hotels come out in the wilds of Retezat (in all honesty, it's the only hotel). In the jaws of Buta Gorge in the park's southeast, the complex divides itself between a modern building and more traditional log cabins, and it's a popular launchpad for hikes up to Bucura Lake. Its little luxuries, like warm water, wi-fi access, TV and a restaurant, are far from ubiquitous in the park – but the sports pitches are a Retezat one-off. Open year-round.

Do this!

Hiking
Tramping through ancient forests, you emerge into a striking glacial landscape: lunar-like boulder fields bejewelled by lakes, punctured with calderas and crested by some of Eastern Europe's most extensive high-altitude mountain country. The treks from Poiana Pelegii or Cabana Pietrele chalets up to Bucura Lake and then Peleaga are Retezat at its most ravishing.

Lakeside camping
Camping up at Bucura Lake, the largest glacial lake in Romania, is a Retezat rite of passage. The mountains sheer up in every direction, mirrored in the glimmering water, and you're perfectly positioned for the park's premium trails.

⬦ Nature lovers will find peace in the pristine forests and waterways of Retezat National Park.

What to spot...

Retezat has a savage climate, with 275 days of snow or ice annually. Bears, wolves and 1000-plus plant species (some 60 endemic) are the fauna and flora highlights.

GREY WOLF Romania has Europe's greatest grey-wolf population by a distance. This largest (but still shy!) member of the canine family uses its long legs to negotiate the thick snow often covering the park.

Itinerary

Hike into Retezat's sublimely beautiful heart, camp at its best lake and scale some surrounding peaks.

01

Three days

From Petroșani drive 40km northwest on the E79 to Ohaba de sub Piatra, then 16km southwest on road 667A to Cârnic village. Park here to start the 1½-hour tramp up to Cabana Pietrele, a pleasant gaggle of chalets in the forest foothills. Your main target for today, the glittering glacial Bucura Lake, is another 6km. But the vistas will take your breath more than the climb, and halfway is the idyllic chalet of Cabana Gentiana (good for beer and snacks). Once camped lakeside (by now the mountainous magnificence has opened up like a *Lord of the Rings* set), stack boulders around to block out the winds.

Trails to try on day two include those up to Peleaga or Retezat peaks. Weary? Spend tonight in more comfort down at Cabana Pietrele.

On the last day, when returning from Cârnic, it's worth stopping at the ancient capital of Roman Dacia, Ulpia Traiana Sarmizegetusa, on the park's northern edge.

48

Sarek National Park

In Sweden's north, Sarek's inhospitable mountain peaks, raging rivers, dense woodlands and glaciers challenge experienced trekkers who like to be at one with the wild.

A primordial landscape of glacier-covered mountains, lakes and valleys strewn with erratic rocks, cirques, moraines and drumlins – some of the last vestiges of the most recent ice age to have held northern Sweden in its cold grip – Sarek is one of the largest wildernesses in Europe. Stark, sharp shoulders of dark rock rise above the wide Rapadalen valley, its boggy greenery bisected by a tangle of icy waterways as the Rapaätno river surges down from the glaciers of Sarektjåkkå.

The ice sheets receded from northern Sweden as recently as 10,000 years ago, leaving behind deep, U-shaped valleys that hint at the passage of the moving glacial masses that carved them. The land, as if finally breathing freely after being relieved of its icy burden, is still rising by almost half an inch a year.

Around 8000 years ago, these frozen boreal wastes were settled by nomadic hunters, whose remains – old hearths, dwelling sites and rock paintings of reindeer – are plentiful. These were the ancestors of the present-day Sámi, whose lives revolve around the rhythm of the reindeer herd, as they have done for centuries. Sarek was designated a national park in 1909 and together with three other national parks it makes up the Laponia World Heritage Site, a vast swathe of wilderness that preserves the traditional Sámi way of life. Every year the reindeer follow thousand-year-old migration paths across the valleys of Sarek in search of forage grounds. For the Sámi communities of Tuorpon, Jåhkågaska tjiellde and Sirges, Sarek's calving grounds, foraging areas and reindeer corrals are an essential part of their livelihood. 'Mountain Sámi' move their

herds large distances from the forest to the mountains and back again, while the 'forest Sámi' follow their beasts from wetland to forest.

⬆ Sarek's wild and mountainous terrain makes it prime hiking country. Previous page: Rapadalen valley.
➡ Nijak Mountain reflected in a tarn.

Getty Images | Johner Images

When to go
Hike under the midnight sun in May and June. July and August bring berry picking and fishing but mosquitoes aplenty. Autumn boasts wonderful colours and clear, cold days. Winter is strictly for snow sports.

Getting there
Sarek stretches along the wild border with Norway in a northern corner of Sweden's Lapland. There are no roads or towns nearby; the only way in is on your own two feet/skis/snowshoes or by helicopter drop.

Park in numbers

1977

Area covered (sq km)

2089

Highest point: Sarektjåkkå (m)

8000-10,000

Years that humans have been active in the park area

Stay here...

Camping wild

One of Sarek's biggest attractions is the liberty to pitch your tent anywhere in the wilderness before you. Whether you choose a splendidly scenic spot at the foot of the mighty Sarektjåkkå or on the banks of a river teeming with fish, you must be completely self-reliant and prepared for the extremes of terrain and volatile weather conditions. Bring plenty of food.

STF Saltoluokta Fjällstation

In Stora Sjöfallet National Park at the northern border of Sarek, this timber building and five satellite guest houses sit on the bank of Stora Lulevatten lake. The restaurant serves northern Swedish specialities, and guided ascents of nearby Lulep Gierkav mountain are on offer.

STF Kvikkjokk Fjällstation

This mountain station has a superb location on the bank of a roaring river near Sarek. The simple rooms and dorms and well-equipped guest kitchens cater to self-sufficient hikers; there's an on-site restaurant. It's closed October to mid-February and May to mid-June.

Do this!

Wildlife watching

Sarek is the 'Alaska of Europe'. Exploring it with a guide in winter gives you a proper appreciation of its glacial wilderness. Strap on a pair of skis, follow animal tracks in the snow and pitch your tent nightly under the northern lights.

Ski touring

Sarek's vastness, remoteness from civilisation and visits from just a few hundred hikers a year mean that the chances of animal spotting are very high. Bring binoculars and scan the narrow valleys for reindeer; the park doubles as pastureland for several Sámi families. In summer you can see bears with cubs hunting for berries (give them a wide berth), while in September giant moose are out, looking for mates. If you're particularly lucky, you may spot a lynx near the Rittak and Laitaure lakes and in the Rapadalen valley.

Helicopter trekking

Getting dropped off or picked up by helicopter at the Sarek border of your choice is easily doable in summer with Fiskflyg. En route you get a remarkable aerial view of the narrow glacial valleys, glistening glaciers, dense forest and barren mountains.

What to spot...

◄ The northern lights provide a spectral backdrop to any Sarek hike.

Sarek is distinguished by its brief, warm summers and dark, harsh winters, when temperatures drop to -40°C. Habitats include subarctic forests, taiga, glaciers, mountains, and alpine rivers and grasslands. Ample precipitation means that wading-bird species thrive, while golden eagles nest in the mountains. Diurnal mammals like reindeer, brown bears and unusually large moose roam the remote valleys, while predators such as lynx, wolverine, the critically endangered grey wolf and the Arctic fox hunt by night.

BROWN BEAR Sweden's largest predator subsists mostly on roots, plants and berries, as well as moose and rodents. Brown bears hibernate from October until May. Keep your distance in summer, when they have cubs.

EURASIAN LYNX Europe's largest cat is a nocturnal, extremely efficient hunter that can bring down prey much larger than itself – mainly reindeer. Cubs accompany their mother on hunts from the age of three months.

ARCTIC FOX Found in remote, mountainous areas, Arctic foxes live in large family groups in underground dens. They prey on rodents and their thick white fur allows them to camouflage themselves well against the snow.

See this...

O1 Rapadalen
Numerous ribbons of steel-grey water wind their way along the wide valley floor between craggy, bare cliffs, snow-capped mountains and countless oxbow lakes.

O2 Kåtokkaskatjåkkå
One of Sarek's more accessible mountains and the park's most picturesque peak, Kåtokkaskatjåkkå has a vast cirque glacier spilling down from its summit and feeding a tributary of the Rapaätno river.

O3 Pårtetjåkkå
Ice fields cover the steep flanks of one of the tallest mountains in Sarek (2005m), with a cluster of pristine oxbow lakes in the valley below.

⬆ In winter, ski-touring is one of the best ways of exploring Sarek.

Itineraries

Be an intrepid explorer by heading into uncharted wilderness, fording icy rivers, revelling in the lack of trails and relying on no one but yourself.

➡ Every year, reindeer follow thousand-year-old migration paths through the park in search of foraging grounds.

01

Four or more days

Starting in Kvikkjokk, just outside Sarek, this is the easiest way to taste the Sarek wilderness without getting lost, as it follows a 73km stretch of the 440km Kungsleden (King's Trail) through part of the park. From Kvikkjokk, hike north through pine forest until you reach a large lake. Skirt its western side and stay overnight in a cabin at Pårtestugan. You're in Sarek proper now, and the day's hike will take you across bare, mountainous terrain, with excellent views of the Pårtetjåkkå and

Kåtokkaskatjåkkå massifs to your left. You'll reach the vast Laitaure lake, which you cross using the rowing boats provided. Here you can use the cabin at Aktse as a base for venturing off the trail and into the wilds of Sarek's Rapadalen valley, home to numerous elk and bears. In the valley mouth you can camp around the many oxbow lakes and branches of the river for a couple of days before making your way back to Aktse and trekking north across a boggy stretch of land, with wooden

boardwalks to help you across. Traverse another lake using the boat service run by a caretaker to the cabin in Sitojaure. From here, it's a steep descent to the village of Saltoluokta, a short bus ride away from the town of Gällivare.

02

Two weeks

A real off-the-beaten track adventure, this 200km, two-week hike stays largely within the boundaries of Sarek. You'll be completely off the grid and venturing into the wilderness with no trails and no mobile-phone coverage, so compass, map and GPS are essential. The only thing you don't have to worry about is water.

Start the trek in Kvikkjokk, the closest settlement to Sarek's borders, and head into the mountains bordering Sarek to the south by following the river valley west and

skirting the southern flank of Tarrekaise mountain (1829m). It'll take at least two days' hike to reach the Sarek border, passing three cabins en route. Then you'll enter Vallevágge valley and spend the next few days making your way across rough terrain in between bare Sarek massifs. Head east towards the mighty Pårtetjåkkå peak, and then continue north into Njåtjosvagge, a narrow glacial valley. Be prepared to ford several tributaries of the main river. Passing a string of lakes, and

skirting yet another massif, head north towards the vast Alkajaure lake before following the course of the Rapaätno river around the northern side of the glacier-topped Akkatjåkko mountain. Keep to the right side of the river until you reach the confluence of the Rapaätno and another river. To finish, head south into the spectacular Rapadalen until the mighty Rapaätno dissolves into myriad waterways and flows into Laitaure lake. From here, take the Kungsleden back to Kvikkjokk.

49

Saxon Switzerland National Park

Hang out with the rock stars at one of Germany's most soul-stirring national parks, where the sandstone is convoluted and stairways lead to free-climbing heaven.

Getty Images | Franz Waldhäusl

You're striding along a forest trail or shimmying up an iron-rung ladder through a mossy crevasse when suddenly your gaze lifts to fluted sandstone pinnacles, columns, tabletops and cliffs that rise like the ruins of a fantasy fortress. A peregrine falcon dips and rises with the breeze. In the distance you fancy you can spy the turrets of a medieval castle. As day fades into dusk, the rock formations take on an other-worldliness below a bruised pink-purple sky.

Inspired to paint or write? You're not the first. Creative souls have long extolled the beauty of Saxon Switzerland, and none more famously than the 18th-century Swiss double act that gave it its moniker: Adrian Zingg and Anton Graff. While teaching at Dresden art academy, they fell hopelessly in love with the region that so reminded them of their homeland, Jura. Hot on their heels came inspiration-seeking Romantics, including 19th-century landscape artist Caspar David Friedrich, who thrashed out forbidding paintings of wild, mist-ensnared crags.

Starkly eroded over 100 million years, these rocks might look as porous as honeycomb or as fragile as wax candles, but they've been around since dinosaurs walked the planet. They rose up from the Cretaceous ocean, and the Elbe River has helped to sculpt them into the spires, gorges and mini mesas you see today.

It's not only geologists who have a field day here. These rocks are the cradle of free climbing – the rules were written right here in the early 20th century – and there are more than 1000 pinnacles to clamber up and jump across (yes, really). Hikers are in their element, too, on trails that plunge deep into citadels of stone, and on tracks that flirt with mountaineering, with rungs

and steps leading up and down millennia-old cliffs like a primeval game of snakes and ladders.

⬆ Exploring Saxon Switzerland's sandstone towers.
Previous page: the Basteibrücke offers a channel through the rocks.

Getty Images | Westend61

Toolbox

When to go
Each season has its charm. Spring and autumn are quieter and bring a splash of colour to the landscape. Crowds peak during summer, prime time for activities like rock climbing, hiking and water sports. Occasional snow dusts the pinnacles in winter.

Getting there
Saxon Switzerland straddles the Czech border; the closest airport is in Dresden, 50km north. Towns like Bad Schandau, Königstein and Rathen are linked to Dresden by the B172, B6 and A4 roads, and regular trains.

Park in numbers

93.5
Area covered (sq km)

562
Highest point: Grosser Zschirnstein (m)

1990
Year the park was established

Stay here...

🏠 **Burg Alrathen**
It's not every night you get to stay in a medieval castle. This one in Rathen is the real McCoy, perched on a rocky outcrop and featuring plush, warm-hued digs with pine trappings. Opening onto a panoramic terrace overlooking the Elbe, the restaurant cooks up hearty meals such as pork roast with sauerkraut and dumplings. It's in a fabulous position, with the Bastei's striking rock formations right on the doorstep, meaning you can get there before the masses.

⛺ **Boofen**
Take the lead of local climbers and get that bit closer to nature by *boofen*. This practice of sleeping below a rock overhang goes back aeons in Saxon Switzerland. With bivvy or sleeping bag, you're good to go – just check the designated sites with the park authority first.

🏠 **Elbresidenz**
Fancy a dash of luxury after a hard day's hiking? This grand pile on Bad Schandau's main square delivers. Rooms are slick and contemporary (Elbe-facing ones cost more), and you'll welcome some chill time in the huge rooftop spa after a day on the trail.

Do this!

📷 **Bastei**
Even the most fervent Romantic painter couldn't have dreamt up a landscape as wondrous as the Bastei. Rising like a giant's gnarled fingers above the village of Rathen, these crags and fluted pinnacles soar 194m above the Elbe River. Just try to suppress a gasp when you first eye the 19th-century Basteibrücke, a sandstone bridge that leaps photogenically between the bizarre rock formations. Goethe waxed lyrical about this view, and whether seen in swirling mist, snow flurries or dazzling sunshine, it really is something else.

🚲 **Exploring the Elbe**
Snaking through the national park's heart, the Elbe is one of Germany's greatest rivers. Discover it by paddle steamer or rowing boat or by pedalling part of the Elbe Cycle Route.

⛰ **Free climbing**
Saxony wrote the rulebook on free climbing (no artificial aids; ropes and carabiners only for protection etc), and you can see why. The weathered buttes and pinnacles are a vast playground for climbers, with 17,000 routes, graded I to XII, scrambling up 1100 rocks. Inexperienced? Go with a pro.

What to spot...

Saxon Switzerland pieces together a jigsaw of habitats: tabletop mountains, deep canyons, moors, primeval forest, plateaus and rugged, rocky terrain. Ferns, mosses and lichens thrive in its cool, damp ecosystem, as do flowers and herbs such as gelbe Veilchen (yellow violet) and Sumpfporst (wild rosemary), which usually only grow in tundra climates. Wildlife thrives in its hard-to-reach corners, including eagle owls, otters, dormice, black storks, peregrine falcons and lynx.

EURASIAN EAGLE OWL *Bubo bubo* is the Latin name for this tufty-eared, mottle-feathered owl with distinctive orange eyes. Females are bigger than males and can have wingspans of nearly 2m. This nocturnal predator likes the cliff ledges and gullies of the park's remoter corners.

SALMON Dams and diminished water quality decimated the Elbe's once-healthy salmon populations, but they have bounced back. At 1165km, the Elbe is Germany's second-largest river.

EURASIAN LYNX This wildcat prowls park forests. Europe's third-largest predator, it is carnivorous (stalking and pouncing on prey) and solitary, and changes its coat from golden-brown to silver-grey in winter.

Hike this...

01 Malerweg (Painter's Way)
Got a week to spare? This phenomenal 112km circular hike offers mazy gorges, ladders teetering up sheer cliffs and hilltop fortresses with giddy views. Follow the 'M'.

02 Bastei
Give day trippers the slip on this panoramic 5km loop to Schwedenlöcher – 700 steps unravel to a ravine where local troops dodged the Swedes during the Thirty Years' War.

03 Schrammsteinaussicht
The 6km, two-hour hike to the viewpoint above the park's densest rock labyrinth requires surefootedness for the final ascent straight up the rocks via a network of steel stairs and ladders.

Getty Images | Tobias Richter/LOOK-foto; Bernard van Dierendonck/LOOK-foto; Getty Images | subtik

Itineraries

Thrill to the morning sun spilling across knobbly spires of sandstone, free climb or clamber up Heaven's Ladder for celestial views, and map out medieval German history at high-on-a-hill Königstein.

◀ Strict rules govern rock climbing ethics on the sandstone towers of Saxon Switzerland.
▶ Königstein Fortress sits above the Elbe River and is well placed for defence and stunning views.

01

A weekend

Begin on a high at the Bastei, where rock pinnacles thrust up like a petrified forest above the broad curve of the Elbe River. The Romantic artists longed to paint it, and at the very least you'll want your camera handy, especially when the gracefully loping Basteibrücke slides into frame. Cross it to reach the remnants of a partly reconstructed medieval castle, Felsenburg Neurathen. From here, take a ramble on the circular trail to Schwedenlöcher. Slotted into the cliffs, this mossy ravine is where troops hid from the Swedes during the Thirty Years' War. Count the 818 steps leading to the Amselgrund Valley.

Round out the day with dinner at Bastei Berghotel's restaurant. Snag a window table for views while digging into fish or game paired with local wines. Burg Alrathen's rooms offer fine panoramas and peaceful slumber.

On the following day, rise early to beat the crowds to Königstein Fortress. Lifted high on a tabletop mountain, 260m above the river, it commands sweeping views across Saxon Switzerland's forest of rock pinnacles. The 13th-century citadel looks every inch the fairy-tale castle and is Germany's biggest. Highlights include the Brunnenhaus, with its seemingly bottomless well, and Georgenburg, once Saxony's most feared prison, whose inmates included Meissen porcelain inventor Johann Friedrich Böttger. During WWII, it served as a POW camp. Linger to see sunset backlight the distinctive tabletop mountain of Lilienstein in the distance.

02

Four days

Follow the weekend itinerary, then on day three get yourself over to the Schrammsteine first thing – this rocky wonderland of weirdly eroded sandstone formations is most striking in the morning light. The big deal here is the head-spinning two-hour hike to Schrammsteinaussicht (417m), which threads along a sandy track, through cool, damp gorges and up a seemingly never-ending one-way staircase, the Himmelsleiter (Heaven's Ladder). The view at the top? Just wow. Here you're just a hair's breadth from the Czech border. Back in Bad Schandau, go for dinner at Barthel's on the Marktplatz – sit on the terrace if weather permits. The kitchen dishes up a gutsy feast of old-fashioned Saxon grub like *Sauerbraten* (braised beef in spiced vinegar). Spend the night at the spa-topped Elbresidenz.

Your last day in the national park presents you with choices. You could walk a chunk of the Malerweg, contemplating the great Romantic painters who went before you. Or perhaps you'd prefer a spin along the Elbe River by bicycle. If free climbing is more your scene, the park really is your oyster. Pick your pinnacle and go for it. Should you want to feel closer to the elements, spend your final night *boofen* – wild camping under a rocky overhang, with nothing but the starry night as your curtain.

50

SPAIN

Sierra Nevada National Park

You've seen them before: Spain's snowcapped Sierra Nevada mountains provide the much-loved, much-photographed backdrop to La Alhambra in Granada. But they're even better up close.

Getty Images | Antonio Luis Martínez Cano

Sierra Nevada National Park

Home to mainland Spain's highest mountain, a miracle of snow rising above the baking plains of Andalucía, the Sierra Nevada is one of Spain's most unlikely attractions. Where else in Europe can you stare up at dazzling snows through a cloud of heat haze? Or be almost guaranteed a sighting of extravagantly horned ibex? Or see almost one-third of Spain's entire portfolio of plant species in one place? Or experience all of these things on the same day?

Formed at the same geological moment as the Alps and Morocco's Atlas Mountains, the Sierra Nevada stretches 75km west to east, and its foothills and high valleys bear echoes of one of Spanish history's grand epics. In 1492, with the Christian armies of the Reconquista in control of Granada, ending eight centuries of Islamic rule in southern Spain, Boabdil, the last Muslim ruler of Al-Andalus, crossed the Sierra Nevada on his way into exile. As he did so, he turned for one last tearful look at his beloved city, only to be scolded by his mother: 'Do not weep like a woman for that which you were unable to defend like a man!' Boabdil and his followers settled in Las Alpujarras, a high-altitude cluster of villages on the southern downslopes of the sierra, villages that even today seem more Arab than European.

And in the same way that the Sierra Nevada provides the backdrop to La Alhambra and Granada, so, too, does this history provide backstory to these mountains' excellent selection of activities – winter skiing at Europe's southernmost ski station, summer hiking through flora- and fauna-rich high country, as well as horse riding, climbing, mountain biking, paragliding and some seriously good eating.

Toolbox

When to go
The mountains are accessible year-round, but the time to go depends on what you want to do. Las Alpujarras are best April to mid-June and mid-September to early November. The ski station is open roughly November to March. High-altitude hiking trails usually open late June to October.

Getting there
The park spans the Granada and Almería provinces of Spain's southeast in the triangle between Granada, Málaga and Almería.

Park in numbers

862
Area covered (sq km)

3479
Highest point: Mulhacén (m)

5000
Number of wild ibex roaming free within the park

Getty Images | Bruno Abarca

Stay here...

Carmen de la Alcubilla del Caracol

Granada makes a fine base for visiting the Sierra Nevada, although it's so fabulous that it can be hard to tear yourself away. Hidden behind white walls in the lee of the Alhambra hill, this heavenly *carmen* strikes an eloquent balance between history, romance and modern comfort – and it's backed up by attentive personal service by host Manuel. The rooms perch over a flowery terraced garden, and an open deck is the scene of leisurely breakfasts that involve far more than just tostadas and coffee.

Hotel Maravedi

Above Pitres in the hamlet of Capilerilla (and along the E4 footpath), Hotel Maravedi is a rustic, mountain kind of place, but that vibe is combined with home comforts, plus satellite TV and a private bar-restaurant for guests.

L'Atelier

In an ancient village house in Mecina, in the heart of Las Alpujarras, welcoming French-run guesthouse L'Atelier serves gourmet vegetarian/vegan meals (lunch Saturday and Sunday, dinner Wednesday to Monday) that might just be a highlight of your visit to the region.

Do this!

Hiking

Nowhere else in Spain can you walk this high. Trails wind across the mountains, linking the villages of Las Alpujarras, and you could easily spend a week or more crossing from one end to the other, with many a pleasurable diversion en route. But most people come here to attempt the ascent of mainland Spain's two highest peaks: Mulhacén (3479m) and Veleta (3395m).

Skiing

The Sierra Nevada ski station sits up at Pradollano, 33km from Granada on the A395, and its 85 marked downhill runs and numerous cross-country routes cover more than 80km, often with better snow conditions and weather than northern Spanish ski resorts.

Village touring

Exploring Las Alpujarras – a long jumble of valleys, arid hillsides split by deep ravines, and oasis-like white villages set beside rapid streams and surrounded by gardens, orchards and woodlands – is one of the premier pleasures of visiting Spain.

◄ The narrow, vertiginous streets of Capileira.
Previous page: Pradollano.

What to spot...

The park has a high-altitude ecosystem all its own. Andalucía's largest Spanish ibex population may get most of the attention, but you've also a chance to see wild boars, martens, badgers and, if you're really lucky, European wildcats. Scan the skies also for bird species that include the golden eagle, Bonelli's eagle, Eurasian eagle-owl and red-legged partridge. Remarkably, the Sierra Nevada boasts close to 2100 of Spain's 7000 plant species, with 60 of these endemic.

SPANISH IBEX Also known as the Iberian ibex or Spanish wild goat, the ibex has short legs and flexible hooves that make them perfectly adapted for bare rocky outcrops. The males have marvellously curved horns.

SNOW STAR Endemic to the Sierra Nevada, the snow star grows beneath overhanging rocks and in rocky crevasses and cracks. When in flower, it resembles a white starfish.

BONELLI'S EAGLE This mountain specialist is a large brown-and-white bird of prey with a 1.5m wingspan, brown-flecked white chest and yellow feet.

Hike this...

O1 Mulhacén
Take the shuttle bus from Capileira in Las Alpujarras. From where the road ends at the Mirador de Trevélez, it's a 6km climb to the top of Mulhacén.

O2 Veleta
Take the bus 3km beyond the ski station to the national-park information post at Hoya de la Mora, then hike the final 4km to the summit of Spain's second-highest peak.

O3 GR7
Of the long-distance footpaths that traverse Las Alpujarras, the GR7 follows the most scenic route; you could walk it from Lanjarón to Pampaneira (20km) in a long day.

Shutterstock | Luna Vandoorne, 500px | Javier oliva, Getty images | Westend61

Itineraries

The Sierra Nevada's stirring landscapes and timeless villages will leave you longing for more no matter how much time you spend here.

◀ Bubión's 16th-century Mudéjar church.
▶ The Sierra Nevada is home to some world class downhill mountain bike trails.

01
A day

If you've only allocated a day for the Sierra Nevada, treat it like a reconnaissance mission to help you plan your return – a single day is never enough here. If you're coming from Granada, drive up past the ski station at Pradollano, then on to Hoya de la Mora – to reach here you may need to take the shuttle bus, depending on the season, then either ski back down (in winter) or climb to the top of Mulhacén for immense views, not to mention the cachet of summiting mainland Spain's highest mountain; watch for ibex on the high slopes and silhouetted atop rocky outcrops. If, on the other hand, you're starting the day on the southern side of the range, spend the morning exploring the villages of the Poqueira Gorge – Pampaneira, Bubión and Capileira. These are quintessential Las Alpujarras hamlets: whitewashed clusters with 16th-century Mudéjar churches and a real sense that you've strayed into North Africa. From Capileira you can push on to approach (and then climb) Mulhacén from the south.

02
Two days

An extra day, well spent, allows you to deepen your experience of the Sierra Nevada, although be warned: every day that you spend in the area only deepens its hold on you. Stay in any of Las Alpujarras' villages on the first day to soak up the silence and enable an early start. To your ascent of Mulhacén on day one add a hike up its spectacular deputy, Veleta. If climbing two such towering peaks proves too daunting, consider climbing either peak on day one, then walking the 20km from Lanjarón to Pampaneira on the second day. Shorter day hikes are also possible, while you could expand your vehicular exploration of Las Alpujarras by adding the villages of La Taha sector and throwing in a visit to Trevélez for good measure. The latter's reputation for fine *jamón*, produced from pigs kept in pristine surroundings, makes it an excellent lunch stop as you continue into the park's southern reaches through the Trevélez gorge.

03
Three days

OK, now you're talking. Begin in Granada by admiring the Sierra Nevada from afar (with the peerless Alhambra in the foreground, of course), then picture yourself standing on the range's highest point within hours. To make that a reality, take the A395 from the city outskirts to the Mulhacén trailhead. As no roads cross the mountains here, return to sleep in Granada at the end of day one. Early on the morning of day two, rush south along the E902 as far as Tablate, from where the A348 leaves the world of haste behind, twisting across the southern flanks of the Sierra Nevada. Wherever you encounter a side road disappearing off to the north, take it. Whenever you find yourself in a beautiful village, park the car to get out and walk. And by the end of day two, make sure you've visited as many villages as you can, and have factored in the Veleta ascent. On day three, leave your wheels in Lanjarón or Pampaneira, then walk between the two.

51

Slovenský Raj

Get drenched by waterfalls, cling to ladders and shiver inside an ice cave: exploring Slovakia's Slovenský Raj is not for the faint-hearted.

Shutterstock | Milosz_M

Naming this national park 'Slovak Paradise' was no idle boast. A web of crystal-clear streams thrashes through Slovenský Raj, and two dramatic mountain ranges, the Low Tatras and the Slovak Ore Mountains, cradle the park. The Hornád River carves out deep canyons, overlooked by towering beech trees. Rare wolves, wildcats and boar trot silently through the forests that cover 90 percent of the park. With countless waterfalls drawing butterflies to their swirling mists, Slovenský Raj feels like a paradisiacal place indeed.

The park conceals much beneath the surface, too. Hundreds of caverns are secreted away in limestone cliffs, visited only by bats, while the karst plateaus are pockmarked with sinkholes. The most remarkable subterranean discovery occurred in 1870, when mining engineer Eugen Ruffínyi first slid down into Dobšinská ice cave. This frosty grotto is in a state of eternal winter: warm air cannot percolate down to the cavern, while cold air sinks like a stone through its narrow crevices. Within a year of its discovery, the cave was open for visitors. It remains the most popular sight in Slovenský Raj.

Since the late 19th century, pockets of eastern Slovakia have been ring-fenced for protection. This gradual process created a patchwork of 11 national nature reserves and eight nature reserves, some of the most unspoilt corners of the park. The park's 'paradise' moniker stuck in the early 20th century, though the area wasn't officially classified as a national park until 1988.

Today, more than 300km of hiking routes extend across the park, and cycling trails link its major sights and villages. But the terrain has kept its rough charisma, from moss-scented trails to perilous gorges and tempestuous waterfalls. After all, no one ever said paradise was easy.

⬆ The park's most scenic lookout, Tomášovský Výhľad. Previous page: paths line the sparkling streams.

Toolbox

⚙ **When to go**
May and June bring sunshine, wild flowers and hikers, though crowds truly arrive in July and August. Come in winter for frozen waterfalls and skiing, though hiking options are limited.

🧭 **Getting there**
The park is 100km northwest of Slovakia's second city, Košice, along the E50. From Slovakia's capital, Bratislava, take a train to Smižany or Spišské Tomášovce (via Poprad). From Budapest, travel by train via Košice. Airports in Košice and Poprad have direct flights to UK airports.

Park in numbers

197
Area covered (sq km)

450
Number of caves and sinkholes

70
Height of Závojový, the park's tallest waterfall (m)

Stay here...

Ranč u Trapera
Horse around in this homely wooden guesthouse with attached stables, located in Hrabušice village in the northern part of the park. Walking trails are only 500m from your door, while in winter you're within easy reach of ski areas like the Levočská Valley. You can arrange a canter on the owner's horses for an extra fee. The location feels as wild and ranch-like as the hotel's name promises, and major park drawcards like the ice cave and Kláštorisko hiking trails are a short hop away.

Penzión Pod Guglom
Slalom to your door at this welcoming guesthouse near Gugel ski area in Mlynky, in the southern part of the park. The on-site sauna soothes stiff muscles, plus there are kid-friendly perks such as play areas, bike hire and a trampoline.

Park Hotel Čingov
Each of the 20 rooms in this superbly located hotel, on the eastern side of the park, has a balcony overlooking the park or the spiky High Tatras. The vibe is old-fashioned, and menus groan with roasted meat and dumplings drowned in sour cream.

Do this!

Ice-cave exploring
While most of Slovenský Raj's caves hide from view, you can walk beneath stalactites in Unesco-listed Dobšinská ice cave. Find the entrance to this cavern of ice floors and frosty pillars on the north slopes of Duča hill, near the village of Dobšina, and watch your breath turn to mist along 515m of walks (open mid-May to September) – one-third of its total length. And if the setting isn't surreal enough, picture ice skaters pirouetting through the grotto: it was a year-round pastime until the 1940s.

Skiing
After hikers tramp out of Slovenský Raj, skiers arrive. Gugel Mlynky, usually open from January to mid-March, has 5km of runs, including a freeride area and snow park. Wilderness seekers tend to ply its 35km of cross-country trails.

Cycling
More than 110km of cycling trails thread the park. From Podlesok, Green Path 3 (6.5km) reaches the Carthusian monastery ruins in Kláštorisko. For a longer ride, Blue Path 4 (20km) zigzags towards the ice cave; turn right onto Green Path 1 at the end.

What to spot...

Shaded woodlands dominate Slovenský Raj, so it's no surprise that 40 species of mammal forage here. Look out for the park's rarer denizens: endangered squirrels and otters at ground level, and the saker falcon soaring above. But much likelier to tiptoe into view are martens, foxes and deer. The few wolves and wildcats prowling through the park will likely bolt at your scent, but look out for their prints, especially in muddy banks along the Hornád River.

BROWN ARGUS BUTTERFLY This chocolate-brown butterfly with amber markings is one of many winged things in Slovenský Raj, which boasts more butterflies than anywhere else in the country. You'll spot them fluttering from May until September.

SAKER FALCON Evolution honed this tawny raptor into a killing machine, with a powerful beak and a diving speed of up to 360km/h, but only small birds need fear its beady glare. Slovenský Raj is one of its few remaining European habitats.

PINE MARTEN Bright eyed, bushy tailed, with pointed ears and downy brown bodies, these omnivorous mammals scamper through Central Europe's woodlands. They're plentiful in Slovenský Raj, where they have river fish, birds and fruit to nibble.

Hike this...

O1 Suchá Belá
The park's most popular gorge makes a scenic two-hour hike from Podlesok along 4km of moss-lined rocks and wooden stairs – you'll need a good sense of balance.

O2 Prielom Hornádu
This river canyon is exhilarating but not for the timid: over roughly four hours, you'll grapple 12km of climbing irons and ladders, from Hrdlo Hornádu in Podlesok to Maša Bridge.

O3 Veľký Sokol circuit
Only hardened hikers should attempt this 21km round-trip. Seven calf-stiffening hours of hanging off chains and climbing against the stream are rewarded with views of Sokol's waterfalls.

Itineraries

Let Slovenský Raj set your pulse racing, whether you've a single day or several: balance along gorgeside trails, gawp at an ice cave, and feel the cooling mist of waterfalls.

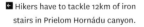 Hikers have to tackle 12km of iron stairs in Prielom Hornádu canyon.
 The gleaming interior of Dobšinská ice cave.

01

A day

See the national park's icons in the space of a day: you just need your own wheels and a thirst for adventure. Drive into the park from the northeastern entrance through Hrabušice village, in the Podlesok area. From here, embark on one of the park's most beauteous walks: Suchá Belá gorge. The journey involves chains, ladders and footbridges, so expect to emerge river splashed, mud streaked and elated. You'll get wetter in spring or autumn, when the waterfalls are at their most spectacular. We don't

recommend clutching a *trdelník* pastry in one hand, and hanging on to a wooden ladder with the other, so save your appetite for a late lunch in Hrabušice – try Restaurant Rumanka for Slovak specialities like *bryndzové halušky* (little dumplings with sheep's cheese).

After lunch, it's a 17km drive southwest to the most unusual sight in the park, Dobšinská ice cave. Summer tours take you into this sub-zero grotto, where 110,100 cubic metres of ice are amassed into gleaming

turrets, and icicles drip from the walls. From here you can drive south out of the park, but you might want to stop to see Palcmanská Maša, the park's largest reservoir, glowing in the sunset, with views of pretty Dedinky village across the water.

If, in the golden light, you realise a day wasn't enough in Slovenský Raj, Dedinky is a fine starting point for excursions to the park's southern reaches, while nearby Mlynky is a superb base for winter sports.

02

Four days

Drive into Podlesok (or take a bus from Poprad to Hrabušice) for four days of waterfalls, ruins and stellar hikes. Start with one of the park's favourite treks, to Suchá Belá, followed by a meal back in the village. A few guesthouses here offer horse-riding; check in (you'll need two nights) and spend your afternoon riding around fields of daisies.

The next day, swap your steed for a rental bike. From Podlesok, pedal along Blue Path 1 (about 20km), stopping at Vernár village for lunch. Continue the

trail towards Krivian, then cycle south via Green Path 1, which leads to Dobšinská ice cave. After your visit, take an alternative route back to Podlesok, scenic Blue Path 4.

On day three, pack a light overnight bag and set out for Kláštorisko's crumbling Gothic monasteries, via the hour-long Prielom Hornádu trail. Spot seven waterfalls along the way. Spend the afternoon exploring 14th-century monk's cells and the haunting 'symbolic cemetery', which commemorates climbers

and other adventurers who died in the park. You can spend the night in cabins here (open in summer only).

Awakening in Kláštorisko puts you at the centre of some of the park's very best hiking routes for your last day. Experienced hikers should start early and trek north along Red Trail 4, then east along Blue Trail 2 to the park's most scenic lookout, Tomášovský výhľad. Just be sure to leave energy for the final hour clambering back from Kláštorisko to your starting point in Podlesok.

52

Snæfellsjökull National Park

An array of Iceland's most captivating features, Snæfellsjökull promises all the trappings of the 'Land of Fire and Ice' at the tip of a mesmerising peninsula.

L ush fjords, haunting volcanic peaks, dramatic sea cliffs, sweeping golden beaches, and crooked, crunchy lava flows make up the diverse and fascinating landscape of the 100km-long Snæfellsnes Peninsula. The area is crowned by the glistening ice cap Snæfellsjökull, immortalised in Jules Verne's fantasy tale *Journey to the Centre of the Earth*. In his proto-sci-fi tale, the brooding ice mound covers a massive volcano whose magma chamber doubles as the gateway to the planet's core. And although the author never travelled to the mountain himself, news of Snæfellsjökull's majesty was undeniable, and it captured both his attention and his imagination.

Snæfellsjökull and its surrounding area – now a national park – have been immortalised in literary works for over a thousand years. Several of Iceland's most crucial sagas – legends captured in the writings of the island's first settlers – took place among the peninsula's lava fields. Stories of battling trolls and seafaring adventurers originated here and helped form the modern conception of Norse history. It was along the shores of the Snæfellsnes that the first Europeans embarked on expeditions to the Americas, their achievements proven by compelling archaeological evidence gathered on the banks of Canada's Newfoundland. Christopher Columbus, reportedly aware of the Icelanders' accomplishments, is said to have stopped within the preserve's confines to seek navigational advice while planning his famous voyage to the New World.

Today, New Age practitioners attribute Snæfellsjökull National Park's millennium of veritable fame to the energy and

magnets tucked away below the Earth's surface – like a planetary chakra akin to those of Sedona (Arizona) and Ubud (Bali). Some visitors come to Hellnar to feel the intangible forces of nature and rebalance their minds. For others, the reserve casts a much simpler spell: Arctic vistas so compelling that you'll be frozen in awe, unable for a moment or two even to photograph the splendour before you.

⬆ Lava fields line the landscape in front of Snæfellsjökull volcano.
Previous page: Arnarstapi township.

Toolbox

☼ **When to go**
June and July benefit from long days (midnight sun!) and generally warmer weather. October is a fun time to partake in the *réttir* (the rounding up of roaming sheep for winter). March gets a reasonable amount of daylight but snow remains on the fjord peaks – a very charming combination.

🧭 **Getting there**
The park occupies the western recesses of the long Snæfellsnes Peninsula, about two hours northwest of Reykjavík.

Park in numbers

440
Area covered (sq km)

1446
Height of the park's active volcano (m)

1477
Year Christopher Columbus reportedly visited Iceland, landing within the park's borders

Stay here...

🏠 Hótel Egilsen
This might just be the cutest inn in all of Iceland. The 10 rooms at the Egilsen occupy a lovingly restored timber house – once owned by a wealthy Danish merchant – that creaks in the most endearing of ways when the fjord winds come howling off the bay. The perfect amount of rustic Scandinavian charm (wooden slatting and handwoven quilts) is effortlessly married with stylish accent pieces (copper lamps and a flashy yellow runner up the stairs), as though Jonathan Adler and Martha Stewart have had an Icelandic baby. Heaping portions of homemade breakfast sweeten the deal.

🏠 Hótel Buðir
Windswept, lonely and incredibly romantic, Buðir is the fjord-side bolthole of your dreams, complete with baronial furniture, infinite views and an incredible dinner menu of local cuisine served in the candlelit dining room.

🏠 Icelandair Hotel Reykjavík Marina
For those basing themselves in the capital, this boutique establishment in a converted factory is a fine choice. It sits right along the harbour in the middle of town, offering fjord views, sleek nautical-themed decor and a hip cocktail bar in the lobby.

Do this!

🤿 Hot-spring swimming
Wading through piping-hot water is practically Iceland's national pastime, and these 'hot pots' are everywhere – from downtown Reykjavík to the isolated fjords of the north. Head to Lýsuhólslaug, a swimming pool at the local primary school that taps into a natural artery of steaming liquid. The pool has a green tint from the algae that thrives in the gurgling carbonated waters – you'll emerge with glowing, dolphin-like skin after a relaxing dip.

🧲 Horse riding
The Icelandic horse is a special breed of equine that bears many noticeable differences from other horses, including its stout pony-like stature and two extra gaits in addition to the walk, trot, canter and gallop. Visit Lýsuhóll, just a hop beyond the park's southwestern boundary, for a chance to trot along the barren beaches nearby.

❄️ Snowmobiling
When the moody weather mellows over the crown of the glacier, you can explore the snowy expanse by snowmobile or snowcat. Tours are based out of the township of Arnarstapi and run during the warmer months of the year.

What to spot...

Iceland's harsh landscape, bombarded by Arctic winds and seismic blasts nearly without respite, makes a relatively inhospitable environment for living creatures. The country has a noticeable dearth of trees and is home to only a handful of mammals, but several species of migratory bird pass through.

TERN The beautiful white tern, with a black cap and a red beak, is notorious for swooping at humans who are nearing its nest. If you spot one, defend yourself by holding a walking stick (or similar) above your head.

GUILLEMOT Making its home along the jagged cliff walls at the tip of the peninsula, the guillemot nests in large groups. In breeding season, each female lays a single egg within the craggy escarpments.

GREY SEAL Considerably larger than the common (or harbour) seal, the grey seal grows to around 3m in length and is most frequently found in Iceland's west and north.

Hike this...

O1 Hellnar to Arnarstapi

This 2.5km walk passes frozen lava flows and eroded caves once home to saga heroes. In stormy weather, waves pound through the rocky arches, creating a blowhole effect.

O2 Öndverðarnes

The westernmost tip of the peninsula forms a spit hosting golden Skarðsvík beach, with an ancient Viking grave, and the dramatic Svörtuloft bird cliffs.

O3 Djúpalónssandur and Dritvík

Stamp along the black-sand shore, passing rocky stacks that look like petrified trolls, until you reach a smaller cove with the haunting wreckage of the fishing vessel Eding, destroyed here in 1948.

Itineraries

Like a wondrous microcosm of the entirety of Iceland, Snæfellsjökull and the peninsula surrounding it offer fjords, glaciers, volcanoes and waterfalls, yet they draw a mere fraction of the visitors who go to the nearby Golden Circle.

◄ Weathered Gatklettur (Arch Rock) at Arnarstapi.
➔ Hardy Icelandic horses are bred from stock brought to the country in the 9th and 10th centuries.

01

A day

One full day in the park is doable by following the circular seaside route (165km) all the way through. Along the way you'll score a sampling of what the park has to offer, but beware: once your appetite is whetted you'll regret that you only have a single day to explore. Start on the southern stretch of the peninsula's Rte 54, where the land is low and the beaches are broad. Just before entering the park, try an hour of horseback riding at Lýsuhóll, followed by a dip in a neighbouring geothermal pool to soothe your weary muscles after all that galloping through the lava fields. Park at Arnarstapi for a 40-minute cliff-side hike to Hellnar, spotting birds nesting among the ochre earth, then drive into the heart of the national park for another short stroll down to the pebble-strewn shore of Djúpalónssandur. In the summer months, a hearty fish stew awaits in the northern recesses of the park at Gamla Rif, a cafe run by two fishermen's wives. Spot the small church bearing an elaborate painting that depicts Christopher Columbus' reputed voyage to the peninsula to gather information from the local Norsemen about their journeys to the New World. Continue along the northern track of Rte 54 as the central peninsular ridge towers above like the spine of a stegosaurus. Pull into the charming village of Stykkishólmur for the night, staying at Hótel Egilsen.

02

Three days

With a long weekend of exploration, you'll want to follow the same coastal loop as the day-long itinerary, but you'll be able to move much more slowly as you venture off the pavement and into the hidden, forest-like expanses of craggy lava. Start on the northern side of the peninsula, basing yourself at Hótel Egilsen in Stykkishólmur. On your first day, swing by Leir 7, a local ceramicist's studio where the artist uses clay from the nearby fjord, then see the Library of Water, an art installation housing tubes of glacial liquid. Hit Grundarfjörður to try one of the whale-watching excursions with Láki Tours that follow the peninsular coast in search of orca pods (the best months are January to April, during which you can see hundreds of orcas on a single trip).

Spend your second day solely within the park's official boundaries by zipping along Jules Verne's infamous glacier by snowmobile, then traipsing below the surface on a guided tour of the park's Water Cave. Don't miss a hike out to the peninsular tip at Öndverðarnes, where birdlife thrives among the inhospitable cliffs. As Rte 54 ploughs beyond the preserve's borders, diversions include horse riding, hot-spring bathing and a rocky ledge covered with blubbery sunbathing seals. Hótel Buðir is just beyond, with a sumptuous dinner menu of delicious local produce, and a lonely black church the size of a postage stamp outside – both perfect fodder for your Instagram.

53

Snowdonia National Park

Carved by glaciers, wrapped in mist and lost in legends, beautiful Snowdonia is as Welsh as Tom Jones, cheese on toast and dragons.

500px | callum wright

Rugged Snowdonia is the heart and soul of Wales. The rocky Snowdon massif has protected not only unspoilt nature but also a way of life. Two out of three people speak Welsh as their first language in this rugged corner of the British Isles, where the ancient kings of Eryri once held court. It's as firmly tied to the Welsh identity as male voice choirs and Arthurian legend. Indeed, King Arthur is said to have killed a monstrous beard-tugging giant and buried the body somewhere on the summit. Most modern visitors, though, are drawn by the landscapes: big, bold and elemental, the remains of prehistoric volcanoes remodelled by passing glaciers.

Used as the training ground for the first ascent of Everest, Snowdon is the most climbed mountain in Britain, though for many, the 'climb' is actually a leisurely ride on the rack-and-pinion Mountain Railway. That's the easy route; the hard way is the direct ascent of the cliffs at Clogwyn Du'r Arddu. At 1085m, Britain's second-highest peak has been a testing ground for thrill seekers since 1798, when Peter Bailey Williams and William Bingley completed the first recorded rock climb in Britain on the face of old 'Cloggy'.

The rough-and-ready terrain is far from uninhabited, but there's plenty of proper wilderness, providing a haven for all sorts of endangered critters. Rather amazingly, this all used to be under the sea, as demonstrated by the fossilised seashells that crop up at the summit. There's still plenty of standing water – somewhat inevitable considering the Welsh climate – creating still and silent lakes in the bottom of bowls scooped out by prehistoric ice. It's stunningly beautiful in good weather,

and solemn and moody in bad, but you can always retreat to the cafe at the summit for a warm cuppa.

🏔 Tryfan's rugged summit.
Previous page: steam trains have chugged their way up Snowdon since 1896.

Getty images | joe daniel price/Moment RF

Toolbox
When to go
Snowdon in winter is not for the faint-hearted, with strong winds and blankets of snow. Most visitors come in summer, when blue skies are reflected in Snowdon's lakes. Autumn and spring bring fewer crowds, but not less rain, which belts down at these times.

Getting there
Bangor and Caernarfon are the nearest towns, and domestic flights drop into the tiny airport on nearby Anglesey. The Conwy Valley railway line runs through the park; the Mountain Railway departs from Llanberis.

Park in numbers

2170
Area covered (sq km)

1085
Highest point: Snowdon (m)

1920
Year the first cafe opened at the summit

Stay here...

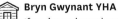

Pen-Y-Gwryd Hotel
Snowdonia has no shortage of heritage hotels, but we think the history of the 1953 Everest expedition is rather more interesting than the etchings of Lord So-and-So. Edmund Hillary and his follow mountaineers set up camp at Pen-Y-Gwryd Hotel, in Nant Gwynant, in 1953 before heading to Nepal, and not a lot has changed since. A gong still announces dinner every night, and memorabilia from the 1953 expedition encrusts the walls. The hotel was built as a farmhouse, but crossed ice axes have been its emblem since the first stones were laid in 1810.

Bryn Gwynant YHA
If you're serious about summiting Snowdon on foot, this quintessentially Welsh YHA occupies a moody grey-stone mansion on the shores of placid Llyn Gwynant, just a couple of miles from the start of the Watkin Path.

Coed-y-Celyn Hall
Set in the grand former home of a local slate-mining magnate, these self-catering apartments in Betws-y-Coed are perfect for independent-minded explorers, with a fine location on the edge of the Gwydyr Forest, much loved by walkers and mountain bikers.

Do this!

Mountain walking
There's really no buzz like summiting Snowdon, but how you do it depends on your head for heights. The easiest trail is the 8km Llanberis Path, but this means a crowd. You'll have less company on the 5.6km Watkins Path, but we say go all in, and tackle the 6.5km Crib Goch track, which picks its way along a knife-edge arête, with perilous drops on either side. People have been known to crawl the whole way...

Riding the railway
Now that the upper station and cafe have been remodelled, riding the Mountain Railway to the top of Snowdon feels like an excursion in the Swiss Alps. The rack-and-pinion railway opened in 1896 and charming steam locos still gently push carriages to the summit, offering stunning views all the way.

Mountain biking
Outside the summer months, the paths climbing Snowdon double as mountain-bike trails, offering a bone-shaking but undeniably direct route to the valley floor. There's plenty of free-wheeling on the way down, but going up is a mix of riding and carrying.

What to spot...

Hill farms sprawl over the Snowdon massif, but the higher ground provides shelter for all sorts of rare Welsh beasties. Scan the skies for peregrine falcons, red kites and rare ospreys, or look out for wild goats gambolling on the slopes – they were domesticated by the ancient Britons but have been running wild here since at least the last ice age. In early summer, seek out the Snowdon lily, an alpine flower that is common in the Alps but incredibly rare in Britain.

POLECAT These ferret-like mustelids were almost wiped out by Victorian gamekeepers, but two World Wars and legal protection allowed populations to recover. Look out for sinuous shapes scampering around the higher ground.

OTTER Waterlogged Snowdonia is a natural home for the elusive otter, which roams all the way from the high *llyns* (lakes) to the coast. Your best chances for sightings are at Tal-y-Llyn in the south of the park.

RED KITE The national bird of Wales, the heraldic-looking w can be spotted floating effortlessly on the updrafts that rise over the Snowdon massif; look for the distinctive forked tail.

Hike this...

01 Llanberis Path
The easiest of the many trails struggling up the slopes of Snowdon, this 8km path tacks alongside the Mountain Railway.

02 Crib Goch path
This tough 6.5km track veers off the Pyg Path onto a Grade 1 scramble that becomes increasingly exposed as you gain the razor-thin Crib Goch ridge.

03 Welsh 3000s
You'll get to bag the summits of Snowdon and 15 other 3000ft (914m) peaks on this epic 48km trek, completed in a single stint lasting anything from four to 24 hours.

Itineraries

Claim the summit of Snowdon, mountain-bike down rocky trails or watch the clouds slide over the mirrored surface of a glacial lake; to know Snowdonia is to love Snowdonia.

◀ A mountain biker grinds his way up Llanberis Path to the summit of Wales' highest peak, Snowdon (1085m).
▶ The ruins of Dolbadarn Castle, which was built in the 13th century by Welsh prince, Llywelyn the Great.

01
Two days

Even with just a few days in Snowdonia, you'll be able to bag the summit, but it pays to earn it by coming up here on foot. Start day one with a scenic drive to Bala to enjoy the watery pleasures around Llyn Tegid. This finger-like glacial lake is licked by scouring winds, providing excellent conditions for sailing and windsurfing, and you can rent everything from kayaks to catamarans. Nearby Tryweryn and Dee rivers offer Wales' most reliable white water; the water-sports centres at Bala and

Frongoch will strap you into a life vest faster than you can say *iechyd da* (good health). Continue on to Dolgellau, which boasts the impressive distinction of having the highest concentration of listed buildings in Wales. The Dolgellau Trail will take you on a nostalgic trip past historic wool mills and relics from the short-lived Dolgellau gold rush, or you can drop into the silent depths at the Corris Mine. If you still have energy, the 5.6km Precipice Walk offers sweeping views towards Snowdon and Cader Idris.

Snowdon gets its chance to shine on day two. From Betws-y-Coed, a favoured destination for Victorian holidaymakers, follow the winding road up to Pen-y-Pass, starting point for the Pyg Path, Miners' Track and Crib Goch trails to the summit of Snowdon. Which one you choose will depend on your taste for sheer drops and loose scree. At the top, reward yourself with lunch at the summit cafe. Moving on, either scamper down the Llanberis Path or make the trip on the puffing Mountain Railway.

02
A week

A week opens up all sorts of interesting ways to explore the national park, from mountain trails to the beaches of the Snowdonia coast. Start in Betws-y-Coed and devote a day to strolling around local landmarks such as Gwydyr Forest and the Ugly House, built from boulders by bandits, according to local legend. On day two, hit the slopes of Snowdon, walking up via the knee-knocking Crib Goch trail, and down via the Pyg Path or Miners' Track. Take another day in Llanberis

for a cruise on Llyn Padarn or a ride on the summit railway, and an afternoon at the more-exciting-than-it-sounds National Slate Museum, devoted to the tough lives lived by Welsh slate miners. For a more hands-on approach, go for a scuba dive in the village's submerged slate quarry. Slingshot through Caernarfon on day four to complete the circuit of Snowdon and reach Beddgelert, where Welsh prince Llywelyn the Great reputedly buried his dog after a mix-up involving

his baby son and a hungry wolf. The town copper mine has been operating since Roman times, and the ruined fort of Dinas Emrys was allegedly home to two dragons who were liberated by the wizard Merlin! Yes, there are a lot of legends in Snowdonia...

Finish your Snowdon odyssey by rolling downhill to Portmeirion, whose kooky pottery factory was the setting for cult TV show *The Prisoner*, then soak up the salty sea air across the estuary on the beach at Harlech.

Shutterstock | Peter Wey

Swiss National Park

A spectacle of nimble-footed ibex, crevassed glaciers, topaz lakes and dolomitic peaks, the Swiss National Park is a glimpse of the Alps before the dawn of tourism.

Swiss National Park

Striding in quiet exhilaration through high pastures freckled with wild flowers, suddenly you stop dead in your tracks. Not because of the arresting view of moraine-streaked mountains, their summits dappled with honeyed morning light. Not because a podgy marmot has just emerged to keep watch over its rocky burrow. But because you have found the Holy Grail of Alpine flora: edelweiss, the delicate, fuzzy white bloom which folk once risked life and limb to pick for their sweethearts.

Even the most ardent Alpine hiker can go years without clocking edelweiss, but such rarities abound here, where nature is left to its own devices. Perhaps it's the first time you've seen the flower in the wild, but then the Swiss National Park is all about firsts. This was the first national park to be established in the Alps, in 1914, and over a century later it still keeps a tight grip on its conservation ethos: no trees are felled, no meadows are cut, no animals are hunted, and human intervention is scant – almost non-existent.

Nudging the Italian and Austrian borders in a remote corner of the Engadine Valley in eastern Switzerland, the park is often hailed as a 'Canada in miniature' – and it lives up to the hype. Whether you're watching ibex leap from rock to rock on the trail to the jewel-like Lakes of Macun, rambling through sap-scented forests with the roar of rutting stags echoing through the Val Trupchun, or gazing up to raw, glacier-capped peaks of dolomite, which originated in an ocean 200 million years ago, this pristine pocket of wilderness will linger in your memory long after your footprints and photos have been erased.

← A cyclist climbs Umbrail Pass (2501m).
Previous page: the Inn River flows swiftly.
↑ Swiss National Park is a walking paradise; hikers at Fuorn Pass (2149m).

Shutterstock | Tim Graham, Getty Images | Bruce Yuanyue Bi

Toolbox

When to go
Go June to October, after the park shakes off its long winter hibernation and the first wild flowers are popping up. July and August are hiking heaven, with long days and all trails open. Forests kindle into colour in autumn, and mid-September to early October is stag-rutting season.

Getting there
The closest airport is in Zurich, a 2½-hour drive northwest. Frequent trains serve Zernez, S-chanf and Zuoz. Hiking buses provide an eco-friendly means of reaching trailheads.

Park in numbers

170.3
Area covered (sq km)

3174
Highest point: Piz Pisoc (m)

80
Marked hiking trails (km)

Stay here...

Chamanna Cluozza
Slip back to nature by overnighting in the park's thickly forested heart. Situated at 1882m, the chalet is basic: there are no showers, and dorms and bunks are bare bones (bring or rent a sleeping-bag liner), but the setting in the off-the-radar Val Cluozza is phenomenal. A three-hour walk from Zernez, it's open mid-June to mid-October.

Hotel Parc Naziunal Il Fuorn
Once a retreat for smugglers, pack trains and iron-ore miners en route to the Ofen Pass, this 16th-century inn is now the park's only hotel. The generous-sized rooms are comfy, and the restaurant dishes up grub like game and *Capuns* (chard-wrapped dried meat) and *Spätzle* noodles.

Hotel Bär & Post
Going strong since 1905 and run by the kindly Patscheider family, this sweet chalet-style hotel in Zernez harbours pine-heavy rooms and a little spa. The restaurant menu swings with the seasons – from *Bündner Gerstensuppe* (creamy barley soup) to venison with chestnuts.

Do this!

Guided ranger hikes
Sure, you can go it alone, but you might get more out of one of the guided hikes run by the Swiss National Park Visitor Centre in Zernez from late June to mid-October. These skip from Val Trupchun wildlife-spotting treks to high-altitude hikes to the Ofen Pass and Lakes of Macun. Most are in German, but guides usually speak some English. The visitor centre also has a 1:50,000 map covering 21 walks in the park.

Wildlife spotting
With a little luck and a decent pair of binoculars, you can sight some fantastic Alpine wildlife. Hot spots include Alp Stabelchod at 1958m, where you might spot red deer and chamois and almost certainly marmots. Lammergeiers (bearded vultures) can often be glimpsed from the nature trail near Il Fuorn, ibex around the Lakes of Macun.

Rafting the Inn
If you want to ramp up the adrenaline, take to the thrashing white water of the Inn River as it pummels through forest-flanked, waterfall-ensnared gorges. Engadin Adventure in Scuol is a good bet, offering half- and full-day tours.

What to spot...

The Swiss National Park is the Alps in a nutshell, with dolomitic peaks rearing above high pastures, subalpine grassland and mixed forests of cembra pine, larch and spruce. Edelweiss and trumpet-shaped gentian, Rhaetian poppies, bellflowers and the bright-pink puffballs of Alpenrosen (Alpine rhododendrons) brighten mountain slopes in summer. Wildlife has a field day in this remote environment, including sprightly chamois, ibex and mountain hares, and burrowing marmots. Keep your eyes to the skies to sight lammergeiers and golden eagles.

LAMMERGEIER No bird elicits such excitement here as the *Lämmergeier* (bearded vulture), reintroduced to the Stabelchod valley in 1991. This carrion-gnawing predator has a near-3m wingspan. They colour their feathers by bathing in ferric oxide–rich waters.

IBEX With their distinctive curved horns, proud stance and deeply cleft hooves, these wild goats are natural-born rock climbers. You'll often spot them leaping around the heights of the national park at elevations above 2000m.

MOUNTAIN HARE Well adapted to the park's harsh winters, these stocky, short-eared hares hang out among the pines and boulders. Their coat changes from greyish brown in summer to purest snow-white in winter.

Hike this...

01 Val Trupchun

Brushed gold in autumn and crowned by ragged peaks, this wild, wooded valley is accessed by an easy three-hour hike from S-chanf. The stag rutting is at its most spectacular here.

02 Macun

It's a tough, sensational 16km hike from Lavin to Zernez, with views deep into the Bernese, Silvretta and Ortler Alps. The highlight is the 2500m plateau of Macun, sprinkled with glittering lakes and tarns.

03 Val Mingèr

The two-hour uphill hike from Pradatsch takes in weirdly eroded rock formations, and you might spot chamois and deer.

➜ The 17th-century ruin of Fortezza Rohan sits above the village of Susch.

Itineraries

Listen for whistling marmots at Stabelchod, hike over rugged peak and flower-flecked pasture to the jewel-coloured Lakes of Macun, and immerse yourself in the culture-rich villages of the Engadine.

■→ A newborn chamois is greeted by its mother; one of the main reasons for the creation of the park was to protect chamois.

01
A day

Get the inside scoop on the park's wildlife, geology and hikes at the Swiss National Park Centre in Zernez. The village's cluster of stone houses is outlined by the profile of its baroque church and the tower of its medieval castle, Schloss Wildenberg. Stock up on picnic supplies – *Bergkäse* (mountain cheese), *salsiz* (air-dried sausage) and the like – for your hike. Or snag a table on the terrace of Hotel Parc Naziunal Il Fuorn for an early lunch.

Devote the afternoon to the three- to four-hour *Naturlehrpfad* (nature trail) for instant immersion in the park's compelling Alpine scenery. From the Ofen Pass, trudge up to Stabelchod (1958m). Continue on up to a crystal-clear stream, pausing to glimpse a glacial moulin in the rock face. If you're lucky you'll see the park's most famous resident – the lammergeier. The jagged summit of 2328m Margunet commands some soul-stirring views across starkly eroded, moraine-streaked peaks. From here you descend through the wild Val dal Botsch.

02
Three days

With three days on your hands, explore the park's tremendous hiking territory further. Follow the day itinerary, then on your second day hook on to an outstanding ranger-guided hike, where you'll become a minor expert on the park's Alpine geology and wildlife. Enjoy a well-earned Engadine-style supper back at Hotel Bär & Post.

Day three is a biggie: a tough, full-day hike to the Macun Basin. Begin in Lavin (trains run here from Zernez), where you'll cross the swift-flowing Inn River to ascend through forest. Arrow-shaped peaks like 2889m Piz Macun slide into view as you approach Alp Zeznina Dadaint, a meadow where scenes from *Heidi* were shot. From here it gets rough and rocky en route to Macun, a cirque ringed by craggy 3000m peaks and sprinkled with Alpine lakes. Clamber up to the exposed ridge of Fuorcletta da Barcli (2850m) for top-of-the-world views, before dropping out of the national park. Look for ibex having a sundown snack as you zigzag down.

03
Five days

After following the three-day itinerary, spend day four culturally by taking in Romansch-speaking villages that punctuate the Engadine Valley. Scuol, Guarda and Zuoz are particularly lovely, with Hobbit-like, sgraffito-decorated houses, cobbled lanes and fountains spouting pure spring water. Dig into local specialities like *Pizokel* (stubby wheat-and-egg noodles with parsley, speck, cheese and onions), *Bündnerfleisch* (air-dried beef) and *Nusstortorte* (caramelised walnut tart). To up the adventure, drive over the spectacularly lonely Ofen Pass to Müstair. Tucked away on the Italian border, the town is one of Europe's early Christian treasures and its Benedictine monastery is a Unesco World Heritage Site.

On your final day, go on one of the park's excellent half-day hikes. Try Val Mingèr, where deer and chamois roam, Val Trupchun, and the four-hour hike from Buffalora via Munt la Schera through a one-of-a-kind steppe landscape. Spend at least one night in the heart of the park, either at Il Fuorn or Chamanna Cluozza.

55

Tatras National Park

Eagles soar above 2000m peaks, while lynx and bears stalk valleys below. Sprawled across Poland's southern border, Tatras National Park is as untamed as they come.

Getty Images | Michał Sleczek

Surveying the panorama from Kasprowy Wierch lookout, mountains consume your entire field of vision. This serrated skyline is where two ranges meet, the High Tatras and the Western Tatras, on Poland's southern border with Slovakia. Peaks higher than 2000m vie for attention, like bare Świnica and three-peaked Rysy. Beneath these geological giants, Poland's Tatras National Park (Tatrzański Park Narodowy) encompasses 23 glacial lakes, as shiny as beaten steel, clasped by forests of spruce and silver fir.

The Tatras mountain ranges were formed more than 65 million years ago. As ice-age glaciers receded, the region's mountains gained their saw-tooth silhouette of plunging ravines and sharp summits, as well as broad moraines dusted with silt. Beneath your feet, a goblin underworld of 650 caves and karst formations lies undisturbed (except by the occasional salamander).

However sublime the views, this Polish reserve has a workaday history. Herders have led flocks among these valleys for hundreds of years. Mining and ironworking plundered local timber during the 18th and 19th centuries. Shortly after, hikers arrived and skiers created a tourism boom in Zakopane, which is slightly north of the park, while Góral (highlander) communities began to captivate visitors with folk music and distinctive 19th-century wooden architecture.

Some fear the park may become a victim of its own success, but 'tread lightly' initiatives are guarding its natural wealth. Since 1992, the Polish side has been twinned with Tatranský Národný Park across the Slovakian border, forming a Unesco biosphere reserve.

So after skiing, horseback riding and trekking to glacial lakes on the Polish side, and then energised by steaming *grzaniec* (hot beer), you might feel inspired to extend your adventure. And across the Slovakian border, hundreds more kilometres of hiking trails await…

⬆ The glacial lake of Morskie Oko is surrounded by peaks that rise for more than a thousand metres above its surface.
Previous page: the Tatras mountains are over 65 million years old.

Getty Images | merc67

Toolbox

⚙ **When to go**
Mid-June to October is excellent for hiking. Spring brings colour to crocus-filled Kościeliska Valley, August hosts Zakopane's highland-folklore festival (expect horse-and-carriage parades and singing contests), and September is your best chance to dodge the crowds. From December to February, winter-sports fans flock to Zakopane.

🧭 **Getting there**
Zakopane, home to the park headquarters, is the best base. The town is a 100km drive south (via the S7) of Kraków, whose airport serves numerous European cities.

Park in numbers

212
Area covered (sq km)

2499
Height of Rysy's tallest Polish peak (m)

270
Total length of hiking trails (km)

Stay here...

Pokoje Gościnne Chochołów

This guesthouse in Chochołów is snug within a traditional wooden building, whose sharp eaves and decorative woodcarving beautifully showcase Góral style. Inside, rooms are made cosy with rugs and shaggy blankets. At the height of summer, the soundtrack to this heritage village is horses galloping across wild-flower meadows. Winter is equally pretty: the guesthouse owners can arrange sleigh rides up Gubałówka mountain.

Hotel Bukovina

Peering over 1000m-altitude Bukowina Tatrzańska village is this wellness hotel, which channels mineral waters into its slinky spa and serves up highlander cuisine with a health-conscious twist. Rooms have an alpine-chalet feel, with sloping ceilings and wooden beams.

Hotel Art&Spa

This newly revamped Zakopane hotel (formerly the Marilor) is housed in a mansion dating to 1912. There's a whiff of nostalgia about its design, but service is trim and the seasonal dishes served in its classy restaurant are among the best in town.

Do this!

Skiing and snowboarding

A century of skiing in the Zakopane area gives this snow hub serious pedigree. Start early to make the wildly popular cable-car ascent up Kasprowy Wierch, at the park's southern edge. When winter pads these heights with pillowy snow, this is Poland's best-loved ski area: the Gąsienicowa side has the speedier lift, though Goryczkowa has a longer slope to thunder down. Between them, there's a thrilling 1km of vertical terrain. Off-pisters, beware: venturing away from the runs isn't permitted on these perilous peaks, and you could be fined (or worse, cause an avalanche).

Horse riding

Canter across meadows and woodland trails: Kościeliska Valley, in the park's northwest, is a popular location for guided horse-riding excursions. Family-friendly pony trips are available, while sleigh rides operate in winter. Book well ahead.

Climbing

Does clinging to granite walls while clouds swirl above you sound like your idea of a good time? If you're an experienced climber, head for the challenging ridges of the Hala Gąsienicowa area. Record details of your route in the Murowaniec refuge before setting out.

What to spot...

Wildlife in this region is a snapshot of the primeval past, when wolves, bears and lynx crept through Europe's valleys. Their numbers have dwindled, but these razor-toothed (though shy) predators have one of their last refuges in the Tatras, alongside golden eagles (also increasingly rare). Easier to spot are deer and Tatra chamois, clambering on precipitous outcrops above forests of fir and beech. Above the treeline sprawl wild-flower meadows; look out for edelweiss peeping from limestone crags.

GREY WOLF Sleek in summer, shaggy in winter, and omnipresent in fairy tales, this wolf's sense of smell means she'll flee before you spot her. Wolf hunting was banned across Poland in 1998, allowing these canines to grow in number.

TATRA CHAMOIS The population of this localised species of goat-antelope, with chocolate-brown coat and striped face, is exceedingly fragile. Only about 250 have been counted on the Polish side of the Tatras.

EURASIAN LYNX These magnificent felines, their ears adorned with distinctive tufts of black fur, are far too stealthy to be spotted by casual wildlife seekers. If you do see one, a delicious red deer can't be too far away...

Hike this...

01 Kościeliska caves

This 14km circuit from Kiry bypasses monuments to Polish luminaries en route to Mroźna and Mylna caves. Including time to visit the caves, the route takes about five hours.

02 Hala Gąsienicowa

Follow the easterly blue route from Kuźnice on a 14km-return trip via forested Boczań ridge, part of the so-called 'Lenin Trail'.

03 Five Ponds Valley

This 25km trek takes a solid nine hours across demanding terrain. Rewards are seeing the Wodogrzmoty Mickiewicza waterfalls, 70m-high Wielka Siklawa cascade and gem-blue Morskie Oko lake.

Itineraries

Cable cars, horses or your own two feet: there are plenty of inspiring ways to explore the Tatras, from its loftiest heights to its deep, shady valleys.

◀ Traditional life continues in the stunning Kościeliska Valley.
➡ Zakopane is Poland's premier ski resort.

01

A day

Looking for a family-friendly day in the park? From Zakopane, drive 8km along Rte 958 to Kiry, gateway to Kościeliska Valley. Trails abound through its meadows and spruce-lined cliffs, but best of all is an equestrian adventure with Kiry-based Stajnia Konsul (book ahead). After a couple of hours trotting through the valley astride a horse, seek out a hearty lunch in Kiry: potato pancakes with sour cream, pork with cabbage, and 'Highland tea' (less innocent than it sounds).

After lunch, head back towards Zakopane, but instead of stopping in town, take the southern exit towards Rondo Jana Pawla II (John Paul II roundabout). Permits are needed to drive the next stretch of the road, so get a taxi or walk for 40 minutes to Kuźnice. This is the base station of one of the oldest functioning cable cars in Europe, Kasprowy Wierch lift. In summer, it's advisable to book online in advance, otherwise buy tickets here. They are timed to allow you 1½ hours at the 1987m summit – snap some

photos and tramp up to the observatory before taking the cable car on the way down. Your sighs of wonder are likely to continue well into your evening meal back in Zakopane.

This summer itinerary can be adapted for winter: simply swap the morning horseback riding for a leisurely horse-drawn-sleigh ride into the valley (possible with advance bookings only). In the afternoon, bring skis so that you can glide down 3400m of pistes from the top of Kasprowy Wierch.

02

Four days

Use Zakopane as your base for four days of hiking and folk culture. Limber up on day one with a five-hour circuit of Strążyska Valley. Armed with *kabanosy*, the near-indestructible air-dried sausages beloved of Polish hikers, walk from Krupówki in Zakopane to the valley, following the Ścieżka nad Reglami pathway to a viewpoint overlooking the town.

On day two, strike out early for Morskie Oko lake. Buses from Zakopane reach Palenica Białczańska, 5km southeast of town, from

where you can walk to Wodogrzmoty Mickiewicza waterfalls and onwards to Morskie Oko, a trout-filled lake 50m deep. The circuit takes around six hours; for a longer trek, walk via Wielka Siklawa waterfalls, the highest in the park.

On day three, experience highlander culture. Drive to Bukowina Tatrzańska at the park's northeasterly edge to see the Dom Ludowy ('People's House', or Folk Culture Centre), one of Poland's largest timber buildings; just north, seek out Białka Tatrzańska's

church, dating to the early 1700s. In the afternoon, get toasty in 38°C waters at the village spas.

Spend your final day in the Kościeliska Valley, an 8km drive west of Zakopane. It's especially beautiful in springtime when covered in crocus blooms. Spend your final afternoon in Kościelisko village, after which the valley is named; it's a short detour on Rte 958 back to Zakopane, and a quaint place to toast the end of your trip with chewy *oscypek* sheep's cheese.

56

Triglav National Park

Slovenia's tallest mountain presides over an Alpine playground for hikers and rafters, made all the more enchanting by fairy-tale beasts and ancient gods.

Triglav National Park

Rippling east from Italy to Slovenia, the Julian Alps comprise hundreds of lofty mountains. But all of them cower before Mount Triglav, the tallest in the range and the focal point of Slovenia's sole national park.

Three-peaked Mount Triglav enjoys an exalted status in Slovene folklore and history. The mountain's distinctive shape has long associated it with a triple-headed Slavic god of the same name, said to rule over the three kingdoms of heaven, Earth and underworld. In more recent history, WWII partisan fighters sported *triglavkas*, triple-peaked caps inspired by the silhouette of Slovenia's highest mountain. To this day, Triglav graces Slovenia's coat of arms and flag.

Surrounding mighty Triglav, forest cloaks more than two-thirds of the park. The Soča River tumbles between these tangles of beech and spruce, while a labyrinth of underground springs carves out hidden caves. Occasionally waterfalls burst forth: Savica and Peričnik cascades are favourite hiking destinations, while temperamental Govic only gushes when rain floods a subterranean chamber.

The limestone and dolomite bedrock of glacial lakes such as Bohinj, the largest in the country, was laid down 250 million years ago. Triassic-era fossils of ammonites are easily glimpsed, especially in Studor Pass. Considerably younger are horseshoe-shaped valleys scooped out by glaciers, and moraines dusted with boulders deposited by glacial movement. Slovenia's most famous fairy tale, *Zlatorog*, offers an alternative origin story: moraines strewn with rocky rubble were kicked up by a golden-horned chamois, guardian of a treasure concealed on the slopes of Mount Triglav.

Though it's one of Europe's oldest national parks (first ring-fenced in 1924), Triglav is an outlier on travel itineraries. Fortunately, Slovenia's tourism trump card, Lake Bled, is just outside the park's eastern boundary. These swan-speckled waters and dramatic cliffs are a gateway drug to wilder Triglav: let yourself be lured in.

⬆ Spectacular Peričnik waterfall.
Previous page: a variety of boats on the water's edge at Lake Bohinj.

Getty Images| Guy Edwardes|/robertharding

Toolbox

When to go
May to September is hiking season, but mid-September brings an extra dash of creamy local flavour: the Bohinj cow parade fêtes the return of cattle from the pastures.

Getting there
From Slovene capital Ljubljana, home to an airport serving numerous European destinations, the park is a 70km drive north along the E61 and west towards Bohinjska Bistrica. From Salzburg, drive 240km south along the A10; from Venice, it's 170km along the E70 and A23.

Park in numbers

880
Area covered (sq km)

2864
Highest point: Mount Triglav (m)

45
Depth of Lake Bohinj (m)

Stay here...

Vila Mila
This mustard-yellow hotel is perched at the top of Bled village, just 4km south of gurgling Vintgar Gorge. Rooms and apartments within the century-old building have been spruced up to airy, light-filled perfection: beds are comfortable, furnishings are dove-grey, and there's a pleasing vintage feel throughout. In summer, the private garden has barbecue equipment available, plus sunloungers to stretch out on. This friendly hideaway is only a 400m walk from postcard-perfect Lake Bled, the tourist magnet just beyond Triglav National Park's eastern edge.

Hotel Gašperin
Sigh at mountain views from this chalet-style hotel in Ribčev Laz village, within the national park's southeastern boundary. Most rooms have flower-filled balconies with Alpine views. Breakfast buffets laden with cheese and cakes ensure ample calories for hikes around Lake Bohinj.

Apartments Koblar
For a quieter, more low-key feel than busy Bled and well-known Bohinj, try these great-value lodgings in Kranjska Gora, north of the park. Apartments are cosy and well kept, and there's ski storage if you fancy schussing through snowy fields.

Do this!

Rafting
The Soča River dances across the western third of Triglav National Park. Take a white-water-rafting trip along the river's prettiest stretch, starting from 136m-high Boka Waterfall. Not that you'll have time to snap photos: you'll be too busy being splashed by chilly spring water. In between rapids, the river widens into calm, glass-green water; here you can draw breath, taking a moment to admire limestone crags and thick forest along the banks.

Canyoning
Abseil rocky creeks, slide down cascades and get delightfully drenched on a canyoning trip to Fratarica Canyon, carved out near Log pod Mangartom in the park's northwestern corner. The tallest waterfall you can tackle is Parabola, a pulse-quickening 45m high.

Cross-country skiing
Between January and early March, the well-groomed pistes of Vogel, off Lake Bohinj's southwestern shore, are suited to beginner and intermediate skiers. But the most majestic views can be found along its cross-country skiing trails, which wend through snow-kissed meadows.

What to spot...

Wildlife thrives in Triglav's arid cliffs, woodlands and river rapids. Foxes, martens and badgers scamper in oak and beech forests, while butterfly orchids peep above tree roots. Meadows bloom with gentians and geraniums each summer. The Soča's tributaries teem with trout, though the otters in pursuit are now rare. Mountain goats, chamois and Alpine ibex defy gravity on cliff walls. Eighty-four bird species nest here, too: gracing the avian A-list are golden eagles and ultra-rare capercaillies (black grouse with scarlet eye markings).

GOLDEN EAGLE Look out for the broad, brown wings of this masterly hunter as it skyrockets after small mammals and glides to lofty nests, usually perched halfway up cliffs.

MARBLE TROUT These freckled freshwater fish are abundant in the Soča but only frolic in a handful of river systems outside Slovenia. The burliest found so far weighed 24kg.

BADGER These earthworm-guzzling mammals, at home in meadows and woodlands, are easily recognised by their fuzzy, black-and-white-striped faces. Badgers are creatures of habit, reusing old setts (burrows) across many generations.

Hike this...

O1 Vintgar Gorge
Crouch under overhanging cliffs and step gingerly over wooden boardwalks on this trail along the Radovna River, whose waters glow a glorious aquamarine. It's 4km there and back.

O2 Soča Trail
Follow the gurgling Soča River from its source to Bovec via 25km of easy walkways and creaky bridges through the verdant Trenta Valley.

O3 Mount Triglav ascent
This tough two- or three-day hike covers 38km from Lake Bohinj up to the three-peaked mountain's summit, before descending through the idyllic Triglav Lakes Valley.

Itineraries

Whether you have hours or days in Triglav National Park, you can sweat on gorge-side walks and valley biking trails before cooling off by lakes and waterfalls.

◄ For a dose of adrenaline, try white-water rafting the Soča River.
➔ Lake Bohinj, the largest permanent lake in Slovenia, makes a great base to explore the park.

01
A half-day

Lake Bohinj is the best base for a half-day taster of Triglav National Park. Direct your satnav to the village of Ribčev Laz, at the park's southeastern corner; from here drive west along the lake's southern bank towards Ukanc. Follow signs to Slap Savica, one of the park's prettiest waterfalls. From Savica car park, it's a 40-minute hike past hulking boulders and charming glades to a lookout over Savica Waterfall, whose waters plummet 78m from their underground source.

In winter, hikers nonchalantly squeeze past the trail's 'closed' sign, but slush makes the path exceedingly treacherous. Instead of the waterfall hike, winter visitors should head to the Vogel ski area, also on the road to Ukanc. Vogel's pleasant tree-fringed runs, up to 6km long, might not be challenging, but the views are magnificent.

After lungfuls of pine-scented air, drive back to Ribčev Laz for lunch (or an après-ski Laško beer) at one of the cafes by Lake Bohinj.

02
A weekend

Cycling is a superb way to see the park. On day one, arm yourself with picnic supplies in Bled village (not forgetting local vanilla cream cake *kremna rezina*) and hire a bike. Cycle 4km from Bled to Vintgar Gorge, one of the park's most scenic journeys. Chain your bike and tiptoe across the wooden boardwalks above churning turquoise swells before returning to picnic near the information centre.

Pedal west along the park's fringe to Krnica, northwest of Lake Bled, where you'll embark on the 16km Radovna Valley cycling route. Take breaks to peruse information boards about local flora along the route to Zgornja Radovna (follow the signposted detour if your quads can't handle the final ascent) and return to Bled for the night.

On day two, catch a bus to Lake Bohinj, in the shadow of emblematic Mount Triglav. Enjoy lunch near the water's edge before a long lakeside amble. Stay overnight in Hotel Jezero, clinking glasses of fruity Sava Valley wine as the sun dips behind the Julian Alps.

03
Four days

On day one, seize trail maps in Ribčev Laz before undertaking a hiking circuit to Mostnica Gorge. Along 12km of pathways you'll see the weather-beaten 18th-century Devil's Bridge and Mostnica Waterfall.

On the second day, follow the shore road west from Ribčev Laz to Ukanc (5km). Bike rental is available here, so check in and hire some wheels to cycle around this epic glacial lake.

Drive west on day three. Bovec and Soča are popular bases for water sports, and you can combine canyoning and rafting into a full day of waterfall-tumbling, river-riding thrills.

Your last day is a road trip north through the park. Farmland rushing past your window will be punctuated by *kozolec* (hayracks), a symbol of national identity. The zigzagging drive takes longer than its 40km suggest. Aim to end in Kranjska Gora, at the park's northern boundary, but break up the journey with a lunch stop in Trenta. In Kranjska Gora, several spa hotels are waiting to steam your weary muscles.

57

Valbona Valley National Park

In northern Albania, the magnificent Valbona Valley National Park is better known to locals as the home of 'the accursed mountains', the name given to the region by its neighbours, for whom conquering this extraordinary landscape was always tantalisingly out of reach.

Despite being a national park for little more than 20 years, the terrain here remains stunningly wild: just a handful of remote mountain villages dot the otherwise virtual wilderness, and getting about beyond any of these hamlets is by foot or on horseback only. This is the Albania of legend: blood feuds, ancient mountain codes of conduct, wolves and bears, but it's also extremely friendly, surprisingly accessible and easy to explore for anyone who makes the trip here. Walking options are almost endless, and while paths are still being created and signed, guides are cheap and tourist infrastructure is growing fast.

Perhaps the best thing about Valbona Valley National Park is that it can be visited on a wonderful loop from the town of Shkodra: visitors take the magnificent Koman Ferry down the valley of the Drin River (created by a hydroelectric dam), an extraordinary succession of gorges that leads to the town of Fierzë, before taking transport up to the village of Valbona, and then hiking the following day to the village of Theth, from where a daily bus takes you back down to Shkodra. Anyone seeking wilderness, scenery and wildlife that can rarely be found elsewhere in Europe today should seriously consider a trip to the Valbona Valley.

Toolbox

When to go
Valbona is primarily a summer park, though more skiers are visiting in winter. In July and August temperatures remain mild due to the altitude, but May–June and September–October are also wonderful times to visit, when you'll find yourself almost totally alone.

Getting there
The best nearby airport is Tirana, from where there's a daily minibus to Valbona. Many people base their trips in Shkodra, which has better transport connections to both the Koman Ferry and Theth.

Park in numbers

80

Area covered (sq km)

2694

Highest point: Jezerca (m)

1996

Year that the park was created

Hike this...

01 Çerem Path
A good introduction to walking in the valley, this gentle four-hour hike up the western bank of a river takes you through wild landscapes but involves some scrambling.

02 Rosi Mountain
A full-day hike from Valbona takes you up to superb views of Rosi Mountain in neighbouring Montenegro, as well as to two delightful lakes if you hike an hour longer.

03 Gjarpëri Trail
This 10-hour walk is a local favourite: you will have breathtaking views for much of the day, and in summer there's the possibility of spotting bears gorging themselves in disused orchards.

Stay here...

🏠 Hotel Rilindja
This gorgeous little home-from-home is a hotbed of local ecotourism and a hugely popular base for hikers and backpackers exploring the national park. Run by the formidable and enthusiastic Catherine, an American who has made the Albanian highlands her home, this cosy lodge a couple of kilometres before the village of Valbona itself is the best base for walkers in the area, due to the excellent information, maps and other general advice Catherine is able to give. Book ahead in summer.

Do this!

🥾 Hiking
Valbona's star attraction is the wonderful six-hour hike between Valbona and Theth, which can be done without a guide as the signage is pretty clear. It's largely an easy walk, with just a few steep ascents and descents, and it takes walkers through the exceptionally beautiful Valbona River valley before climbing the mountainside to the Valbona pass and then descending gently through beech forest to the gorgeous village of Theth. There are several small shacks along the route serving drinks and snacks, but aside from the odd shepherd you'll have this spectacular landscape all to yourself.

◄ The Albanian Alps provide a spectacular backdrop to Valbona Valley.

What to spot...

Alpine Valbona is dominated by beech forest. It's home to wolves, bears, jackals, foxes, bats, lynx and more than 80 species of year-round bird.

WILD BOAR You're more likely to hear these giant creatures snuffling in the bushes than actually see them, though they're a fairly common sight too. Avoid approaching them if you do cross paths, as they can be dangerous.

Itinerary

Just getting to the valley is a great adventure, and the most enjoyable way is aboard the Koman Ferry.

01

Three days

The incredibly picturesque three-hour ferry cruise travels through a succession of gorges. From the final stop at the town of Fierzë, minibuses whisk visitors up to Valbona village, a stunning journey through the mountains. In Valbona itself you'll have a choice of locally run guest houses, all with amazing mountain views and tasty lamb dinners on the menu. On day two, do the famous hike to Theth, which takes you over the Valbona Pass, with soaring views in all directions. The still very isolated village of Theth – seemingly forgotten by time – is dominated by its old stone church and chilling 'lock-in tower', a refuge for those fleeing blood feuds. Here the accommodation is more traditional, in stone houses that have been family homes for generations. On day three, after some more walking in the gorgeous countryside around Theth, take the bus back to Shkodra, via the newly surfaced road that winds majestically through the mountains back to the coast.

58

Vatnajökull National Park

Born of ice and fire, Vatnajökull is everything Iceland should be: wild and exposed, ice capped and volcano scarred, but always ruggedly handsome.

Vatnajökull National Park

Europe's largest protected area, Vatnajökull National Park is a stunning sample platter of pretty much every dramatic natural landscape Iceland has to offer. As you roam this vast reserve, you'll find calving glaciers, geothermal springs, rocky canyons, snow-capped mountains, featureless ice sheets, silent lagoons, buried volcanoes, eerie ice caverns, surreal basalt formations and even wandering herds of reindeer. Sprawling over 13,600 sq km, the park takes up a good-sized chunk of eastern Iceland, so most people take small bites from the edges – from Ásbyrgi in the north, or from Rte 1 as it sneaks between the ice sheet and the eastern seaboard.

With such unforgiving terrain, access is always a consideration. Public transport will take you to the fringes, but it's more thrilling to get out into Vatnajökull on foot. The two-day trek from Ásbyrgi to Dettifoss – Iceland's most impressive, ground-shaking waterfall – will bring you right into the middle of this elemental landscape. You may recognise Dettifoss from the movie *Prometheus* as soon as you see it. In fact, you may recognise bits of Vatnajökull from *Interstellar*, *Batman Begins*, *Lara Croft: Tomb Raider*, *Game of Thrones* and multiple James Bond flicks. What can we say – this is one photogenic place.

You'll need a 4WD or snowmobile to get to the higher reaches of the ice sheet and feel the full elemental force that is Vatnajökull. As you stand amid the silent snows, you can muse on the rather satisfying thought that there's a kilometre of ice between you and the bedrock below... depending, of course, on the goodwill of the molten magma that feeds the Grímsvötn volcano. The last time Grímsvötn blew its top was 2011, with an ash plume that grounded 900 flights – that's a vivid image, but fire and ice are probably what lured you to Iceland in the first place.

⬆ Crampons are mandatory while exploring Svínafellsjökull glacial tongue.
Previous page: one of the many ice caves.

Getty images | Henn Photography;

Toolbox

⚙ **When to go**
The 4WD tracks that cross the frozen centre of the park are only open when the snows melt from July to September, but the park fringes and the northern lowlands are open year round.

🧭 **Getting there**
Vatnajökull National Park takes up most of the southeastern corner of Iceland, with the easiest access from Rte 1 as it follows the east coast. The town of Höfn, just off the Ring Rd, is the most convenient hub.

Park in numbers

13,600

Area covered (sq km)

1

Maximum thickness of the Vatnajökull ice cap (km)

2011

Year of the last, earth-shaking eruption of the Grímsvötn volcano

↓ A surreal landscape greets visitors onto the Vatnajökull ice cap, the largest in Iceland.

The power and the majesty of Dettifoss – no other waterfall in Europe matches the volume of water running over it.

Stay here...

🏠 Hólmur
Backing on to the tongue of glacier at Fláajökull, this family-friendly farm in Hornafjörður has a surprisingly epicurean restaurant, serving everything from local langoustine to crème brûlée made with farm-raised duck eggs. It also has its own reindeer herd and petting zoo, as well as homely farmhouse accommodation. From here, you can ramble down to Jökulsárlón to watch calving icebergs, or join evening tours in summer to the beaches near Höfn, to sip Brennivín and eat air-dried Icelandic shark under the midnight sun.

⛺ Vesturdalur campsite
There isn't much more at Vesturdalur than flat ground for your tent, and a toilet, but the setting is what you pay for. Around the campsite, rainbow-coloured sands and twisted columns of basalt create eerie obstacles to the wind amid the water channels.

🏠 Hoffell
The big attraction at this old-fashioned country guest house is the chance to plunge into the outdoor geothermal pools, which steam contemplatively in front of snow-capped crags. The cheerful owners offer quad-bike tours on the Hoffellsjökull glacier.

Do this!

❄️ Snowmobiling
Getting out onto the ice sheet is what everyone wants to do in Vatnajökull, and the sinuous slither of glacier at Skaftafellsjökull offers the easiest access. Easy is, of course, a relative term. A steep 4WD track is the only way to reach the departure point for snowmobile and super-jeep tours out to the ice sheet, but the reward is being transported into a silent sea of snow, punctuated by outcrops of vivid blue ice – the kinds of views normally reserved for mountaineers.

⛑️ Ducking into an ice cave
On a caving tour beneath the glaciers that slip down from Vatnajökull, you'll clamber through ice tunnels to reach awesome natural cathedrals of blue ice, bathed in surreal light. You'll need a local guide to safely find the chambers among the dangerous crevasses.

🥾 Hiking the Jökulsárgljúfur path
The trail from Ásbyrgi to Dettifoss is an Icelandic classic, taking in a broad sweep of volcanic landscapes and finishing at a thundering waterfall. You're off the ice sheet, so the track is open year-round.

What to spot...

At first glance, the ice sheet and its rocky surroundings seem almost devoid of life, but plenty of animals make their home in this harsh and inhospitable environment. Herds of reindeer roam the higher ground and seals surface along the shoreline, but the plentiful birdlife is what most people come to see, from puffins and pink-footed geese to gyrfalcons and rock ptarmigan. You might also spot an Arctic fox – black in summer, white in winter – scampering among the outcrops.

REINDEER Descendants of Norwegian herds imported in the 1770s, reindeer run wild on the ice sheet. The deer stick to the higher ground in summer but roam close to the coast road in winter.

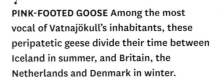

PINK-FOOTED GOOSE Among the most vocal of Vatnajökull's inhabitants, these peripatetic geese divide their time between Iceland in summer, and Britain, the Netherlands and Denmark in winter.

PUFFIN Everyone loves a puffin, and these ground-nesting scamps can be spotted on the sea cliffs at various spots around the Ring Rd, particularly in the nature reserve at Ingólfshöfði.

Drive this...

O1 Eastern Ring Rd

The section of the Ring Rd between Skaftafell and Höfn offers some of the most impressive coastal views in Iceland, taking in everything from puffin-dotted sea cliffs to iceberg-filled lagoons.

O2 Road to Skaftafellsjökull

This spur of the Vatnajökull ice cap is reached via a challenging 4WD scramble, but at the top you can slip out onto the glacier on foot or by super-jeep or snowmobile.

O3 Route to Dettifoss

Two summer tracks run along the Jökulsárgljúfur canyon, with the best views of churning Dettifoss from Road 864 on the east bank of the river.

Itineraries

The largest protected area in Europe is its own winter wonderland of ice and snow, with calving glaciers, plunging waterfalls and an almost unearthly collection of hidden caverns and volcanoes.

← Watch Vatnajökull calving mighty icebergs at Jökulsárlón glacial lake.
→ The glacial lagoon of Fjallsárlón, where icebergs calve off Vatnajökull ice cap.

01

Two days

For a small taste of Vatnajökull's elemental wonders, the two-day, 35km trek along Jökulsárgljúfur, the valley of the Jökulsá á Fjöllum river, is hard to beat. This route through the northern reaches of the national park serves up a menu of waterfalls and weird volcanic formations. Starting from Ásbyrgi, follow a rugged trail along a sculpted canyon to Dettifoss, Europe's most powerful waterfall, which you can feel pounding in your chest long before it comes into view. Day one climbs the side of

the Ásbyrgi canyon, passing through a sepia-coloured landscape of scorched heath and basalt outcrops, before reaching the hallucinogenic coloured sands of Rauðhólar and the honeycombed basalt outcrops of Hljóðaklettar. It's a surreal setting, with more than a hint of alien planet. After an overnight stop in the crude campsite at Vesturdalur, day two continues along the channel of the gorge, skipping over spring-fed tributaries to reach the 27m-high Hafragilsfoss cascade. The final approach to the falls is

cinematic in scale – which is appropriate, really, as the falls appeared across the full screen in the opening frames of sci-fi romp *Prometheus*. At this phenomenal waterfall, an incredible 193 sq metres of water thunders over a 45m cliff with each passing second, kicking up miniature rainbows in a churning cauldron of white water. Stand and be humbled by the forces of nature before continuing onwards to Reykjahlíð, gateway to the pseudocrater-pocked waterlands around the Mývatn lake.

02

A week

With a week to spare, you can roam all over the ice cap. Start with the two-day hike from Ásbyrgi to the Dettifoss cascade, where you can indulge your *Game of Thrones* fantasies standing on the edge of a thundering precipice. Rte 1 will whisk you east to the coast; stop in Höfn to sample the local *humar* (Icelandic lobster) and wash it down with a bottle of locally brewed Vatnajökull lager, made from melted icebergs. From Höfn, duck inland to meet the Vatnajökull ice

cap face to face on the icy tongue of Fláajökull. Keep following the coast road south, to play midwife to a calving glacier at iceberg-dotted Jökulsárlón and creep through mint-blue polar tunnels on an ice-cave tour. To get right on the top of the ice cap, you'll have to join an organised trip, as the authorities are understandably twitchy about tourists coming to harm in this unforgiving environment. The most popular destination is Skaftafellsjökull, another Gene Simmons–esque

tongue of ice snaking down from the main ice cap, reached via a steep 4WD track from the Ring Rd. Fill up on Icelandic grub at the survival hut–like Jöklasel restaurant before hiking out onto the ice, or making your way by snowmobile or super-jeep instead. The sensation of being out among the silent snows is other-worldly – the planet Hoth from *The Empire Strikes Back* is the best approximation we can come up with. 'Oh no', – skkkkrr – 'more AT-ATs; look out, Luke!'... you get the picture.

59

Vikos-Aoös National Park

Search your soul among slate-roofed villages in Vikos-Aoös National Park: the spirituality of this northwestern Greek reserve is as enriching as the sight of its mountains and gorges.

Experiencing Vikos-Aoös National Park can morph from tranquil to high-octane in a matter of minutes. On one hike, you'll stand by the shore of Drakolimni, a lake as still as polished marble. The same day, your senses will whirl at the spectacle of Vikos Gorge, plunging 1km deep. By car, you'll trundle over serene stone bridges and then moments later clutch the steering wheel around needlepoint bends.

The park nestles in northwestern Greece's overlooked Epiros region, among the Pindos Mountains and close to the Albanian border. Its centrepiece is 20km-long Vikos Gorge, so deep it graces the Guinness World Records list – though this claim is contested. But you won't feel the urge to reach for a tape measure when confronted by the ultramarine Voïdomatis River ribboning between keen-edged granite cliffs and past ash orchards and stone-and-slate villages. North of here, the lesser-visited Aoös Gorge weaves through the park's periphery, all in the shadow of Mount Tymfi (2497m at its highest point).

Human civilisation in Vikos-Aoös dates back well over 10,000 years. In the ancient world, settlements here were outposts for hunters and firewood gatherers. From the 15th century, spiritual seekers fled here. Communities of monks built monasteries whose weathered facades can still be admired around villages like Aristi and Ano Pedina. The Zagorohoria ('beyond the mountain') villages prospered as centres of learning under Ottoman rule, awarded special status in return for guarding mountain passes, but they later faded back into the quiet villages you see today.

The Greeks treasured the area long before its 1973 designation as a national park. Meanwhile the ecotourism potential of fragile Vikos-Aoös – vulnerable as it is to landslides and wildfires – is only gradually being tapped. Visit now to see this majestic realm before the crowds catch on.

Toolbox

When to go
July and August are most popular, but June and September bring the ideal balance between sunshine and fresh, hiker-friendly temperatures. Ski touring is possible from late December to February. November, March and April are quiet and many amenities close their doors.

Getting there
The park is a 55km drive north along the E853 from the closest major city, Ioannina; its airport has links to Athens. Konitsa and Aristi, fringing the western edge of Vikos-Aoös, are convenient bases.

Park in numbers

126
Area covered (sq km)

46
Total Zagorohoria villages in and around the park

2
According to legend, the number of dragons

Hike this...

01 Vikos Gorge
Take the precipitous path from Monodendri to Agia Paraskevi monastery, overlooking Vikos Gorge, before venturing along the canyon to Mikro Papingo. It's a tough four hours over roughly 15km.

02 Drakolimni lake circuit
Leaving from the Papingo villages, this steep 21km-return hike to the high-altitude lake of dragons, home to warring reptiles of legend, takes a solid eight hours.

03 Vradeto Plains
Over a full day, hike from Tsepelovo village to the dizzying gorge viewpoint at Beloi, before tottering down the Skala Vradetou stone ladders to Kapesovo village.

Stay here...

Primoula
Feel right at home in this cheerful, eco-friendly guesthouse in Ano Pedina village. Each room in the traditional stone building has a distinct character, and breakfasts overflow with local cheeses and honey. Staff members are bursting with tips about hikes and outdoor activities.

Zagori Suites
Sink into a sofa with mountain views at one of the luxurious suites at this hotel near Vitsa village. All needs are catered for with a smile, whether you need ideas for family excursions or an urgent mushroom-picking tour.

Do this!

Rafting
As well as riding the foamiest stretches of the Voïdomatis River, rafting excursions bypass romantic and ancient architecture. From Aristi village, your boat will bob and whirl beneath elegant stone bridges and float past centuries-old monks' caves and monasteries.

Mountain biking
Konitsa, on the park's northwestern edge, is the starting point for superb biking trails into the park. To enjoy a gentler pace, pootle through the Papingo villages, pausing to bathe your aching feet in the rock pools.

← The vertiginous path to the Hermit's Cave, near abandoned Agia Paraskevi monastery.

What to spot...

Ash and chestnut woodlands conceal foxes, and storks and kingfishers hunt in shallow waters, but the only dragons at Drakolimni are speckly alpine newts.

WHITE STORK These wader birds with black-tipped wings cut an elegant silhouette as they soar above lakes and strut in the shallows. Look out for their large nests perched on trees and pylons.

Itinerary

Cling to the side of the gorge or ride the river's rapids to seek out ancient monasteries and feasts to break any fast.

01
Four days

Begin in Ano Pedina to admire an icon-strewn 18th-century church before hiking on towards Lilliputian Dilofo. Unwrap a picnic at Koukouli bridge, a historic span over the Voïdomatis, and then press northwest to Monodendri, where you can visit Agia Paraskevi monastery; its 15th-century frescoes dazzle as much as the Vikos Gorge views.

After a cosy night in one of Monodendri's rustic guesthouses, strike out early along the Vikos Gorge trail. Your reward is reaching the twin Papingo villages, backed by the spectacular 'Towers' rock formations.

On day three, meander the 2km path between the two Papingo villages, pausing to bathe in natural pools along the way. Hike or call a taxi from Papingo to Aristi village, pausing at 17th-century monastery Panagia Spiliotissa on the way, before settling in for a feast of roast lamb.

On your final day, join one of Aristi's rafting operators for a day tumbling over the Voïdomatis' swells.

60

— DENMARK —

Wadden Sea National Park

At Denmark's coastal wonder, tidal rhythms expose a seabed teeming with life. Bumper birdlife flocks here, as do humans with a penchant for oysters.

Mudflats and salt marshes don't sound as sexy as alpine peaks, but Denmark's west-coast national park demonstrates how endlessly appealing (and fun!) they can be, with tractor-bus rides to salty offshore islands, fat harbour seals lolling on sandbanks, and the chance to put on waders and pluck and shuck oysters. Plus birds – so many birds!

In Wadden Sea National Park, the seabed meets the horizon twice daily, when low tide exposes flats of sand and mud, and birds swoop to hoover up the buffet on offer (tasty morsels like worms, cockles, crabs, shrimp and snails). Annually, some 10 to 12 million feathered friends use this region as a feeding place, or to rest, on their migrations. That's a boon for birdwatchers, who tick off dozens of species including geese, ducks, waders, gulls and terns. Starlings draw a crowd for their stunning, balletic dances across the dusk sky.

The history of humans in the region is also on show, with dykes and polders evidence of the struggle to master the watery landscapes. Denmark's oldest town, Ribe, is the perfect base for exploring the park. It dates from around AD 700, and its meandering river, lush water meadows and cobbled streets make it a delight to wander.

Although Denmark's national park stretches from Ho Bugt (near Esbjerg), south to the German border, the bounty of the Wadden Sea continues further west, across the great river estuaries of Germany and into the Netherlands. It's a total length of some 500km and a total area of about 10,000 sq km. There are coastal national parks in Germany and the Netherlands, and the entire region is inscribed on the Unesco World Heritage list as the largest unbroken system of intertidal sand- and mudflats in the world.

⬇ At low tide a tractor-bus takes visitors across mudflats to the tiny island of Mandø.

Toolbox

When to go
The Wadden Sea islands are summer-holiday hot spots, with beach crowds and family-friendly activities from June to August. Oyster safaris run in cooler weather; starling flocks mesmerise in spring and autumn.

Getting there
The park stretches along the southwestern coast of Jutland. The region's biggest city is Esbjerg, but Ribe is a far sweeter base. Rail and road links are plentiful. The prime islands are accessed by causeway (Rømø), ferry (Fanø) or tractor-bus (Mandø).

Park in numbers

1466
Area covered (sq km)

10-12 million
Migratory birds, visiting twice yearly

3
Countries sharing the Wadden Sea eco-region

Walk this...

01 Mudflats meander
At low tide, the mudflats are ripe for exploration (bring rubber boots or shoes, or go barefoot). Note: the difference between high and low tide is 2m, so get tide times straight or go with a ranger.

02 Walk to Mandø
Guided walks lead 8km across the seabed to the island of Mandø, with expert commentary. You'll get close to tidal life, and you can take the tractor-bus home.

03 Nightwatchman
Take a living history lesson by joining the Nightwatchman on his evening stroll around the cobbled lanes of Ribe.

Stay here...

Danhostel Ribe
Stay in a prime position in Ribe, a chocolate-box idyll of cobblestones and crooked houses. Rooms in this functional hostel are simple and affordable (all have private bathroom); they're ideal for families, groups and backpackers. Knowledgeable staff members rent bikes and promote sustainable travel in the region.

Sønderho Kro
On the island of Fanø (reached by a 12-minute ferry ride from Esbjerg), this thatched-roof *kro* (inn) exudes the prized *hygge* (cosiness) for which Denmark is famous. It dates from 1722 and has antique-filled suites (some with Wadden Sea views) and an acclaimed restaurant.

Do this!

Going on an oyster safari
October to April, join an oyster safari, where mussel beds are combed and shellfish appetites sated. Pacific oysters don't come fresher than self-harvested and shucked on the spot, and the setting couldn't be more natural: wind in your hair, water lapping your legs (waders provided).

Visiting Mandø
At low tide, a tractor hauls a bus 8km over the flats to deliver visitors to wee Mandø. This peaceful island is a microcosm of the park – follow walking paths or hire a bike to discover dykes, birdlife, sunbaking seals and cosy inns.

What to spot...

The sea itself and the mudflats, sandbanks, marshes and islands support a rich ecosystem. Harbour seals are plentiful, but the bounteous birdlife really wows.

EUROPEAN STARLING Each spring and autumn, starlings visit the park. Close to the marshes, just before dusk, up to a million birds gather in formations that dance across the sky (Danes call the phenomenon *sort sol*: 'black sky').

Itinerary

Paddle in the shallows, inspect mudflats, count birds and seals, and slurp oysters from their shells.

01

Two days

Visit the Wadden Sea Centre (VadehavsCentret), 10km southwest of Ribe, to get an overview of the park and check out the guided activities – options usually include birdwatching, seal spotting and mudflat exploration. From here, jump on the tractor-bus that runs across at low tide to the small outlying island of Mandø. Hire a bike to get the full experience, and set off on the 10km trail around the island; dykes, mussel beds and seals await, as does a lunch of regional specialities like *marsk lam* (salt-marsh lamb). Take the bus back to the mainland and, if your timing is right, a dusk viewing of the starling murmurations is unforgettable. On the second day, visit an island: Fanø is postcard pretty and reached by a 12-minute ferry ride from Esbjerg. Or drive the causeway to Rømø and sign up for a horse ride along the beach, or a kitebuggy race across the huge expanses of sand, where your go-kart has a parachute-like kite to harness the cracking winds.

Index

Published in April 2017
by Lonely Planet Global Limited
CRN 554153
www.lonelyplanet.com
ISBN 978 1 7865 7649 1
© Lonely Planet 2016
Printed in China
10 9 8 7 6 5 4 3 2 1

Managing Director, Publishing Piers Pickard
Associate Publisher Robin Barton
Commissioning Editor Matt Phillips
Art Direction Daniel Di Paolo
Layout Lauren Egan
Editors Ross Taylor, Nick Mee
Wildlife illustrations Holly Exley
Spot illustrations Jacob Rhoades
Cartographer Wayne Murphy
Print Production Larissa Frost, Nigel Longuet

Written by: Abigail Blasi, Alexis Averbuck, Anita Isalska, Anna Kaminski, Anthony Ham, Brandon Presser, Carolyn Bain, Clifton Wilkinson, Emilie Filou, Etain O'Carroll, Joe Bindloss, Kerry Christiani, Luke Waterson, Marc Di Duca, Neil Wilson, Regis St Louis, Tom Masters, Vesna Maric **Thanks to:** Branislava Vladisavljevic, Anna Tyler, James Smart and Gemma Graham

STAY IN TOUCH lonelyplanet.com/contact

Front cover image: Picos de Europa. © Justin Foulkes/Lonely Planet.
Back cover image: Corniglia and Manarola from the Sentiero Azzurro, Cinque Terre. © Justin Foulkes/Lonely Planet.
Back cover inset images, l–r: © Miguel Castans Monteagudo/Shutterstock; © Matt Munro/Lonely Planet; © Matt Munro/Lonely Planet; © Miguel Sotomayor/Getty Images; © ueuaphoto/Getty Images.

AUSTRALIA
The Malt Store, Level 3, 551 Swanston St,
Carlton, Victoria 3053 T: 03 8379 8000

USA
124 Linden St, Oakland, CA 94607
T: 510 250 6400

IRELAND
Unit E, Digital Court, The Digital Hub,
Rainsford St, Dublin 8

UNITED KINGDOM
240 Blackfriars Rd, London SE1 8NW
T: 020 3771 5100

1	2	3	4	5	6	7	8	9	10
11	12	13	14	15	16	17	18	19	20
21	22	23	24	25	26	27	28	29	30
31	32	33	34	35	36	37	38	39	40
41	42	43	44	45	46	47	48	49	50
51	52	53	54	55	56	57	58	59	60
61	62	63	64	65	66	67	68	69	70
71	72	73	74	75	76	77	78	79	80
81	82	83	84	85	86	87	88	89	90
91	92	93	94	95	96	97	98	99	100
101	102	103	104	105	106	107	108	109	110
111	112	113	114	115	116	117	118	119	120
121	122	123	124	125	126	127	128	129	130
131	132	133	134	135	136	137	138	139	140
141	142	143	144	145	146	147	148	149	150
151	152	153	154	155	156	157	158	159	160
161	162	163	164	165	166	167	168	169	170
171	172	173	174	175	176	177	178	179	180
181	182	183	184	185	186	187	188	189	190
191	192	193	194	195	196	197	198	199	200
201	202	203	204	205	206	207	208	209	210
211	212	213	214	215	216	217	218	219	220
221	222	223	224	225	226	227	228	229	230
231	232	233	234	235	236	237	238	239	240
241	242	243	244	245	246	247	248	249	250
251	252	253	254	255	256	257	258	259	260
261	262	263	264	265	266	267	268	269	270
271	272	273	274	275	276	277	278	279	280
281	282	283	284	285	286	287	288	289	290
291	292	293	294	295	296	297	298	299	300
301	302	303	304	305	306	307	308	309	310
311	312	313	314	315	316	317	318	319	320
321	322	323	324	325	326	327	328	329	330
331	332	333	334	335	336	337	338	339	340
341	342	343	344	345	346	347	348	349	350
351	352	353	354	355	356	357	358	359	360
361	362	363	364	365	366	367	368	369	370
371	372	373	374	375	376	377	378	379	380
381	382	383	384	385	386	387	388	389	390
391	392	393	394	395	396	397	398	399	400